CAMDEN MISCELLANY
VOL. XXV

CAMDEN MISCELLANY VOL. XXV

CAMDEN FOURTH SERIES
VOLUME 13

LONDON
OFFICES OF THE ROYAL HISTORICAL
SOCIETY
UNIVERSITY COLLEGE LONDON, GOWER ST.,
LONDON, WC1E 6BT
1974

DA
20
.C17
V.13 / 38,484

Printed in Great Britain by Butler & Tanner Ltd., Frome and London

CONTENTS

I

THE LETTERS OF WILLIAM, LORD PAGET OF BEAUDESERT, 1547–63

edited by

BARRETT L. BEER, Ph.D.
and SYBIL M. JACK, M.A., B.Litt., F.R.Hist.S.

CONTENTS

ABBREVIATIONS

Anglesey MSS	Manuscripts of the Marquess of Anglesey, Plas-Newydd, Llanfairpwll, Anglesey
BM	British Museum
Cecil MSS	Manuscripts of the Marquess of Salisbury, Hatfield House, Hertfordshire
CSP Spanish	*Calendar of State Papers, Spanish*, ed. G. A. Bergenroth *et al.* (London, 1862–)
DL 42	Public Record Office, Duchy of Lancaster, Miscellaneous Books
E 315	Public Record Office, Court of Augmentations, Miscellaneous Books
Ellis	*Original Letters Illustrative of English History*, ed. Henry Ellis, 1st ser., 3 vols. (London, 1825)
Haynes	Samuel Haynes, *A Collection of State Papers . . . Left by William Cecil, Lord Burghley . . .* (London, 1740)
PLB	Paget Letter Book, Fitzwilliam of Milton Manuscripts, Northamptonshire Record Office
SP 10	Public Record Office, State Papers, Domestic, Edward VI
SP 12	Public Record Office, State Papers, Domestic, Elizabeth
SP 68	Public Record Office, State Papers, Foreign, Edward VI
SP 69	Public Record Office, State Papers, Foreign, Mary
Strype	John Strype, *Ecclesiastical Memorials . . .* , 3 vols. in 6 (Oxford, 1822)
Tytler	Patrick F. Tytler, *England under the Reigns of Edward VI and Mary*, 2 vols. (London, 1839)

INTRODUCTION

THIS edition of the letters of William, Lord Paget of Beaudesert, covers the period from the accession of Edward VI in 1547 to Paget's death in 1563. His correspondence from the earlier period has been omitted because the larger part of it has been calendared in the *Letters and Papers of Henry VIII.* The editors have attempted to include all surviving letters from 1547 forward as well as the most important papers relating to Paget's political career. In addition a short selection of letters written to Paget has been included in the Appendix. All materials pertaining to his household and landholdings have been excluded. Also omitted are various Privy Council minutes and official correspondence which includes Paget as only one of a number of signatories. Because of this selective process, the present edition falls short of the ideal of completeness cherished by editors of earlier generations. But the goal of completeness is itself illusory since historical research is a continuing process. No doubt new Paget letters will be found and papers identified whose authorship has not yet been established. Paget's thirty years' service, partially spent in diplomatic work, make it scarcely an exaggeration to say that any archive whether in Britain or in Europe might conceivably yield additional materials, though the present editors' inquiries have yielded very little.[1] If the items included here stimulate further work and interest, the objectives of the editors will be fully satisfied.

I. *Paget's Political Career*

Paget's political career is remarkable primarily because he held high office under Henry VIII, Edward VI, and Mary with only a brief interruption in 1552. Among his contemporaries, he possessed a talent for survival rivalled only by William Paulet, marquess of Winchester. Paget has usually been characterized as a 'master of practices', a shrewd and calculating opportunist who managed to avoid the pitfalls of politics and religion under the early Tudors.[2] An examination of his writings, however, reveals him to be a

[1] For example, an attempt to locate Paget's missing commonplace book has not yet succeeded; see *Notes and Queries,* n.s. xix (1972), p. 467.
[2] The only modern biography of Paget is S. R. Gammon, *Statesman and Schemer: William, First Lord Paget, Tudor Minister* (Newton Abbot, 1973).

statesman of considerable stature. Paget understood the realities and limitations of politics perhaps better than any of his contemporaries, and his letters are filled with sound advice that all too often went unheeded.

His political and social philosophy was essentially conservative; and, although he disliked the harshness of Henry VIII's regime, he came to realize that many of the reforms promoted by Protector Somerset encouraged discontent and threatened the stability of society. Paget, like the Tudor monarchs whom he served, feared rebellion and held that the maintenance of law and order was the highest priority of government. He was also one of the most able diplomats of his day, frequently consulted on financial questions, and an articulate proponent of conciliar government. On religious questions he favoured caution and moderation. His writings reveal very little about his own religious views, but it appears that he preferred the Henrician settlement though he was sufficiently flexible to serve Somerset and Northumberland as well as Philip and Mary.

Born in either 1505 or 1506, Paget was educated at St Paul's School, London, and at Trinity Hall, Cambridge, where he came to the attention of the Master, Stephen Gardiner. Entering the service of Henry VIII as a protégé of Gardiner, Paget advanced through a number of minor offices, including the clerkship of the Privy Council, to become secretary of state in 1543. He served as a diplomat in missions to Germany, France, and the Low Countries. During the last years of Henry VIII, Paget was numbered among the king's closest and most trusted advisers.[1]

Paget was at the height of his influence when Henry died in 1547 leaving the throne to his nine-year-old son, Edward VI. Serving as confidential adviser to the duke of Somerset, Paget was instrumental in the creation of the Protectorate and intimately connected with the formulation of policy in 1547 and 1548. His letters to Somerset in 1549, however, reveal increasing apprehension about the protector's leadership. Paget remained active as a diplomat negotiating with Charles V in 1549 and with the French in 1550. He survived the fall of Somerset in 1549, but in October 1551 was imprisoned, at first allegedly for insulting the emperor, and was later convicted for misconduct as chancellor of the Duchy of Lancaster. After a period of imprisonment in the Tower and the imposition of a heavy fine, Paget made a complete submission and was readmitted to the Council in

---

[1] For Paget's career under Henry VIII see J. J. Scarisbrick, *Henry VIII* (London, 1968), and especially L. B. Smith, *Henry VIII, The Mask of Royalty* (London, 1971).

1553 in time to sign the devise of Edward VI transferring the crown to Lady Jane.[1]

With many fellow councillors, however, Paget turned as soon as it seemed feasible to promote Mary's cause, and the queen retained him as one of her chief councillors. He helped to promote the Spanish marriage, leading the faction in the Council that opposed his old master, Gardiner, who favoured Edward Courtenay. Paget, however, would have no dealings with those who, after Wyatt's rebellion, would have taken extra-legal steps against Elizabeth or who would have re-established the Catholic religion in haste. He certainly incurred Mary's displeasure at this time, and the only consistent explanation of his conduct is to assume that he was logically pursuing a line of conduct indicated by his convictions about the nature of government and council. Despite residual distrust Mary employed him extensively particularly because he was highly regarded by Philip.[2]

On Elizabeth's accession it was reported that she had sworn Paget as a councillor, but this was not apparently so, and Paget, whose health was deteriorating, held no formal office again despite his attempt to obtain the presidency of the Council in the Marches. His relations with the queen's government are curious and call for further study. Elizabeth apparently intended to send Paget to Spain as ambassador in 1559 had his health not prevented it and may have continued to use him to feed information to the Spanish ambassador in London.

II. *Paget's Letters*

Paget's letters are dispersed among a large number of manuscript collections and archives. Important materials are included among the manuscripts of the Marquess of Anglesey at Plas-Newydd, but this collection is disappointingly incomplete. A considerable portion of Paget's official correspondence is predictably to be found in the State

---

[1] The most detailed account of Paget's activities under Edward VI is contained in W. K. Jordan, *Edward VI: The Young King* (London, 1968), and *Edward VI: The Threshold of Power* (London, 1970). Also important are A. F. Pollard, *England under Protector Somerset* (London, 1900), Conyers Read, *Mr Secretary Cecil and Queen Elizabeth* (London, 1962), and Mary Dewar, *Sir Thomas Smith* (London, 1964). For Paget's relations with Somerset see B. L. Beer, 'A Critique of the Protectorate', *Huntington Library Quarterly*, xxxiv (1971), pp. 277–83, and 'Sir William Paget and the Protectorate, 1547–1549', *Ohio Academy of History Newsletter*, ii (1971), pp. 2–9.

[2] See J. A. Muller, *Stephen Gardiner and the Tudor Reaction* (New York, 1926), E. H. Harbison, *Rival Ambassadors at the Court of Queen Mary* (Princeton, 1940), and F. G. Emmison, *Tudor Secretary, Sir William Petre at Court and Home* (London, 1961).

Papers Foreign and Domestic at the Public Record Office. Other items are found at the British Museum, at the Northamptonshire Record Office, among the records of the Duchy of Lancaster, the Cecil manuscripts at Hatfield, the Hengrave and Corpus Christi College manuscripts at Cambridge, the Loseley manuscripts at the Folger Library in Washington, D.C., as well as in archives at Vienna and Brussels.

The letters survive in a variety of forms. First and fewest are the original letters sent, whose survival depended upon the fortunes of the archives of the recipient; then there are the final drafts or minutes of letters, which Paget would himself have retained; and there are also early drafts and copies of some papers. Several letters survive in a variety of forms, but for the most part we are dependent on a single text. Some of the most important letters written during the reign of Edward VI are found in letter books prepared either by Paget or by the recipient of the letter. These letter books have never been fully identified and are listed below:

1. Northamptonshire Record Office, Fitzwilliam of Milton, 31. Contains 31 items including a collection of Paget's letters to Somerset. No foliation. Cover vellum leaf cut to size. 3 gatherings of 8 leaves, one of 4 and 1 single leaf stuck to back of last 4 leaves.[1]

2. BM, Cotton MS, Titus B. v, fos. 28–38. Fragment of a letter book including Paget's letters to Somerset, Smith, Petre, and some in-letters from the Council. Watermark: gloved hand with flower on fos. 31, 34, 35, 36, 38. Original foliation 423–33.

3. BM, Cotton MS, Caligula E. iv, fos. 201–18. Fragment of an inward and outward letter book including correspondence of Paget's embassy of January–February 1550. Damaged so that original gatherings are impossible to establish. Starts with final paragraph of last letter of previous embassy; on dorse of this are instructions of 1550 embassy.

4. BM, Harl. MS 523. Evidently a copy of all of Sir Philip Hoby's letters received and issued during reign of Edward VI. Contemporary index. Watermark: gloved hand with flower; quaternion gatherings, irregular.

5. BM, Cotton MS, Galba B. xii. Contains some of the original minutes of Paget's 1549 embassy, plus other original documents collected at the time or concerned with Hoby's period as ambassador, interfoliated with which is the much separated and disordered abbreviated letter book for a good part of Hoby's embassy, from which the copies in Harl. 523 were apparently made. The letter book, which has two separate papers with different watermarks, runs fos. 3–21, 33–4,

[1] For a listing of the contents of the letter book see B. L. Beer, 'The Paget Letter Book', *Manuscripta*, xiv (1970), pp. 176–9.

gloved hand watermark; 92–118, 238–56, catchwords and watermark anchor. An exceedingly misordered volume, a disorder which dates back to the original binding of the volume as the contemporary numeration of groups of pages runs continuously A–Z.

Detailed attention must be given to the Northamptonshire Record Office letter book as it is the major source for Paget's correspondence with Somerset, and the reasons for its compilation are not self-evident. The volume was deposited at the Northamptonshire Record Office in 1946 as part of the family correspondence of Earl Fitzwilliam of Milton. While there is no obvious reason why a Paget letter book should be among these records, it has been suggested that it came into the hands of Sir Walter Mildmay, whose daughter married Sir William Fitzwilliam in 1569.[1] Most of the letters to Somerset are not extant elsewhere, although minutes of two are among the Anglesey manuscripts and copies of others are in the State Papers and the Cotton manuscripts. In addition to the letters to Somerset, the volume includes an almost complete documentation of the letters written at the time of the fall of Somerset in October 1549. Also written at this time is a pleading letter to Paget from the duchess of Somerset and a defensive letter from Sir Thomas Smith, both of which have been included in the Appendix. At the end of the letter book is a copy of Paget's opinion concerning foreign affairs in August 1546 which is described as a 'consultation' and a detailed account of the proceedings with regard to the will of Henry VIII. Whether or not Paget normally kept non-diplomatic correspondence in letter books, the fact that this letter book is not arranged in perfect chronological order suggests that it was prepared at a subsequent date to the chronologically last letter, presumably for some specific purpose.

Unfortunately one may only conjecture about the exact circumstances that led to the preparation of the letter book. Two poems at the front strongly imply that it was prepared at a time when Paget was in disgrace and excluded from public office. One poem is in English on the wisdom of treating people well when one's fortune is at its zenith so that the turning of the wheel of fortune will not find one with many enemies; the other, in Latin, shows clear signs of its classical model and relates the greater joys of domestic as opposed to public life.

It is unlikely that Paget needed the letter book to justify his actions at the time of the overthrow of Somerset. On this occasion the Council sought to restore harmony as quickly as possible with Somerset himself returning to the Council board early in 1550. Paget

[1] Mr P. I. King, archivist at the Northamptonshire Record Office, was kind enough to provide this information.

faced a greater crisis when Somerset fell for the second time in 1551 and was subsequently executed for conspiracy. One of the key witnesses at Somerset's trial deponed that the place of conspiracy was Paget's house in London. Another witness against Somerset was Sir Thomas Palmer, a man for whom Paget claimed great affection. Whether Sir Thomas was related to the Palmer who married Paget's daughter is uncertain because of the multiplicity of Palmers at this time. In any case it would be no more reasonable to take this as evidence of Paget's complicity than it would be to assume that he was involved in Wyatt's rebellion in 1554 because another son-in-law, Sir Henry Lee, was Wyatt's nephew. Paget was himself imprisoned on a different charge, and so far as can be seen no attempt was made to implicate him directly in Somerset's fall. Moreover, the charges against Somerset were concerned with the alleged plot to overthrow Northumberland, and no mention was made of Somerset's fall in 1549. A collection of letters designed to provide a defence—if that is the purpose—against the accusation that Paget had earlier been the mind behind Somerset's actions, designed in fact to prove that Paget's advice fell on deaf ears and that he was himself suspected by Somerset, seems inappropriate at this point.

After 1552 Paget faced no similar crises. He was among the first of the signatories of Edward's devise for the succession to declare support for Queen Mary. In any event Mary would have had little interest in Paget's activities during Somerset's protectorate. The possibility remains that the letter book was prepared for some less urgent situation than that of 1551–2 or that it was compiled as a protective or defensive measure for actions that were never called into question. Throughout his long career, Paget was quick to protect his honour and justify his political and diplomatic decisions. His later correspondence was often written with a view towards defending his reputation, and at the beginning of Elizabeth's reign he drew up an outline justifying his conduct toward Lord Clinton, the lord admiral.

More crucial than establishing the reasons for the compilation of the letter book perhaps is the need to determine how selective Paget was in choosing letters for inclusion. Letters dated 1549 are heavily represented, though several letters to Somerset of that year are not included. The problem is to ascertain how frequently Paget would have needed to write major policy letters to Somerset before that year, since minor letters of routine might legitimately be excluded. One may assume that when the two men were together Paget would deliver his advice verbally rather than on paper, except in particular circumstances such as those surrounding the 'overthrow of horsemen' (no. 7) and the 'schedule or glass' (no. 12). Paget was absent in

Staffordshire for about a month in April 1547, and for a similar period on one or two other occasions. Whether these absences produced letters of significance is impossible to judge as there is no independent evidence that any were written. The letter of 30 August 1547 (no. 3), however, written to Somerset when he was away fighting against Scotland while affairs in London were in Paget's hands, is independently attested by both the French and Spanish ambassadors, while the 'glass' is referred to by Paget in an original letter dated before Somerset's first fall. It was apparently only at the end of 1548 that Paget found it necessary to write Somerset letters when the two could have seen one another face to face, and it seems reasonable to explain this as much by a deterioration both in the political situation and in the relationship between the two men as by any conscious censoring of earlier correspondence. The survival of the minutes of two of the letters among the Anglesey manuscripts, and of separate copies of other individual letters among the State Papers and elsewhere, which, judging from minor textual differences, were almost certainly not copied from the letter book, is evidence enough both of the authenticity of the letters and, in the case of the copies, of the fact that from the start the letters attracted some contemporary attention. Moreover, when the letter book was compiled, it would probably have been possible to find the originals among Somerset's correspondence. The collection as a whole does not appear to have circulated widely as there appear to be no copies or partial copies of the whole in the collections or works of antiquaries who were only too eager for letters of this sort. In short, much editing seems unlikely.

As a diplomat, Paget wrote to some of the most prominent men in Europe, but unfortunately few of the original letters have survived. On the other hand, it appears from surviving indications that Paget was careful to preserve copies of his own letters. On more than one occasion, both in the letters here printed and in those from the reign of Henry VIII, he asked, quite urgently, for a copy to be made or sent back to him of a letter that he had dispatched without retaining a copy of it. Although it is rare to possess his letters in a whole range of forms, there are interesting exceptions from his embassy of June–July 1549. The minutes of these letters are in BM, Cotton MS, Galba B. xii, and the originals among the State Papers Foreign. In addition we have the fragmentary letter book in Cotton MS, Titus B. v. The letters were also entered in an abbreviated form in Sir Philip Hoby's original letter book, also in Galba B. xii, and soon after copied with various other correspondence kept by Hoby into another volume, Harl. MS 523. At some later stage, after the last letters of the embassy had been lost from the state paper collections, a further copy was made from the original letters then surviving, which is now in BM, Add. MS 5935.

This abundance is not repeated for the negotiations of Paget, Bedford, Petre, and Mason with the French between January and March 1550. No original correspondence has survived among the State Papers, and Paget's letter book, Cotton MS Caligula E. iv, is badly damaged, apparently as a result of the Cottonian fire. The letter book is also incomplete, for it contains only 18 items of at least 26 indicated by the numbering scheme at the end of each letter entered. Professor W. K. Jordan gives the misleading impression that Paget reported only to the earl of Warwick, when, in fact, Paget and his colleagues wrote to the whole Council.[1] The instructions from the Council contained in the letter book, but omitted from this edition, contain the names of Cranmer, Rich, Northampton, Wiltshire, Dorset, and Southampton as well as Warwick. There is one letter from Warwick alone to Paget which is included in the Appendix. The text of this letter demonstrates clearly that Paget and his colleagues negotiated under the direction of the Council. In addition to the Caligula E. iv letter book, there are two other letters from Paget to Warwick pertaining to the French negotiations. One, a copy (no. 55), is in BM, Lansd. MS 2, printed by Strype and widely quoted; the other (no. 58) is a minute in the Anglesey manuscripts.

For the diplomatic mission under Queen Mary, we are even less well served, as letter books, if made, have not survived. For the negotiations at Marcq in 1555 there is only the badly damaged diary (no. 71) in BM, Cotton MS Titus B. v, which fortunately may be supplemented by other sources examined by E. H. Harbison in *Rival Ambassadors at the Court of Queen Mary* (Princeton, 1940). For other missions the one or two surviving original letters or drafts are unlikely to constitute the entire correspondence. Apart from the diplomatic letter books mentioned above, one very long and complete book for the embassy of 1544 during the reign of Henry VIII survives at Gonville and Caius College, Cambridge. The existence of the letter books indicates that Paget, in common with most of his diplomatic colleagues, had his diplomatic correspondence both outwards and inwards copied by one of his clerks.

Among the other items included in this edition are letters and papers showing Paget's interest in rather specialized aspects of governmental administration. The letters from the Duchy of Lancaster records offer a brief glimpse of his work as chancellor but nothing more, and his five-year tenure in that office consequently

---

[1] *Edward VI: The Threshold of Power*, p. 121.

remains largely unexplored. The paper of 1550 dealing with the conduct of business in the Privy Council may be seen as a natural outgrowth of his concern with the concentration of power in the hands of Protector Somerset. The undated papers from the reign of Mary concerned with the repeal of Reformation statutes, and the privileges of the Hanse merchants call for careful study, but clearly underscore Paget's continuing participation in policy-making at the highest level. After the accession of Elizabeth, his correspondence is that of an elder statesman offering helpful, but perhaps unsolicited, advice on monetary and diplomatic matters. His last letter, sent to Archbishop Matthew Parker and signed with a shaky hand requesting favour in securing a minor ecclesiastical position for a protégé— a request that proved unsuccessful—is a sad finale.

Of the surviving letters the greatest number are addressed to Somerset, a total of twenty-three letters and papers between 1547 and 1549, though it is striking that not a single letter has survived from the period following his deposition as lord protector. After Somerset the next greatest number are addressed to Sir William Petre, Sir William Cecil, and Simon Renard, the Imperial ambassador. The letters to Cecil fall into two groups, one in 1551 when Paget's career was in danger, and another after the accession of Elizabeth. No letters to Edward VI, Thomas Cranmer, or any other Protestant reformer have survived. During the reign of Mary there are no extant letters to either Reginald Pole or Stephen Gardiner. Hardly any of Paget's surviving correspondence concerns his family though he makes reference to them in his diplomatic correspondence in terms of affectionate anxiety.

III. *Editorial Procedure*

In the preparation of the text the editors have followed the 'Report on Editing Historical Documents', published in the *Bulletin of the Institute of Historical Research*, i (1923), pp. 6–25. In keeping with these guidelines, the original spelling has been preserved, abbreviations have been extended, and capitals have been introduced according to modern practice. Some modern punctuation has been added, and the full stop, semi-colon, or comma have been used in place of the *virgula*. The sentences themselves, however, have not been shortened but retain the loose flowing style characteristic of the period. Lacunae of uncertain length are indicated by dots. Badly damaged letters have been printed to retain the original wording in each line so that the reader may note how much has been lost along the left and right hand margins. Where more than one copy of a letter survives the important variations have been noted, but insignificant ones have not. The letters have been arranged in chronological order with undated ones placed at the end of the year in which they seem most likely to have been written. The complete text is printed only when the letter has never appeared in print; all others are briefly calendared with references to the printed text.

The editors are grateful to the Marquess of Anglesey and the Marquess of Salisbury for permitting materials from their archives to be included. They are also grateful to the Trustees of the British Museum, the Northamptonshire Record Office and Corpus Christi College, Cambridge, for permission to print documents in their custody. Professor S. T. Bindoff made helpful suggestions for locating Paget letters. Professor I. R. Christie, Mr Christopher Harrison, Mr Peter King, and Mr K. V. Thomas have given assistance that is deeply appreciated. Barrett Beer wishes to thank Professor C. V. Graves and acknowledge grants from the American Philosophical Society and Kent State University. Sybil Jack wishes to thank the University of Sydney for a vacation travel grant.

1. *To Stephen Gardiner, Bishop of Winchester. Westminster. 2 March,*
1546–7.
(SP 10/1, no. 53; modernized text printed in Tytler, i, pp. 24–6.)

Thanks Gardiner for advice in his letter and defends himself against
accusations that he abuses his power. Wishes that bishops and
others might be well ordered and that Gardiner would agree to such
reformation of the estate as might be decided on. Will grant Gardiner's
commission in as ample manner as he has authority.

2. *To John Dudley, Earl of Warwick. Drayton. 22 July, 1547.*
(E 315/475, fo. 52ᵣ.)

It may lyke your good lordship with my most harty commendacions
and the semblable to my good lady your wief to vnderstand that I
am sory I haue not the commodite to satisfye your desyre in your
lettre sent to me by this berar so sone as I woold, for both my lord
protectors grace is absent at London, and I here at Draiton also
absent from the court by reason of the meseles wherwith all my
house is troubled one after another. Nevertheless I think to se my
lordes grace shortly and then to do what lyith in me for the satis-
facton of your lordships desyre which semyth to me not vnreason-
able. Touching your lordships diettes I sayd asmochas I might conveniently. Wheras at the first there was appoynted but v markes
which was to litle and in dede v *li* had bene to the full howbeit your
lordship can wisely shape your cote by your clothe. Elys your man
may tary sumtyme after your lordships departing with whom it may
lyke you to leave your commission and I will see if I can procure
another to be by hym sent after you and hym self also holpen in
sum what to his contentacion or eles I shal want of my wil. Wherof
I wilbe loth eyther in these thinges or any other wherin I might do
you service or pleasure as God knowyth who send you helth with
increase of as moche honor as I wish your lordship. From my cotage
at Drayton the xxij th of July 1547.

Your lordships most assured to commaund
William Paget

3. *To Edward Seymour, Duke of Somerset. No place. 30 August,*
1547. (PLB)

It maye lyke your grace to be aduertised that this daye after the
French embassade[1] had ended with my lordes of the counsaill he
desired to speake with me aparte in my chambre, and there firste
openinge vnto me what had passed lately betwene your grace and
him, concerninge the greate practise for Bulloygne, in suche sorte
poynt for poynt as your grace declared to me and how yow had
ordeyned him to open to me what he shuld further do therein. He
sayd that the constable[2] had willed him to saye vnto me with greate
request for contynuaunce of my good will to thamitie that he was
mervailous glad to here that your grace was so well enclyned to the
devise of suche meanes as might take awaye the suspicions that were
risen betwene bothe the princes in eche one towardes thothers
doinges and that if it shold lyke your grace to worke any thinge
therein, youe shuld fynd him such a mynistre, and of so syncere and
good faith and dealinge to bring the thinge to the desired effecte as
your grace was never matched with in a semblable case. Affirminge
to me also that I shuld fynd the lyke of him in the same practise,
and that he wold be gladde to mete with your grace with all his harte.
Mary, before two such personages shuld convene, it shuld do well
the matter were first somewhat disgrossed to thintent there might
firste appere what successe were lyke to ensue leste not findinge
thoverture agreable either to thone or thother and departinge without agrement both dishonour might folowe to bothe the personages
and also further inconvenience. And therfore seinge your grace
thought yt good that thambassador shuld open to him the communication which passed by your grace in that behalfe he trusteth
that to so godly a beginninge your grace will geve a further perfection and signifie vnto him your opinion for the meanes which
youe thincke wold sette bothe your masters in establishement of
amitie voyd of all jelousie. To this I declared what good wille your
grace had borne always to thamitie of Fraunce, and that I myselfe
beringe no lesse affection had in the kinges dayes that dead ys great
experience therof. And here we felle into a longe disgression of the
love that was betwene oure late two masters and of there proceadinges together and so returninge to oure purpose sayd that I
doubted not but that your grace wold endevoir your selfe muche to
do what soever youe might with preservacion of your duetie to the

[1] Odet de Selve, French ambassador to England, 1546–8. For de Selve's version
of this interview see *Correspondance Politique de Odet de Selve*, ed. G. Lefèvre-
Pontalis (Paris, 1888), nos. 216–18.
[2] Anne de Montmorency.

kinges maiestie your master that might confirme the amitie betwene his maiestie and the Frenche kinge. Of any devise your grace had thought vpon I said I knewe not, but rather loked (I supposed) the devise shuld procede from them and that as he sayd before any metinge. For that we, contentinge oure selfes with suche agrementes as was passed, sought no newe, and they, sekinge quereles to breake that which they sayde at the firste they wold observe, went aboute to have alteracions and newe compositions. Wherfore I sayd they shuld do well before any suche metinge shuld be to breake the matter and as they (like woers) saye thaye wold have this so to tell vs howe we maye do it with honour. To this he aunswered after longe discourses of the conestables good affection to this amitie and greate desire to lyve in peax and what greate benefite shuld ensue to all Christendome yf all thinges were well compounded. Repetinge also the procedinges of Montio[1] whome the conestable had nowe cut of and referred the hole matter to hys mayninge that the conestable desired your grace seing youe had geven so good an entre and that he persuaded him selfe that your grace had not entred the purpose to blere his eyes and to wynne tyme but of an onely good will and godly mynd meaninge that it would like your grace to go further, and to let him knowe your devise for the conducinge the same to good further effecte. And that I wold signifie thus moche vnto your grace, and let him knowe your pleasure therin. I sayd that I could not thynke that your grace had alreadie devised any thinge. Howbeit I wold aduertise your grace, and of your aunswere advertise him agayn accordingly. I send to your grace herewith suche lettres as I have lately receaved from Brewno[2] and the governour of the merchauntes.[3] It may like your grace also tunderstand that we have devided our selfes here into two bandes in suche sorte as in a scedule hereinclosed maye appere to your grace and have appointed that one band shall wayte contynually one weke and the other band the other weke and vpon Sondayes to be alwais together at the courte whereof I thought good to aduertise your grace and havinge written thus farre both of this lettre and of the other from the counsaill well nere at ende (for that Master Secretary [4]is some what diseased). Themperors embassades secretary[5] arryved with me to aske audience for his master which was then accorded by my lordes to be to morowe in the morning.

[1] Ludovic de Monts, agent used by the German princes.

[2] Probably Dr Hans Bruno, a German protestant agent in England.

[3] Merchant Adventurers.

[4] Sir William Petre.

[5] Secretary to Van der Delft, who was recalled in May, 1550 and died later that year.

Wherfore your grace shalbe enformed more at large in the counsayles lettre. And thus &c xxx *Augusti.*

W. P.

4. *To Somerset. No place. 2 February 1547–8.*
   (*PLB*)

A remembraunce to the duke of Somerset at Candelmas. 1547

Fyrste yt maye lyke your grace to calle for a declaration certayne of your debte to all your garrisons at this present and to considre what thordinarye charges of them betwene this and Christmas wilbe.

Item vpon the vieu aforesayde findinge (as certaynely your grace shall) your revenewe shorte for the satisfaction of your garrisons which in tyme of warre must nedes be payed or ells besydes their discouraginge other inconvenience maye growe to forse and provide with diligence the supplement of the wante and that assuredly to thintent youe maye knowe whereunto to truste.

Item to calle vpon the certayne victuallinge (and in that poynte also to knowe the very state) your selfe as nere as maye be of all your peces aswell on thother syde the seas as in Scotland.

Item yt maye like your grace for the loue of God to waie what dishonour besides daungier shuld ensue yf any the peces which youe now haue or shall take a freshe in hande nowe to fortefie in Scotlande shuld be loste agayne, and therfore seinge the Frenche men sende no small ayde to them, and that the time of the yere for to begynne to fortefie ys farre onwarde, and but two monethes at the moste lefte for that purpose (for your grace seethe now adaies thinges enterprised by prynces and at suche times as excedeth the common expectacion of the world). I besech your grace for Goddes sake to passe ouer this sommer with out newe fortificacions and by your good wisedome and experience to appoynte suche a nombre of horsemen and footemen to serve for the northe, as maye be hable to defende your owne and helpe to kepe that youe haue taken in Scotlande, which shall sounde more to the kinges maiesties honour and your owne, then if buyldinge tenne fortresses youe shuld fortune vpon the commynge of Fraunce to lose but one, and in stede of fortifications to waste the countrey before youe to your enemies handes.

Item to appointe to everie quarter of the realme suche personages as youe thincke mete to haue the staie of the countreys and to sende home suche of them as be absent from thence.

Item besides those horsemen that your grace will pike out to be sent northeward to take a vieu and give commaundement for the same with what horsemen and footemen euery man of the counsaill and of the chambre with the reste of the courte and suche other officers and men of reputacion nere at hand shalbe readie to serue either about ye kinges maiesties person or to be sent to any place for relief vpon any soddaine of thennemye.

Item to cause my lorde admirall[1] to geve ordre for the description of two or thre thousand mariners I meane not to geve them any preste but to cause a vieu to be taken of so many and byllinge their names in writinge to charge them not to be out of the waie and a like description to be made of a like nombre of souldiers in suche places as where they maye be best taken to furnishe the shyppes.

Item to dispatche Master Bellingham[2] and Master Aleyn[3] into Irelond.

Item to set forthe the proclamation for the callinge in agayne of the testornes.

Item to appointe the nombre of learned men as well for the consideracion of the lawes which are to be contynued and which abrogated as also for the decent ordres to be observed in the churche and stayenge all thinges vnto the parliament tyme, then with advise and consent of the bodye of the realme and the learned men, to contynewe or alter suche thinges as vpon great and depe consideracion and foresight shalbe thought convenient, and agreable bothe to Goddes lawe and to preservacion of the pollicie of the realme and this shalbe my lorde beste for your graces discharge bothe towardes God, the kinge, and the realme. And otherwaies be vncertayne subdayne and daungerous, to youe and yours, and God knoweth to what confusion of thinges. And thus I doubt not but your grace, waienge my vnfayned faithfull harte vnto yow, will take yt in good parte.

W. P.

5. *Sir William Paget and Sir Thomas Smith to the Vice-Chancellor [Matthew Parker] and the University of Cambridge. London. 21 February, 1547–8.*
(*Corpus Christi College, Cambridge, MS 106, no. 86. Latin. Text printed in* A Collection of Letters, Statutes, and Other Documents from the MS Library of Corpus Christi College, *ed. John Lamb (London, 1838), pp. 89–90.*)

Paget and Smith are to act as umpires in a dispute between the university and town.

[1] Thomas, Lord Seymour of Sudeley, brother of Somerset.
[2] William Bellingham, lord deputy of Ireland.
[3] Sir John Aleyn or Alen, chancellor of Ireland.

6. [*To an English Prisoner in Scotland*] *No place*, [*July 1548*]
   (*BM, Cotton MS, Caligula E. iii, fo. 63ʳ*).

................you must say to hym[1]......................
...uppon the good wil you haue to the.........................
....how it commyth to passe, that thinges ha...................
these extremites. For the king that ded is bare special.............
and to the bishop and so did and doth my lord protector...........
here as can do most and the rather for that we................
Goddes word and that hering how they had abandoned th.........
doubting that (which is chaunced) God woold therfor.............
sore. And here must you take occasion to set....................
they haue susteyned at our handes what domage.................
of ayde and frendship hath done them and what litle..............
to haue for it. Remembre the bishop of Dunkes[2] (who hath bene
    in F........
of it) that the French set not by them lengre then servith for the.....
it doth appere in all thinges to euery Scotyshman that hath bene.....
appere playnly in a gret matter, for the French king that...........
of the late king our Master made a new league with vs leaving
    the Sco...
knowyng that by vertue of the furst treaty of peax we............
for not comprehended and did refuse to receyve the Scottes.......
in certain and vnsure comprehension, that the French made then...
they promise the gouernor a dukedom in France but what effect..
length he is lyke to fynd to his gret detriment if he prove it....
you may say that the French kyng can gyve no duchy in Fraunce....
of lyfe so as his sone may pipe for it, but you thynk verrly.....
knoweledge god and his trowth he woold set sum good way be-
    tween.........
doubt not but if the gouernor and the bishop woold cum to appoynte-
    ment.........
be not so far past but they myght be redubbed, the gouernor and....
theyre bloode haue as gret credit and authorite with vs as ever...
and be aswell provided for, and here set forth the coniunction
    of our......
of one language, the similitude of our natures the lyklyhood......
fynal agrement, the pryde of the French, the syrvitude they......
them theyr wiefes and chyldern in for ever, thexperience alredy....
therof; eftesones repeting to them the state of the realme at this
    ......

---

[1] Arran, then governor of Scotland.
[2] John Hamilton, bishop of Dunkeld, Arran's brother.

contynuyng in enemite with vs can not but daily wax worse and
......
thus and by all other good ways you can, vse a dexterite to move
......
and the bishop to ioyne with vs. Declare the good nature of my
    lord.......
who vndoubtedly wil vse them honorably how moch it grieues
....
make warre vppon them and how he lamentith sum tyme that
    for......
to themselfes no honor to the realme nor profittes to theyrs but for
    th......
pleasyr of others, willingly as it wer they ar contented to
. . . hamed dishonored, and destroyed. And thus I say you sr devise to
bring . . . to talke with vs and to cum to an accord and offre your
    self to be a worker if they . . . .
herin and of your procedinges herin aduertise by your next lettre a
    part and also who. .
of the thre they wil desyre for you, whervppon further may be sayd
    and done. . .
as the case shall requyre.

Yours William Paget

he that callith youe nephew commendeth him to you and to your
    frend
and so doth. . . .

7. *To Somerset. No place. n.d.* [*July, 1548.*[1]] (*PLB; another copy,
BM, Cotton MS, Titus F. iii, fo. 273ʳ.*)

To the Duke of Somerset when the overthrowe was of horsemen
in Scotland and when Sir Thomas Palmer was taken.

Sir, I beseche your grace moste humbly to pardon my departinge
from yow this night which all thinges consydered I shuld not have
done. But I assure yowr grace my harte was and ys so greate for
the losse of Sir Thomas Palmer that I shuld rather have troubled
your grace then otherwise. I loved the man in particuler frendshippe
which had beginninge of his aptenesse to serve the kinges maiestie.
But the losse of him for the service of his maiestie greveth me moste,
and the rather for that I knowinge his nature, courage and his
desire to please youe, and to be suche as neded no spurre to serve.
We have provoked him to muche forward with lettres accusinge his

---

[1] *Cf.* Jordan, *Edward VI: The Young King*, pp. 285–6.

stillness, slackenes and slepinge, without doinge any thinge. But Sir, for Goddes sake let us never pricke the sturringe horse more then nedeth from henceforthe and thincke, Sir, that yow supplie the place of a kinge and to every wise manne every lettre, every word, every countenance of yours, ys enoughe to cause the dulle horse to entre the fire, and the quicke horse to be to busie. Sir, yow are nowe not the Earle of Hertford, nor the Duke of Somerset, but governour of the kinges parson, and protector of his realmes and subiectes, and even so waye althinge in your selfe, and remember by tymes paste, how the wordes of a kinge or cardinall might haue moved youe and so thincke yours move other men. I beseche your grace to pardon me, youe knowe my trewe harte and meaninge to your grace. Sir, yt maye like youe to write vnto my Lorde Graye[1] some wordes of comeforte for him selfe, to whom in his lettre bemoninge him to your grace, I remember not that youe wrate any comfort for him and the man ys somewhat to be comforted with good wordes. I am lothe toffend your grace, glad to please youe, and desirous to tell youe the trouth, because I beleue yow trust me.

W. P.

8. *No addressee. The court. 24 July, 1548.*
   (*DL 42/135, fo. 124ʳ.*)

After hartye commendacions forasmuche as youe enforme me that there are certayn poure peple at Pountfret[2] wiche are not paid there lyuyngs syns the reuenewes came to the kynges handes accordingynge to the fundacion thes shalbe to requyre youe to content euery of them for asmuche as ys all redie due vntyll further order be taken for the contynuaunce therof, from the Court xxiiij July 1548.[3]

Your louynge frend
William Paget

9. *No addressee. Drayton. 21 September, 1548.*
   (*DL 42/135, fos. 124ʳ–124ᵛ.*)

Begins: After my ryght hartie commendacions vnto youe. Theis shalbe to requyre youe to contente and paye or cause to be contented and paide yerly duryng their lyves to the persons herafter named that ys to saie to William Dene nowe incumbent within the

---

[1] William Grey, Lord Grey de Wilton.
[2] Pontefract, Yorks.
[3] *Cf.* Robert Somerville, *History of the Duchy of Lancaster* (London, 1953), i, p. 299.

chappell of Arkendale within the paryshe of **Knaresborough** to do syruice there...xij *s*. xj *d*.

A list of similar entries follows.

10. *No addressee. No place. 26 November, 1548.*
  (*DL 42/135, fo. 58*ʳ*.*)

After my hertie commendacions for asmoche as Sir William Pentith as nowe of late appoynted to be vycar of Manchestre with the stypende of xx *li* and Sir Lawrence Vawse and Sir William Willson to be assistauntes vnto the said vycar wyth the seuerall wages of viij *li*, these shalbe therfore to requyre you to content and paye vnto euery of theym theire seuerall stipendes and wages begynnynge from Ester laste paste, and wheras I vnderstonde there is a pencion of vij *li* assignede vnto the said Wilson by patent and is all redie paid of parte therof, by force of the same, I will you that you resume the said patent into your handes and to delyuer the same into the Corte the next terme to be cancelled and to paye hym from hensforthe after the rate of viij *li* having respect (if yt be trewe) to that whiche he haith all redye receyvid and theise my lettres shalbe vnto you a sufficient warraunte all oder orders taken or lettres hertofore addressed for this purpose to the contrary notwith-standinge. Wrytten the xxvi th of Nouembre, 1548.

Youre frend
William Pagett

11. *To Somerset. No place. 25 December, 1548.*
  (*PLB; modernized text printed by B. L. Beer in* Huntington Library Quarterly, *xxxiv* (*May, 1971*), *pp. 277–83.*)

Believes Somerset has erred by attempting to please all men and has been lax in the administration of justice. Under Henry VIII men feared to speak though the meaning were not evil; now every man has the liberty to speak without danger. Laments war with Scotland and France. Recommends appointment of able officials including Sir Walter Mildmay and Sir Anthony Aucher. Hopes Somerset will not think him presumptuous or rash, for he has great affection and devotion.

12. *To Somerset. Westminster. 2 January, 1548–9.*
  (*PLB; another copy in BM, Cotton MS, Titus F. iii, fo. 273*ʳ*.*)

Because the determinacion to renewe giftes of the newe yere was sodayn I cold not prepare suche a newe yeres gifte for your **grace** as the fashion of the world required me to present to a personage of your estate, and yet consideringe the favour of your grace to be speciall towardes me, and my love the reciproque towardes youe, me thought it beste to sende your grace thoughe no riche gyfte yet a token of my herte which wishethe both this and all other yeres hereafter happie and luckye vnto youe. My token is this scedule here inclosed, wherein as in a glasse if your grace will dayly loke, and by yt youe readye youe shall so well apparell your selfe as eche man shall delight to behold youe. I praye your grace taccepte this token in good parte, which very hartie love and greate carefullnes of your graces well doinges hathe moved me to send unto your grace to whome I wishe as well as I do to myne owne soule.

From Westminster etc, W. P.

The Scedule

Delyberate maturely[1] in all thinges. Execute quickely the delyberations.[2] Do justice without respecte. Make assured and stayde wise men ministers vnder youe. Mainteyne the ministers in their offices. Punishe the disobedient accordinge to their desertes. In the kinges causes geve commission in the kinges name. Rewarde the kinges worthye servauntes liberally and quyckely. Geve your owne to your owne, and the kinges to the kinges franckelie. Dispatche suters shortelye. Be affable to the good, and sterne to the evell. Folowe aduise in counsaile. Take fee or rewarde of the kinge onelie. Kepe your ministres about youe vncorrupte. Thus God will prosper yow, the kinge favour youe, and all men love youe.

W. P.

13. *To Somerset. My chamber. 24 January, 1548-9.*
   (PLB.)

Sir, I beseche your grace to calle to remembraunce how that youe have bene moved diuerse tymes, not onelie by me but also by sondry others of the counsaill to send to discipher thempereur which your grace hath consented to be a thinge necessarye and yet haue semed to differ yt for want of good occasion and oportunitie to put the same in vre. Now Sir, vpon thys chaunce of staye of your shyppes, and also of this your proceadinges with thadmirall beside your determinacions for the yere to come youe haue so good occasion as youe shall never have bettre. Sir, occasion ys bawld behind, yf youe take not hold before, youe shall not after, when your grace wold.

---

[1] Titus F. iii has 'naturaly'.   [2] Titus F. iii has 'determynacions'.

For Goddes sake, Sir, followe thinges when tyme requireth and whiles tyme serveth. I see your grace myche trobled, for the which I am sorye, and therfore I amongest others thincke yt my duetie to put your grace in remembraunce of things necessary to be done, beechinge your grace when yow are put in remembraunce of them to waye whether the thinges be mete to be done or no, and if youe thincke them so mete, then to folowe the remembraunces and do the same without delaye, or at the leste not to forgette an other tyme that your pore frendes haue discharged their dueties towardes youe for your better procedinge in the kinges maiestes service. God send your grace to do as well as I wishe unto your grace. From my chambre &c.

W. P.

14. *To Somerset. No place. 25 January, 1548–9.*
   (PLB.)

A Memoriall to the Duke of Somerset xxvth of January, 1548

To remembre the makinge of the decre and other ordres for the committinge of thadmirall and his complices and your other procedinges against the same.

The depeche for Bulloygne and to appoint who shall go in lieu of thadmirall and to knowe of my lorde greate master[1] how farre forthe he is for money.

The depeche for the northe, and to resolve determinately who shall go thyder, and who shall tarye there, and to considre the state of your vitualls there what nombre of men yow shall have there of all sortes and what nombre yow will have there vppon any occasion more or lesse, and to geve ordre for description of the same, and to consider also your estate for money.

To resolve for the ordringe of your navie in cases.

To provide by espialls or otherwise by your embassadours for knowledge of the procedinges of Fraunce.

To resolve vpon your procedinges in the parliament for money out of hand for the tyme goeth awaye and yt had bene meter to have bene nowe in levienge of yt then about to aske yt.

To geve ordre for the staye of belles, leade, and other ornamentes, and goodes of churches which the people make awaye apase.

To aunswer the fyrste request of the comyns for the sherifes and thexchetours cases &c.

[1] William Paulet, Viscount St John; later earl of Wiltshire and marquess of Winchester.

To send out commissions for the visitacion of hospitalls, cathedrall churches, and vniversities.

To geve ordre for the spedie printinge and settinge forth of the service with speciall charge to see yt trewly printed.

A generall pardon.

15. *Interrogatives for the Lord Admiral. No place. [January, 1548–9.]* *(Cecil MSS, vol. 150, fos. 58ʳ–58ᵛ; modernized text printed in Haynes, pp. 86–7.)*

A series of queries concerning the lord admiral's actions and confederates.

Whether he had 'comoned' with any persons concerning an alteration of the order of the person of the King and of his council? What are the names of those with whom he conferred?

What letters has he received since the late King's death?

Whether he has talked with anyone concerning the marriage of any of the King's sisters?

Whether he reported to anyone before his accusation that he knew he was accused?

16. *To Somerset. The court. 2 February, 1548–9. (PLB.)*

Sir, my very duetie to God the kinge and the realme, knytte with a moste perfect and sincere love to your grace, moveth me so myche that I can not forbeare to wryte to your grace my conscience and poore opinion for your procedinges at this tyme, beseching your grace moste humbly and with all my harte, and for the very selfe same thinges sake that maketh me thus to write, to waye and ponder my wrytinge agayne and agayn; and make me not to be a Cassandra, that is to saie, one that told the trouthe of daungers before and was not beleved, sory wold I be to lyve to be suche a one. But your grace maye do myche that I be not such a one. And now, Sir, lyfte vp, lyfte vp the eyes of your herte, and loke in what termes and in what compases yow stande, and loke not nere at hande onely but also aloofe and farre of and to this your grace muste vse bothe your wisedome and foresighte; and where force will not serve or is not hable, there to vse wisedome and pollicie. Theffectes thereof as they seme to be uncertayne (and so they be indede) for no man knoweth the sequele of his advise or counsayll certaynly. So yet the consideracion and conference of thinges paste of theim, that are to come geveth a light of lykelyhod and maketh a reason for some knowledge for the sequele of that hereafter which we do presently debate, and almoste by none other meanes are we able to judge of thinges to come. First your grace seith youe are in playne warre with the Scottes, and even ready to enter the same with the French. There is cause to doubte themperour abrode and lykewyse some of your owne at home, this your grace seith at hand. Nowe maye it please your grace to loke farre from yow. I meane what will happen hereof if foresighte be not vsed: Mary, daungier wonderfull to the kinges maieste; certayn and vndoubted ruyne and destruction to the hole realme and to your selfe ioyned with an infamy. What reamedye? Let vs see what our force ys. Furste we have no money at all to speake of in a kinges case. No, but youe saye we shall nowe have yt of the subiectes. But if thempereur jarre with youe there can be none levied. For the merchaunt shall haue no vent, the clothier shall haue no vent, nor your shepemaster no vent of his wolle. No, it maye be sayd, yet will every trewe man in case of nede helpe with all that he hath for defence of the realme. I knowe no man but trewe. But yet I thincke all men though they be trewe, be not throughly wise and able to vnderstand and waye his duetie, and that which semeth to one man well, maye seme to an other evell. But lette vs yet consydre whether (that if all men at home wold consente in one) our force were of yt selfe without helpe from other partes sufficient to withstand Scotland, Fraunce, thempereur and the Romyshe, but if thempereur do square with vs, yt is good to se whether here at home some thinckinge yt to be for religion, will peraduenture thincke yt also their duetie for suerty of the kinge and the realme to take his parte, and then your force at home ys to weake, and abroad consider your grace what helpe youe shall have. If youe saye in Almayne, I aske from whome there. The Langrave Fredericke of Saxone, the duke of Wirtemberge, the countie Palantyne, be as prisoners to thempereur, Morice of Saxony, the dukes of Bauiere and marques of Brandenburge be firmelie knit with thempereur, and so is also Denmarke. Pruse ys pore. The cities marytine be pore and afrayd, and the kinge of Poole[1] ys to farre of, and but newlie come into his kingedome, and not yet fully established. If yt be said yet, for religion they will joyne with youe, I answere that thoughe the kinge of Poole be farre of, and therfore (thoughe he had his kingdome vnited with hym wholly, as he hath not, but is therin in the same case and worse then we be, and hath also the Muscovites at his backe to troble him daylye) can do us no good at all. Yet myght we for religions sake make a good partie with some of thalmayns yf we had good store of money, without the which they

[1] *i.e.* Poland.

neyther wyll (and that experience of tymes paste teacheth vs when they were in felicitie) nor nowe are able for their pouertie and infelicitie. And though there were such a league for religion, yet your grace knoweth that thempereur can devise some other cause to falle out (when he lyste) to stoppe theyr mouthes abrode, and nevertheles some here at home will thincke yt to be (and in dede their is none other cause) for cause of religion. All which thinges layde together I conclude to my symple vnderstandinge (remyttinge the same to the better judgement of your grace) youe are not able with your owne force onely, nor with your owne force nor any other that youe can have abrode, withstand the imminent and present daungiers. What then saythe your grace all in desperacion? Nay, by St. Mary, Sir, but where strength fayleth assaye what arte wyll do, and remembre the old sayenge, 'It ys evill havinge of a lordes harte and a beggers purse togethers', and beware of the old sayenge, 'Yt is good beatinge of a proude horse'. Wherfore me thought yesternight your grace beganne to devise well to fayne frendeshippe with thempereur, to seme to yeld to hym, to dalye withe hym, to wynne tyme of hym, by puttynge him in hope that youe will geve eare to hym, and youe haue good meanes to do yt yet, for the thinges that hetherto youe have passed be but formes and facions of service and mynistracion of the sacramentes which ys and hath bene dyverse in dyverse ~~facions~~ places in Christ churche and ordered and altered as pleaseth the governours. So as there ys no cause why thempereur shold be in dede offended with this, yf the matter were well debated with hym. And therfore haue youe hereby (yf youe staie goinge further) good meanes to practyse with hym, and to enduce hym to thincke that as youe myght alter these ceremonyes from their former facion to this they be nowe at, so he maye fortune to enduce youe to alter them from this facion to that they were at before, and in the handelinge of this matter, tyme will passe yf yt be well handeled, and tyme bryngeth forthe many thinges. But by this meane (which is but one) and some other devises yt is possible to wynne a respyte to brethe and to make your selfe hable after to runne the better. It ys now onely arte, pollycie and practise must helpe (for these be the meanes in myne opynion) that God will nowe vse for our helpe. For as yt is trewe that sekinge fyrst the kingdome of God he wyll furnishe vs of all thinges, so yt is trewe that sithens the beginninge yt hathe pleased God to do his thinges by meanes, and the olde proverbe ys not for nought which sayeth, 'Youe maie lye longe ynough in the dytche or God will helpe youe yf youe helpe not your selfe'. As sone as the parliament ys done, sende some notable man Northeward, an other into the Marches, an other into Kente, an other into

Suffolk and Norffolk, an other for Sussex and Wyllshyre, an other into the Weste, or ells some speciall gentleman to be spoken with all that shall reside in Cornewayle and Deuonshire. Let them be well enformed before their goinges in to the countreys of your advise, bothe for the staye of their countreys, and also for the levienge of the reliefe. Let proclamations be sente forthe, declaringe and settinge forthe the gratuities the kinge gevith nowe to his subiectes for their kindenes in releasinge the purveyours and the reste of the thinges. Sende forthe proclamations to staie the churche plate and belles, also commission to gentlemen for that purpose. Commissions also for musters, commaundementes also for the beakons, appoint Sir Edward Wotton (yf he be able to lie at London as I thincke he be aswell as at his house) and Sir Walter Myldemaye to assyste for the money matters. Do as myche as in your grace shall lye after the pardon to se the lawes executed without remission except it be for a very great consideracion. For so shall youe bringe in agayn obedience which nowe ys cleane gone, and therby your grace shalbe feared in the service of the kinge, the noblemen shall be regarded, and everie other man in his place abrode in the world reputed as he ought to be, wherby quyet shall ensue amonge oure selfes, and takinge all disputacions from vs other then by the lawes ys apointed or permytted, we shall no more saie thow papist and thoue heretique, for your lawe the laste yere for the sacrament, and this yere for the ceremonies will helpe moche the matter yf they be well executed. I maye seme to your grace bothe tedious and folyshe, but I beseche your grace to have respecte to the dewtie and love that moveth me thus to do, and for my sake and at myne humble requeste to loke sometyme vpon the glasse I sente your grace which can do youe no hurte yf it shall please youe to vse yt. And thus I leave besechinge the lyvinge God to directe your graces herte to do all thinges for his glorye, the honour of the kinges maieste and of your selfe, and to the benefite of the realme.

From the courte &c.

W. P.

17. *Minute of a letter from the Council to Princess Elizabeth. The court. 17 February, 1548–9.*
   (Cecil MSS, vol. 150, fo. 100ʳ; modernized text printed in Haynes, p. 107.)

Being informed that Lady Tyrwhit, who has replaced Katherine Ashley, has not been sufficiently attendant to her duties to the princess, the council has thought good to say to her 'rowndeley in that

C M—C

beholf'. Expects her to serve better. Asks the princess to accept Lady Tyrwhit's service thankfully and to follow her advice especially in such matters as the council has at this time appointed her to move to the princess.

18. *No addressee. Westminster. 10 March [probably 1548–9].*
   (DL 42/135, fo. 125ʳ.)

After hartie commendacions forasmuche as all the possessyons of the prebendes and vycars of Rypon are come vnto the kinges maiestie and vnderstandyng that ther ar contynued vj vicars and one chauntrie priest havyng cure wherfor the gretnes of the cure cannot well haue lesse then ther accustomed lyuynges which as I perceve was viij *li* to thend that they may more dylygently serue the said cure accordyng to ther duties, I haue thought goode to requyre youe to content and paye vnto them from tyme to tyme ther seuerall wages aboue said. And if eny of them ether refuse to serue the said cure or ells fortune to die that then ye place some other mete and able prest bying a pencioner to serue in that rome forseyng that my aduyse theryn be fyrst had and that his patent be ether surrendred in to the court or elles cancelled. And thes shalbe to youe a suffycyent warrant and discharg in that behalfe. And lykwyse to paie vnto euery suche clerk as hath and dothe serue the vicars ther accustomed wages borne by the colledge so that it exced not the yerly some of iij *li* from Westminster the x th daye of Marche.[1]

> Your louynge frend
> William Paget

19. *To Somerset. The court. 12 March, 1548–9.*
   (PLB; Anglesey MSS, vol. ii, fo. 3ʳ–3ᵛ.)

Sir, I beseche your grace moste humbly for Goddes sake to ende the parliament[2] to thintent yow maye provide for your owtwarde thinges in tyme, wherof youe haue great nede, and so myche as I never sawe in my tyme. All the noble men and others do desire yt, and for my parte I thincke yt had bene beste yf it had bene ended afore Christmas, for then your grace shulde haue had leasure in the dedde tyme of the yere (which is nowe paste in makinge actes not so necessarye, but they might haue bene differred till a more quiet

---

[1] *Cf.* Somerville, *History of the Duchy of Lancaster*, i, pp. 299, 301.
[2] The second session of the first parliament of Edward VI met from 24 November, 1548 until 14 March, 1549.

tyme) to provide for the thinges that shalbe nedefull in sommer. If your forrayne affayres shuld quayle, I meane in the northe and at Bulloygne, it wold be suche a corseye bothe to your grace and your pore frendes, and peraduenture suche a daungier to all the rest, as my harte bledes to thincke vpon, and vndoubtedly wold touche your graces credyt at home and the credyte of all the rest of the counsayle. If your grace aske what remedie, in as myche as a trobled wit can saye, I answere that furst your grace cause out of hand to ende the parliament, which bothe the houses saye, stayes onely vpon your graces pleasure. Next appoint freshe men to the money matters, for if youe do not your grace shall shortely se great[1] daungier followe. Let them certaynely make of the mynte, of the sales, of the admyralles, of Sheringtons[2] money and plate, and of the kinges plate comynge to the Tower, all the money they can possiblye, and make what shyfte they can devise for more, by which I thincke yf wise men maye haue the handelinge, maye be made fourty thousand powndes. And in this case, Sir, and also for the sendinge of a speciall man northewardes your grace must not sticke to vse aucthoritie, thoughe some men will not peraduenture specially for the money matters be beste contented. But for Goddes sake, Sir, spare no man so the kinge maye be well served, and appointe men to serve that can serve what soeuer this man or that man abrode saye. Your grace knowes myne opinion already which of bounden duetie to the kinges maieste I haue already ere this tyme declared to your grace: Master Wotton and Master Myldemaye for money matters, and yf your graces pleasure were to requyre my lorde of Southampton[3] to take paynes therin youe might slepe the quietlier; my lorde greate master might take charge of victualles to occupie him withall; my lorde of Warwicke[4] into the northe as sone as might be possible; my lorde pryvy seal[5] in to the weste, who havinge helpe semes not to myslyke yt. Let so mych money be sent to Bulloigne as maie be gotten conveniently, and the lyke into the northe [and if your graces pleasour be to send me any whither either to the north],[6] east west or south, your grace shall fynde me as readye or readier then the chauncelour of thaugmentacions,[7] and vntill now I beleved ~~my beloved~~ my ladies grace had thought the same. The lyvinge God sende youe bothe as well to do as I wishe to my selfe. From the courte & c.

W. P.

[1] Anglesey MS omits 'great'.
[2] Sir William Sharington, vice-treasurer of Bristol mint.
[3] Thomas Wriothesley, Earl of Southampton.
[4] John Dudley, Earl of Warwick.   [5] John Lord Russell.
[6] Bracketed section appears in the Anglesey MS, but is omitted in PLB.
[7] Sir Edward North.

20. *To Somerset. Drayton. 21 March, 1548–9.*
   (*PLB.*)

Sir, sithens yt pleased your grace to determyne your pleasure vnto me yesterday seuenyght, consernynge my suite to your grace and the parliament, I haue bene enformed that your grace hath conceaved some displeasure towardes me for certaine communication the which hath bene reported to your grace of my mouth touchinge the same matter. Wherfore presuminge vpon your graces goodnesse I haue thought good taduertise your grace, that the failinge of my suyte did not so myche greve me, as yt did to se your grace at that tyme troubled on two sydes, that is to saie beinge lothe to offende your pore frende, and beinge pressed to satisfie other folkes, in respecte wherof vnfainedly I overcame myne owne passion, and as I had bene a suyter in myne owne cause, so (yf your grace be pleased to calle to remembraunce) I sued to your grace to let the matter die. Mary, Sir, to confesse to your grace the very truthe, I beleved vpon information geven to me therin, that my ladyes grace had bene the suyter against me, which (so God helpe me) went to my harte like a dagger. For next to your grace vnder the kinges maieste, I reposed my chefest truste of frendship in her grace, and vpon know- ledge and cleretie of myne owne conscience how myche I honoured and loved youe bothe even with all my harte, I claymed in my harte of very right a love from youe bothe agayne. For of one thinge I am suer, that although many love your grace, I thincke of very frendeshippe, and many beare your grace a love in respecte of your office; yet no man ever hath desired the honour, the vertue, the quietnes of an other, more then I have and do your graces, nor never man toke more care and thought for the well doinge of an other manne, then I haue and do for your grace, God ys judge betwene your grace and me therin, which I promysse your grace procedith of duetie, because of your place of service to the kinges maieste and the realme, and of very love to your person which colde not cease, nor can not, though your office ceased. Now, Sir, when I conceaved that her grace was against my suyte and never voutchesaved to calle me to the reckeninge, it greved me wonder- fully. And I thought there were some prickers forwarde provoked by envye. Havinge herde before that some sayde otherwise of me then I deserved, and herevpon came yt that I sayde, I wold forbeare to shewe my selfe so forwarde in counsaill as I had done before, addinge therwithall that yet neverthelesse as I wolde take awaye the cause of envie, so wold I do as your grace wolde commaunde me, and withdrawe no piece of my duetie neyther to the kinges maieste, ne to your grace, and thus I sayed for speakinge in counsayll, but owt of counsaill I sayde I wolde (yf your grace pleased to knowe myne opinion in any matter) saie alwayes franckely to your grace what I thought. And thys was the somme of my sayenge, wherwith your grace hath no iust cause to be offended and I trust yow are not. Sythens which tyme I have herde from my ladyes grace that vndoubtedly she stirred the matter never to your grace, a thinge to my great reioysinge, and an accusacion of my selfe to be in greate faulte for mistrustinge assured favour and frendeshippe without cause. But herevpon, Sir, I sawe that suche as envied me hadde bene able to prevaile with your grace against me, gevinge suche enforma-tion to your grace as I am sure they were not hable to justefie, and so yt appeared the daye of the prorogation of the parliament, when in the morninge I had shewed them the statute boke in your graces galerye havinge the chefe justice[1] on my parte in the presence of Master Secretarye Smythe[2] whervpon I was sorye, that when in-formacion was geven to your grace agaynste me yt had not lyked your grace to have herde me in the prescence of the informers and thought your grace not to haue bene so good lorde to me, as I persuaded my selfe youe had bene; which thinge proceadinge vpon a greater presumption of your favour towardes me then became me to conceave I beseche your grace to pardon me, and to contynewe to me good lorde, as to him that for dewtie and love sake onely and for none other respecte honor and love from the bottome of my harte yow and all yours, as God can testifie who sende your grace aswell to do as myne owne sowle.

From Drayton[3] &c.

W. P.

21. *To Somerset. The court. 17 April, 1549.*
  (*PLB.*)

Sir, my duetie to the kinges maieste and the realme and my love to your grace vpon whom restethe the greatest parte of the burthen in the gouernement vnder the kinge causeth me to put your grace in remembraunce of such matiers as musinge (sythens your graces departure hence) of the state of the world I haue thought good to enforme your grace of. The one is conteyned in certayn questions grounded vpon certayne occasions expressed before the said ques-tions in a paper here enclosed, which questions in my poore opinion

---

[1] Sir Edward Montague.   [2] Sir Thomas Smith.
[3] For details about Paget's home at West Drayton, Middlesex see S. A. J. McVeigh, *Drayton of the Pagets* (West Drayton, 1970).

(vnder correction of your grace) were good to be proponed to the hole counsayll, to be with some deliberacion considered, debated and resolued vpon. The other matter ys expressed in certayne articles conteyninge the state of this realme, and of the reste with whom we have to do, which your grace maie (yf it so shall like youe) reserue to yourselfe. By them your grace will peraduenture thincke that I put all in despayre and do make the worste of our owne and the best of all oure enemies thinges. Well, Sir, eyther those articles be trewe or false. Yf they be false I am gladde I am deceaved in the knowledge and iudgement of thinges. But if they be trewe your grace knoweth whither their be cause of dispayre or no. And to confesse to your grace the very truthe knowinge by experience that they be for the moste parte or rather all trewe, I am surely in wonderfull perplexitie how we shall be able to do all thinges for the kinges honour in suche sorte as were expedient. I knowe your grace will saye (and I have not tyll nowe misliked yt) yet let vs sette a good countenaunce of yt. But, Sir, our countenaunce ys so well knowen with the reste of owre estate abrode to all the worlde, as the matter will not lenger be holden vp with a countenaunce. And therfore for Goddes sake in tyme devise for remedie. In which parte when your grace shall commaund me eyther in open counsaill, or in this sorte I will declare myne opinion to your grace throughlie and vnfaynedly nothinge doubtinge of your graces good acceptacion of the same as procedinge from one that wisheth youe as well to do as he dothe to his owne harte and that God knowethe who preserve your grace. From the courte &c.

W. P.

22. *Certain Points to Be Resolved Upon in Council. No place. 17 April, 1549.*
(PLB.)

The matter   The Scottes have broken couenaunt made with youe for the mariadge of their quene to the kinges maieste and also an other couenaunt and treatie of peax, for the redresse of which two poyntes we haue bene in warre with the Scottes these viij yeres, and yet contynewe still entendinge conquest of the realme vpon pretence of forfiture.[1]

The question   The question ys whether that this entent beinge not yet brought to passe yt be moste expedient to folowe

[1] Edward VI and Mary, Queen of Scots, were to marry according to the terms of the treaty of pacification and marriage of 1 July, 1543.

the same by warre at this tyme till yt be atcheived or rather to devise and effectually prosecute by some honorable practise to shyfte of the warre either vtterlye or at the leaste for a tyme.

The matter The Frenche have no treatie with youe, but vnder pretence of a treatie lyve in suche a broken frendshippe with youe, as with your honour can not be contynued for they paye not your pencion, they make guerre guerriable vpon your subiectes by lande and sea, and they aide your open enemies the Scottes.

The question The question ys whether that youe shall breake with them, and by force travayle to bringe them to reason, or elles devise by practise and treatie to set thinges betwene youe and them in some more honorable and suer staye, or elles contynewe stille as youe do in suche vncertaine termes.

The Realme

We owe more then we be nowe hable to paye thoughe we had nothinge elles to employe our money vppon but our debtes and ordenarie charges in tyme of peaxe.

We have not nowe nor shall not haue this yere sufficient money to mainteyne vs in the warre honorablie.

We haue great scarsitie of cheiftaynes to conducte the warres.

Our captaines haue learned to geve them selves more to make a gayne of the kinges service, then carefullie to execute their chardges.

We haue great scarsitie of men and those that be are not most willing to serve in the warre but disobedient and slouthfull.

The greater officers not greatlie feared, the people presuminge much of their goodnes.

The inferior officers not regarded but contempned.

The gentlemen despised and so nowe contented to endure.

The common people to liberall in speche, to bolde and licentious in their doinges and to wise and well learned in their owne conceytes.

All thinges in maner goinge backewarde and vnfortunately and every man almoste out of harte and corage, and our lackes so well knowen as our enemies despise vs and our frendes pitie vs.

The Scottes.
They haue good willes to kepe them selfes in libertie out of the thraldome of England.

They want not money, what of their owne at home, what from frendes abroad to do their enterprises withall.

They haue good store of capitaines of their owne and of their frendes and they haue men ynoughe and all willinge to travaile and take payne.

There people in great obedience in all thinges and ready to serve when they are commaunded at all tymes and in all sortes.

Their thinges do nowe prosper and go forwarde.

They haue greate and open succours of the French kinge and secrete aide of the kinge of Denmarke.[1] They are hardy, painefull and faulse, and fynde vs easie to be with their falsehod abused.

The Frenche.

They haue now lyved iij yeres in peax wherby vndoubtedly they are waxen ryche. They have now to do in warres with no other prince.

Their owne people be more esquaryed for the warre then they haue bene in tymes paste.

They are stronger by seas then they were wont to be.

They knowe our myserye and contemne vs.

Thempereur.

Thoughe he seme to favour yow for his owne commoditie yet vndoubtedly he is in his herte displeased with your procedinges in religion.

Thempereur, beinge growne great and knowinge your decaye, can not lyke that youe frame his frendshippe no more then youe do, the rather seinge others do which neyther pretende so myche trust in his frendshippe as we do, nor haue so myche nede of it as we haue.

It is to be doubted leste that thempereur agreinge with Fraunce vpon some composition will then travaill in some purpose aboute vs contrarye to our procedinge nowe, which if he do, yt were good to se what were best to be done.

23. *To Somerset. The court. 8 May, 1549.*
(PLB; SP 10/7, no. 5; BM, Cotton MS Titus F. iii, fo. 273ᵛ; modernized text printed in Strype, ii (ii), pp. 427–9.

Although loving Somerset deeply, he is troubled that no man dares to speak what he thinks. Has himself been sharply nipped for liberal

[1] Christian III.

speech in council. Sir Richard a Lee[1] came weeping after Somerset's rebuke. Reminds Somerset that he would have been pricked at the stomach if a king or cardinal in times past had spoken to him as he speaks to others. Somerset has 'grown into great colericke facions'. Somerset should heed advice when the whole council moves him. Trusts that Somerset will understand that this letter proceeds from a good heart as God can judge.

24. *To George Brooke, Lord Cobham, Lord Deputy of Calais. Newport. 17 June, 1549.*
   (BM, Harl. MS 284, fo. 36ʳ.)

My lord depute, with most harty commendacions and lyk thankes for my god chere at Callais. I fynd here at Newport Hackfort[2] accompanyed with all his band and lxx aboue his nombre whom his request is to haue reteyned with the rest and for myn opinion I thynk it so good beyng both willing men and so well horsed [*two words illegible*] and the rather for that sum of [*two words illegible*] will I suppose fayle in theyr [*two words illegible*] both for theyr nombres and also for thabilite of the men and horses. Charles de Gavara is in prison for levying men without licence. Your lordship shall do wel to write over for knowledge what is to be done for the lxx ouer the part in which case also I haue written to Sir Thomas Smyth to procure my lordes answer to you therin. Thus with most harty commendacions to my lady I pray God send you both well to faire as I woold myself. From Newport this xvij th of June 1549.

Your lordships most assured
frend
William Paget

I pray you my lorde to send this
lettre over to Master Smyth with spede.

25. *[To Somerset.] Brussels. 23 June, 1549.*
   (SP 68/3, no. 167.)

It maye like your grace tunderstande that I haue receaved your graces and others of the counsailles lettres wherein amonges other thinges tooching the state of Scotlande it may appeare that the Frenche king reserueth his greatest force together at home in

---

[1] Sir Richard Lee (1513?–75) was a military engineer who accompanied Somerset into Scotland in 1547. Strype transcribed 'a Lee' as 'Alte'.

[2] Heinrich Hackfort or Hackford, a young gentleman of Gelders in charge of 3000 horse.

expectacion of thempereurs deathe: willing me to sett the same furthe which and the Countie Rangonas[1] mattier I will not faile to do as occasion and oportunitie shall serue for either of them accordingly. And forbecause your grace shall perceave by our comen lettres at this presente our procedinges here I omitt to trooble your grace any further, only praying youe most humbly that of suche thinges as I haue writen to Master Secretarie to knowe your graces pleasour in, I maye be with spede and certainly aduertised from your grace to thende I maye procede thereaftre, and further as your grace shall considre the case to require the same. And thus beseching almyghty God to preserve your grace and send you aswell to do as I wishe to your grace I surcease to moleste you any lenger. From Bruseles the xxiijth of June at mydnight 1549.

Your graces most humbly and hartely at commaundement

William Paget

26. [*To Sir William Petre.*] *Brussels. 23 June, 1549.*
(*SP 68/3, no. 168; BM, Cotton MS, Galba B. xii, fo. 91ʳ, a copy with last page missing.*)

fo. 130ʳ Master Secretary, after my most harty commendacions I thank you for thaduertisementes in your last lettre and forbicause by our comyng lettre it shall appere vnto you how our matters go here I forbeare to write of them. By yours I see that the French make no hast of the meting for that you hauyng vppon theyr request named commissioners they delaye the namyng of theyrs, and I lyke not the sending for out of Scotland of such personages as be in authorite ther seying the sende not only Thermes[2] thither (which might be construed well inowgh) but also that he caryith with him his wief which pretendith no short departure from Scotland, and also is accompanyed of men lernid in the law personages syrving for the gouernement of estate which hath an apparance of contynaunce. On the other side these men here sauour that I haue further to say to them toching Fraunce, for that theyr ambassador[3] there hath bene enformed of that part of my charge as well as of the rest which concernyth a ioynt invasion. And goyng forward in the other partye toching the perpetual establish[ment] of the old treaty will presse the burstyng out of the same. Now one part of myn instructons is to forbeare the vtterance of that poynte til I heare how the commissioners that met with the French do procede in theyr busynes, which I doubt how it can be put of so long here. Wherfor I requyre you to let me be aduertised

---

[1] Pallavicino Rangone, count of Rangone.
[2] Paul de la Barthe, seigneur de Thermes (1482–1562).   [3] Simon Renard.

imediatly wheder I shall procede also to open the forsayd poynt of ioynt enemytie or forbeare til further knoweledge of your procedinges with Fraunce and if I shall forbeare to open it (which I feare wilbe hard to do) then to aduertise me also how I shall procede to put of the same. Also in case they agre to the ratificacon of the treaty by the kinges maieste and the prynce with obligacion in the same that within a tyme the contreys on both sides shall confyrme the same I requyre to be instructed within what tyme the sayd confyrmacion of the contryes shalbe made, and the names of such contreys of themperors as my lordes grace will to confyrme. Also if Bullen cum in to defence with the isles of Aldeney and Silley, to instruct me of my lordes graces pleasyr what places shalbe accepted in to defence in reciproke for themperors part. Also to be instructed in the matter of mariage what is the resolute dote the kinges maieste shall offer with the Lady Mary. When the same shalbe payd; and what dower we shall demande in degrees after the rates of degres in our offres, for the which you shall do well to visit the treatyes with the King Lewes for (*fo. 130ᵛ*) the mariage of the late French quene the king our masters aunte.[1] Also if I shall enter to treate a ioynt enemitie to send me instructions of my lordes graces pleasyr for the particuler poyntes. In what forme we shall ioyn that is to say wheder we shalbe enemye to enemye against almen or against such men as you will name for all causes and querelles or for such certain as you will appoynt and wheder you will appoynt with what nomber the querel shalbe made (as it is alredy in the treaty with viijᵐ) or generally with how few soever the querel be made. Also what you will requyr themperor to do, vppon what part both by land and see; and with what nombres; and lykewise what and where you will offre for the reciproque. These thinges I haue thought vppon; wherin I requyre you ernestly to let me know with spede my lordes pleasyr and that certainly and also of any other thing that his grace there shall consider in these matters mete to be sent vnto me, for they be of gret[2] importance and I haue to do here though not with many not passing thre yet gret wisemen and I haue no speciall instructions for the same. I pray you also to let vs know from tyme to tyme of your procedinges both with Fraunce and Scotland. Wherby we shalbe the abler to furder the kinges maiestes affayres here. And thus I byd you hartely well to fair from Bruselles the xxiij th of June at nyght 1549.

Your very assured frend
William Paget

I pray you remembre to send me a quyck depeche for these folkes here as they vse no delayes so they looke for redy answeres.

[1] Mary Tudor, sister of Henry VIII.   [2] Galba B. xii. ends.

27. *Sir William Paget and Sir Philip Hoby to [Somerset]. Brussels. 24 June, 1549.*

(*SP 68/3, no. 169; copies, BM, Add. MS 5935, fos. 116ʳ–123ʳ, Cotton MS, Galba B. xii, fos. 92ʳ–98ʳ, Harl. MS 523, fos. 57ʳ–64ᵛ.*)

(*fo. 135ʳ*) It may like your grace after the remembraunce of our most humble dueties to vnderstande that I the comptroller being arryved here at Brussels on Wedinsday last the xixth of this instant and having that night and the morowe folowing partely to rest myself and chiefly to conferre the circumstance of my commission with Master Hobby stayed from demaunding of audience Fridaye in the morning I sent vnto Granvele[1] gyving him tunderstande that I was cum hither sent by the king my master to open on his maiestes behalf certain thinges vnto thempereur and therefore I requyred him both to giue his maieste knoweledge therof and taduertise me whenne his pleasyr shuld be to giue me audience, which with many faire woordes and offres he promised to do imediately. The same after none Monsieur de Chantoney[2] Granveles sonne cam to visite me both on thempereurs and his fathers behalf who after sum entretemement and gentle offres for the furniture of any thing that I lacked, shewed me that thempereur being vntil that tyme vnwitting of my cuming had sent him to welcum me, being sory as he said that he had not sent soner to me, and making gret excuse for the same required me to repose myself after my travaill vntil he might haue commodite to giue me audience which he said shuld be very shortely. But bicaus I wold not seme to forget to put him in remembraunce therof I tooke occasion the same night to sende eftsones to Granvele both to giue him thankes for his sons visitation and therewithall to put him in minde of myn audience whenne oportunite shuld serve which neuertheles I referred to thempereurs good commodite. He returned me aunswer with many gentle woordes that as thempereur being empeched about certain maters of Spayn had not that afternone commodite to here (*fo. 135ᵛ*) me so was he sure that his maieste minded the day folowing to send for me till when he desyred me to haue pacience. The next morning Monsieur Darras[3] neither by thempereur nor his fathers commaundement but of himself (as he said) moved by the zeale that his father he and all their house beare vnto the kinges maieste and for his sake vnto his ministres cam to

---

[1] Nicholas Perrenot de Granvelle (1486–1550), Charles V's keeper of the seals and principal minister.

[2] Thomas Perrenot, 2nd son of Nicholas.

[3] Antoine Perrenot, bishop of Arras, elder son of Nicholas.

visite and welcum me offring himself most redy to shewe me all the pleasyr that lyeth in him. Within twoo howres after Monsieur de Bossu[1] le grand esquier well accompanied with diuers gentlemen of the courte cam by thempereurs commaundement to convoye vs to the courte to the empereurs presence. Hereof haue we thought good taduertise your grace that ye maye thereby perceiue the sort of owr enterteinement hitherto: And now, Syr, to the purpose at our cumming to thempereur I, the said comptroller, after the deliuery of my lettres with the kinges maiestes most harty commendacions and your graces and sum other good woordes of office passed to and fro on both sydes concerning the good will and affection that the king my master and your grace beare towardes the contynuance of thamitie and encreace of the same persuading the like at his hande and remembring thold contynued freendeship that hath long sithens bene betwene both their houses and that the commodite of thone dependeth of the welth and saufgarde of thother, his good estate and condition being the kinges maieste and likewise the kinges suretie and prosperite to be not a litle to his benifite. I was I said sent by the kinges maieste and your grace chiefly to travaill to establishe and confirme this amite by such meanes as shuld be thought good on both the partes and the rather at this tyme for that the prince his sonne was nowe here in these low cuntreys to whom (*fo. 136*ʳ) as we thought he minded to leave his cuntreis and dominione so we doubted not also but he woold make him herities of his amites and alliaunces of the which we (I said) reputed ourselfes to be the chiefest and most assured. A second cause of my cumming was (I said) to communicate vnto him the state of the kinges affaires with the Scottes our commun ennemies and also the French his dissimuled freendes and our secret ennemies and the third was to treate if he thought so good vpon a mater of mariage which chaunced to cum in communication vpon occasion of deuising wayes for thencreace and augmentacion of this amitie. And to descende to more particularites I said that touching the furst part your grace had deuised with the counsaill vpon meane to haue it take effect which I thought was so reasonnable as his maieste wold embrace orels shewe to vs sum other waye better for the purpose and more commodious for both realmes. There was a treaty (I said) made betwene his maieste and the late king of famous memorye which they both I was sure ment to haue perpetuel and for that effect caused certain woordes to be couched therin and albeit we doubt not but that both he for his part wold fermely observe the same and that the kinge and your grace for the kinges parte minded noles yet consydering that the prince cannot well bind his successours

---

[1] Jean de Hennin, comte de Bossu.

and their cuntreis without their expres consent to the same as it might appere by a treatie made betwen vs and Fraunce which having a clause to be made perpetuel and we vnmindfull to requyre the confirmation therof was layd vnto us by the French ambassadours before Monsieur Darras, Monsieur de Courcieres[1] and Chapuis[2] at our being to gidre at Callays and we vnable taunswer (*fo. 136ᵛ*) thereto your grace therefore had thought most convenient aswel for his posterite as the kinges to set furth this ouerture that the king and the prince with such cuntries on both sydes as shuld take commodite by this treatie shuld confirme and ratifie the same and that before this ratification which the soner it wer done wer the better the treaty shuld be revisited to see howe one of vs vnderstandeth an other therin and in the debating therof to considre wheder any thing shuld be thought mete to be added that may be beneficial to both parties. Here I staying a while his maieste aunswered me with very gentle woordes that he was right glad to perceiue the good towardnes shewed on the king his good brothers and your graces behalf towardes the conservacion of this amite which for his part he doth most ernestly desyre to enterteyn, and likeas he did take King Henry theight in his lief tyme in place of his good brother and father having at sundry tymes experienced of his firme and stedfast freendship towardes him. So he now for his parte will not (he saith) faile to declare himself in all thinges most redy to requite the same towardes the king my master whom he reputeth as another his sonne and is no les mindefull and desyrous of his maiestes furtheraunce and well proceding thenne of his own, which he affirmed shalbe well declared whensoever oportunite shall serve. And to thende he might more fully perceiue the kinges maiestes and your graces meaning herin he desyred me to descende to the rest. Wherupon touching particulerly by the waye the state of our doinges the last yere in Scotlande (*fo. 137ʳ*) what hath bene done there of late by my lord of Rutland[3] and how my lord of Warwike shalbe shortly sent thither to take a further fote in the cuntrey. I shewed him we wer in no smal hope to growe shortly towardes sum quietnes there so that his maieste wold be pleased to put to his helping hande both in staing the saufconduictes that are giuen out to his subgetes to trafficq thither and also to graunt his consent that his subgetes taken beyond Barwike in their voyage towardes Scotlande may be laufully stayed by our men and their goodes taken as forfaict wherby the Scottes wanting this continuel relief and assistence maye be the soner brought to sum reason. And, Syr, (quoth I) whereas in those warres with the Scottes the French

---

[1] Jean de Montmorency, seigneur de Courrières.
[2] Eustace Chapuys.   [3] Henry Manners, earl of Rutland.

haue by sundry meanes travailed tempeche our procedinges there and also delt on thissue very vnfrendly and vnneighbourly towardes vs the kinges maieste loth to continew in this fained sort of freendeshipp and desyrous to knowe their meaning herin sent lately a gentleman of his to the French king desyring to knowe what he intended by this vnfreendly sort of dealing for if he sought[1] (as by his procedinges it appered he ment) to breake with his maieste albeit he was not desyrous of warre yet if he [the said French king][2] minded the same[3] as it semed by the procedinges of his ministres he did we requyred that like a prince of honour he wold notifie[4] it vnto vs the same and he shuld be aunswered accordingly for after this sort his maieste neither could nor woold endure and that he looked by the same messanger to receiue resolute aunswer herof. Wherupon the French king alledging that these pikes haue bene ministred (*fo. 137*[v]) by ministres vpon the frontiers affirming that he meaneth nothing les thenne to break with vs but rather to contynue peax and amite yea and taugment it also and offred vnto the said gentleman tappoint commissioners to mete with my masters both for the redres of these querels and the establishement if nede be of a further freendeship, or to do any other[5]reasonnable thing that might serve to the purpose. Which offer being so aptly moved of the French part your grace (I said) with thaduise of the rest of the counsaill remembring that we haue nowe these viij yeres (and foure of them alone) without other help contynued in warres both against Scotland and the French king who is a prince of gret power having to do no where els haue thought good not to refuse, and hereupon haue appointed commissioners to mete with the French who shall not conclude any thing preiudicial to the treaties that ar or shalbe passed betwene his maieste and the king my master, neither shall procede to any resolute conclusion but that he shall haue knowledge therof before. And in cace he will (as both nowe and at other tymes it hath pleased him to promies) shewe him-self a freend or rather father vnto the kinges maieste my master and assist[6] him in his right he shall[7] well perceyve we will not let slipp any one jote of his maiestes interest and due, nor yeld in the leest point to the French that may be to his maiestes dishonnour or disauantage. Mary, if we shall now want the good assistence he hath alwaies put vs in hope of; thenne hauing regarde both vnto our masters honnour[8] and proufitt muste we growe to such a bargayn with the French as

---

[1] 'thought' in Add. MS.   [2] Omitted in Add. MS.
[3] Crossed out in State Papers Foreign; included in Add. MS.
[4] 'justify' in Add. MS.   [5] 'other' omitted in Add. MS.
[6] Add. MS omits 'and' and has 'assisting'.
[7] 'should' in Add. MS.   [8] Add. MS omits 'honnour'.

(*fo. 138ʳ*) for his maiestes estimation and surete shalbe thought mete vnto vs. Wherefor that we may the better direct our doinges to the conservacion of thamite betwene the kinges maieste and him I desired that it might like his maieste to declare his pleasyr herin. Hereunto thempereur after his hartie thankes vnto the kinges maieste and your grace for this frendely sort of communicating vnto him the state of our procedings aunswered that he was very glad to perceive our good succes against the Scottes his and our commun ennemies which he wished might go forwarde and contynue and for his parte he woold not faile to shewe the king his good brother all the pleasyr he might. As for the French (quoth he) I knowe they haue delt very vnfrendely with you of late which I am glad ye haue so well encountred, ye knowe (quoth he) it is but their old wont to vse their neighbours this dublely wherof I myself as well as other haue had sum experience howbeit ye do well to gyve care to this their motion of talke wherin as I doubt not but ye will procede as ye saye with respect to my amite so wold I wishe sum good fruit might growe therof to your quiet and satisfaction. Your devise for the revisiting and confirmation of the treaties with those other overtures that ye haue touched vnto me haue a good semblance and be ye sure the king your master my good brother and neighbour shall at no tyme fynde me vntowarde to go through with any thing that may tende to the establishmente and confirmation of this amite like as I also do assure myselfe of the semblable good will (*fo. 138ᵛ*) and shewe of freendeship on his behalf wherunto I knowe there cannot want my lord protectours good furtheraunce who is my freend and old acquaintaunce and hath heretofore bene with me whenne I haue right well perceiued his good affection towardes myn estate and procedinges which I shall not forget to requite as I may. And bicaus (quoth he) these matiers that ye haue moved ar of sum importaunce and therefore require to be aunswered with deliberation I will communicate them to my conseill who afterwardes shall treate with youe herupon, hoping that in the debating therof ye will be content both to here and yelde to reason as I for my part will not faile to be conformable thereto. Herewithall his maieste with most gentle woordes licenced vs to departe. After our being yesterdaye with thempereur, Granuele towardes night sent vnto me one of his folkes declaring that by reason of his sicknes he was not well able to styrre furth of the house and therefore praied me to take paine to mete him at his lodging this morning at viij of the clock as at the tyme appointed we did. When finding him accompaignied with the duke of Alva[1] and his sonnes Darras we entred into consultacion and furst

---

[1] Fernando Alvarez de Toledo, duke of Alva.

Granuele told vs that thempereur vpon the passage that I, the comptroller, had had with him yesterday had willed them to joyne with vs to conferre theruppon and to enter in to further particularites.[1] I, the comptroller, aunswerd him hereto that seing they wer by his maieste appointed to treate with vs I thought it not vnmete topen vnto them as I had done[2] to thempereur the cause of my cumming and here discursed I vnto them the hole (*fo. 139*) circumstance of my charge in these pointes and in like sorte as I did yesterdaye to thempereur. The repeticion wherof bicaus it is superfluous I omitt to trouble your grace withall. Wherunto Granuele after a long protestation of the good will and affection that thempereur beareth to the king my master and his procedinges with sundry offers to do for him in all thinges to the best of his power like a good freende and brother as far furth as may stande with his honnour aunswered first as to the confirmation of the treaties that thempereur thinking the treatie and league that is alredy betwen my master and him to be of sufficient force and strength wherby he taketh himself, his sonne, their successours and countreis sufficiently bounde to thobservacion therof (so as we also for our partes will repute ourselfes in like maner bounde to the same) his maieste supposeth this newe confirmation that we require to be nedeles, adding that though there wer nomaner treaties betwene vs, and that we had not thus fermely bounde ourselfes to gider by this league yet doth thempereur conceiue so good an opinion of our frendeship and beareth so ernest an affection to the king his good brother that he wold not faile to shewe him such freendly pleasyr as might any tyme lye in his power and the rather is he moved to owe the kinges maieste this fatherly love not only for thamite that he alwayes founde in King Henry theight vntil his latter daye but also bicaus it liked him at the howre of his death to will the king that now is to folow his frendeship and to ioyn with the same, who he affirmeth shall in very dede (*fo. 139*) finde him a father whensoeuer cause shall requyre. As to the revisiting of the treaties he saith that the bishop of Winchester[3] and other the kinges commissioners ioined of late yeres with thempereur at Vtrecht for thesclarcissement of such doubtes as wer thought to be in the said treatie, who having to the best that their wittes could serve debated the same and made clere those poinctes that wer ambiguous, he supposeth there is not left nowe either woord or clause that is not plaine ynough and vnderstandable to bothe parties. As to our procedinges in Scotlande thempereur he said was very glad to perceiue the good succes that we haue alredy had and ar like to haue

---

[1] Add. MS inserts 'of the same'.   [2] Add. MS inserts 'before'.
[3] Stephen Gardiner, bishop of Winchester.

C M—D

there. For the furtheraunce wherof his maiestes good and freendly assistence shall not he saith at any tyme want. And for the stayng of their saufconduites and the traficq that thempereurs subgectes vse thither his maieste he said being well enformed of the mater will take such order therin as he doubteth not shalbe to the king his good brothers satisfaction. And how vndesirous we ar to assist the Scottes against youe. It may appere (quoth he) in that we haue bene content to fall out with them for yours sakes betwene whom and the king your masters disobedient subgectes vpon the sees, thempereurs people both of this contrey and Spayn ar so continually travailed and spoyled that it wer much better for them to be at open war. Vnto our procedinges with Fraunce he aunswered me in effect as thempereur did at my being with him with this addition that where it was by me amongst the rest touched that if thempereur woold shewe himself our good freende we wold not (*fo. 140ʳ*) in this present communicacion with Fraunce let slip any one iote of the kinges maiestes right. He said that he supposed we had hitherto nor shuld not haue he hoped hereafter any cause to complain of thempereurs good will and freendshipp who hath already done asmuch ye and more thenne the treaties strayn him to, both in assisting vs with such nombres of men as we haue from tyme to tyme required at his handes and also in staing the Germains with swerd in hande from passing to the French seruice which he gessed was no small help to the furtheraunce of the kinges seruice and abating of the French power who finde themselfes not a litle agreved therewithe supposing thempereur to vse over much parcialite herin. And likeas (quoth he) thempereur doubteth not but ye will at this tyme procede with Fraunce with regard to his amite and the treatie betwene your master and him so if you make him priuey to your doinges with them he will most gladly further youe with his counsaill and advise to the beste of his power hoping that if ye procede to the conclusion of any thing for Scotlande ye will haue in remembraunce to gyve his maieste knoweledge therof as ye ar bounde by the treaty to do. As to the mariage betwene thenfant of Portugale[1] and Lady Mary ye knowe (quoth he) this is no mater to be begon and not gon through withall, and therefore wold we wishe ye descended to sum particularites herin without which we cannot growe towardes any conclusion. I, the comptroller, replied hereto first as concerning the confirmation of the treatie likeas (quoth I) the king my master and his counsaill (*fo. 140ᵛ*) esteming thempereurs frendeship aboue any other do desyre that the same might be contynued without any violation and that the treaties betwen them be left also to their succession. So albeit they doubt not of the reciprocq

---

[1] Don Luis, second son of Emmanuel I of Portugal.

herof on thempereurs behalf yet knowing there can be non amite that is ment to be perpetuel over firmely knit togidre haue they thought meete for the ernest zeale they beare to the preservacion of this amite and to put all doubtes that might herafter arrise apart to require to haue the treatie ratified by the king my master and the prince of Spayn and their cuntreis which we suppose is not to be refused by thempereur. No, (quoth he) and brake my tale I say not that thempereur doth refuse it but I will make a reaport to him again and trust to make you such an aunswer from him as you shall haue reason to be satisfied. As to the revisiting of the treaties, indede, (quoth I) yours and our commissioners haue alredy made an esclarcissement herupon but it is now a good while sithens and sum thinges may perhapp seme now doubtefull that appered theene to be plaine ynough. And in the overlooking and debating of these thinges it might happen that either ye for your profit or we for ours might spye sumthing that ar not conteined in the treaties that wer meet to be added therto at the leest ye knowe that in the viewing therof there can non inconvenience but rather occasion of further amite growe. Ye saye true (quoth he) and so will I put the empereur in minde and make reaport vnto you of his aunswer. As to maters of Scotlande we do not forget (quoth I) that thempereur hath fallen out with them for our sakes as we did also breke with others for (*fo. 141ʳ*) his. And for the spoile that ye saye is made by such rovers as ar abrode on thempereurs subgetes the king my master is right sory therefore his people receyving no les hurt at these mens handes thenne thempereurs, and wer he not otherwayes empeched he woold see a short redres herin, but ye perceiue he hath not presently any apt tyme therto. We knowe that thempereur hath in these warres against ours and his commun enemies shewed vs pleasyr and assisted vs with men for our money wherin he hath shewed much graciousite and don correspondent to the treatie. And we forget it not but wilbe always redy to requite him with the sembable in cace of nede doubting nothing but his maieste will contynue this his good will and freendeship in such further assistence as he shall perceiue to be requisite which is as laufull for him to do towardes vs his freendes without breking his treaties with the French as it is for them tassist the Scottes their freendes against vs without violation of the league that is between vs and the rather for that the same is employed against such as ar aswel enemies to his maieste as to vs. As for the staying of thalmains from passing vnto the French seruice I know (quoth I) the same standeth vs in good stede as it serveth also to thempereurs owne commoditie whom it standeth in hand not to suffre the Frenche to furnishe themselfes with that nation; for although there be not presently any cause of querel betwen the French and him yet who can tel what innovation may happen. As concerning the mariage (quoth I) in dede it (as ye say) mete we came to sum particulerite and likeas we haue power to treate and conclude heruppon so before we entre toffer (*fo. 141*ᵛ) what we think mete to gyve with the Lady Mary me semeth it wer good ye declared to vs the state of thinfant, and here taking that I had demaunded his age, Mary, (quoth he) he is a man of fourty yere old or therabout. Nay, Monsieur Granvele (quoth I) I required not to know his yeres but rather what state he is of and what dower he may be able to assure vnto the Lady Mary. In good faith (quoth he) I am not able to acertain youe therof but as for his personage good witt and qualites I assure you he is a gentleman worthy to be matched with any gret princes. Besides that he is brother vnto the King of Portugall, whereby he shalbe able to shewe frendeship to the kinges maieste and stande your cuntrey to good stede likeas also the good wil that thempereur beareth to this gentleman whom he estemeth as his owne sonne cannot but be a furtheraunce to thentretemement of thamite that we seke on both partes, assuring you that there is not in Christendom so mete a matche as woold be betwen them twayn. And I promise you (quoth I) for our part that the Lady Mary is (as I suppose ye knowe well ynough) both in beauty vertuous and honest qualites nothing inferior to that worthines ye reaport this gentlman to be of and on thother syde she is sister to a king of Englande and nere kyn vnto thempereur and one whom, I gesse, his maieste fauoureth as a daughter of his, and therefor, quoth I, seing the personages ar so mete to matche to gidre and that thempereur reputeth him self as a freende and father to them both (*fo. 142*ʳ) he must in a maner playe both partes and do aswell for the mariage of the Lady Mary as for Don Lowys and with and equal consideracion of their estates order this thing as a mater of indifference for both sydes, not mesuring the demaunde for her dote after thestimation of his own power and estate but after the qualite of them for whom the mater is treated. What think ye mete to bestow with her (quoth Granuele) for I wold be loth to cum empty handed (quoth he) to thempereur and therfor I pray you descend to sum particulerite. I said she had a goodly yerely revenue left her by the kinges maieste decessed, which he making very light I told him that the king, her father, maried his two sisters thone to the French king with ijᶜ thousand crownes and thother to the Scottishe king with a hundred thousande crownes. And I pray you (quoth I) what did the King of Romains[1] offre with his daughter for the king my master. Ye, (quoth he) the King Ferdinande is but a poore prince, but the

[1] Ferdinand, brother of Charles V.

king your master being so riche and puissant cannot but distribute liberally with his suster and according to his honour for his father did offer ones with her to this same man fourty thousand pounde sterling. Ye, syr, (quoth I) my master is as ye knowe and hath ben of long while in warres and hath occasion to be at gret charges and expence of money, howbeit in cace the Infant may assure this lady a convenable dower we will not let to stretche ourselfes to twese asmuch as her father left to her by his testament [*torn*] entured[1] to an hundred thousand crownes. But furst (quoth I) er we can procede to any certain offer herin we must be ioinctely ascertained of this (*fo. 142ᵛ*) gentlemans estate and what habilite he is of to thende we may procede thereafter and not be forced to revocque any thing we shuld offre, for dote and dower must go to gidre arme in arme. Well, (quoth he) I will communicate aswel this as the rest of our talke vnto thempereur and procure his resolucion therin as shortely as may be for I knowe (quoth he) ye woold be loth to folowe the courte, and I have leave to go to my cuntrey but that now I will tary a while to see these maters in sum good point before my going. [We haue bene also with the Quene of Hungarie[2] vnto whom we declared the kinges maiestes lettres with his highnes and your graces most hartie commendations. And for the better furtheraunce of the kinges affaires we thought good in generalite to communicate vnto her certain part of our charge which she tooke in very acceptable part promising with many good woordes to further to the best of her power this or any other thing that may be for thenterteinment of thamite which she hath alwaies furthered to her best knowing the same to be so necessarie for the welth and commodite of both cuntreis.][3] These haue bene our procedinges hitherto which we haue thought good to signifie to your grace in the meane whiles and as we shall hereafter entre further we will aduertise your grace from tyme to tyme accordingly. And thus we beseche God to preserve your grace and send youe well to do in all your procedinges. From Bruselles the xxiiij June in the mornyng 1549. Your graces most humbly at commaundement

William Paget
Phelyp Hoby

28. *To Sir Thomas Smith. Brussels. 26 June, 1549.* (*SP 68/3 no. 171.*)

(*fo. 146ʳ*) Master Secretary. Aftre my right harty commendacions. These maye be to signifie vnto youe that here hath been with me

---

[1] 'peraduentured' in Add. MS.
[2] Mary, queen dowager of Hungary and regent of the Low Countries, sister of Charles V.   [3] Passage omitted in **Add. MS.**

William Damyzell[1] moche dismayed of such lettres as hath been sent vnto him out of Englande sum before my departing thens and sum sythens; he semeth by anything that I can perceave innocent of suche mattiers as ar layde to his charge and offreth to cum home to sett his foote by who soever shall haue accused his procedinges to my lordes grace, or any of the counsaill and if he be proved false in his administracion for the king thenne to lose his goodes and his lief, requiring only that in the prove of his innocencye such as haue labored by wrong informacions to cloke there own conveyaunces maye haue the lesse creditt aftrewarde. Mary, in one thing he sayth he playd the foole that for the gayne of iiij^{xx} xiij^{li} vjs viijd he bownde him self to thadventure of two thowsand powndes besides the penaltie which is dooble and treble the thing forfaited and thimprisonement of his body. Butt hensfurth he wilbe wyser and never slept quietly (he sayth) till he hard it was in Englande for thenne being there arrived he hadde not to do withall. Butt it was Gresshams[2] own bargayn, and he nother in his own name nor the kinges hadde any parte in it. For thoughe he make sumtymes aventure in his own name and sumtymes wynnes thereby and sumtymes losys as he hath lost even now in a bargayn of oode[3] (he sayth) ccc^{li} yett for the king he will not ne dare aventure with out speciall commission. And in this case of Bullyon his commission was to practise ~~for an exchange of lede or bell metall~~ butt at the leest without excepcion for the delyvery of it in London which lettre I saw and myn own hand amonges other at it and I haue seen the minute of his answere which he saythe was delyvered there within three dayes aftre and remayneth with Master Honinges[4] and herd not from youe in a fortenight aftre. And yett thenne none answere to his lettres, during which tyme Tucker[5] sought his proffitt in the sale of it here to suche as woold abide thaventure of it and mett with Gressham to whom it was twise offred or he tooke it. Well theye two be ones (*fo. 146^v*) towght for thaventuring of bullyon for them selfes onlesse theye haue speciall commaundement for the kinges behaulf. And this man seketh only to haue his seruice graciously taken and none otherwise thenne he deserueth. And in dede to saye my poore opinion it is good alwayes to kepe one eare for him that is absent for so shall the trowth be knowen and men that serve abrode be best cooraged. Such a lettre as was written to Damyzell was the death of one of the proprest men that ever served the king on this syde in his feate; as my lorde of Southampton and your fellowe

---

[1] Sir William Dansell, merchant, raised loans in the Netherlands.
[2] Sir Thomas Gresham.   [3] Woad.
[4] Paget's clerk.
[5] Lazarus Tucker, Antwerp banker.

knowe right well. I meane Hutton[1] whom the Lord Crumwell[2] vpon
an vntrew informacion strake to the harte and killed him that he
lyved not three dayes meryly aftre. A kynde herte meaning truly is
easely with vnkyndnes vndeserued sone dispatched. Wherefore
whenne prynces be in soden heates and specially without certaine
grownd, we secretaries must temporise the matter with termes convenyent for elles no man can be able to serve abrode. Thus partly at
the request of the man and sumwhat vppon myn own simple consideracion and also good will to your well doing I haue thought
convenyent to write, doubting nothing butt that youe will take it in
as good parte as I meane it. And thus praying you both to lett me
here sumtyme from youe of your occurrentes and state of thinges there
and to procure quicke dispatches of aunswere to vs here from tyme
to tyme. I bidde you most hartely well to fare with my harty commendacions to my good litle lady your wief. From Brusselles the
xxvjth of June 1549.

Your assured loving frend to my power
William Paget

I praye you do so muche for me as to send me a minute of my lettre
to Master Petre and you of the xxiiijth of this present; it is written
with myn own hand. Master Honinges will copie it out at the furst
for me.

29. *Sir William Paget and Sir Philip Hoby to Somerset. Brussels.
30 June, 1549.*
(*SP 68/3, no. 177; copies in BM, Cotton MS, Titus B.v, fos.
28ʳ–30ʳ, Galba B.xii, fos. 98ᵛ–101ʳ, Harl. MS 523, fos. 64ᵛ–68ʳ,
Add. MS 5935, fos. 123ʳ–126ᵛ.*)

(*fo. 158ʳ*) It may like your grace to be aduertised that vpon the xxvj
of this present cam to the lodging of me, the comptroller, Monsieur
Darras and in his cumpany the twoo presidentes of the counsail
St. Maurice[3] and Viglius[4] who after a few woordes of office passed
betwene them and vs entred the cause of their cumming, saing that
thempereur hauing bene enformed of such conference as passed this
other da[torn] betwene Monsieur de Granuele (for he so nameth his
father) and youe hath to declare his redynes to anything that might
set furth his good will and affection to thamite of the king: sent vs here

---

[1] John Hutton, ambassador at Brussels at the time of Henry VIII's courtship
of Christina of Milan in 1537.
[2] Thomas Cromwell, earl of Essex.
[3] John de St Mauris, uncle of the bishop of Arras.
[4] Viglius de Zwichem (1507–77).

to revisit the treaties, and see howe we do agree vpon thunderstanding of the same. I, the comptroller, aunswered that it was not amisse howbeit I had not so opened the mater nor looked to haue it passed in such ordre, but furst to knowe thempereurs resolution how he can be contented with the confirmation of the treatie in the forme that I had moved, and that agreed vpon, to procede to the revisitation of the same. In good faith (quoth Darras) we did so vnderstand it and so haue reapported to thempereur and this commission hath he nowe giuen vs. Well, (quoth I) seing you ar now here, and haue brought the treatie with youe for that purpose we may do sumthing in it, and afterward be advised further, requiring that in cace any thing shuld be found in this passage of the treatie meet to be considered, that we might before further reading in the mater knowe thempereurs resolution, aswell touching the confirmation of the treaty, as such thinges as nowe might be moved. Which they thought reasonnable and so we beganne to reade the treatie. And whenne we cam to the vjth article wherin (*fo. 158*ᵛ) it is prouided for the commyn ennemite in cace of inuasion, and by thesclarissement set furth with what nombre the inuasion must be made and that both for thinvasion and nombre the prince required to ioyn shall credite the lettres of the prince requiring. I put this cace (quoth I) for thunderstanding of this mater that the king my master will signifie by his lettres to thempereur that such a daye the Scottes our commyn enemies to the nombre of viijᵐ men of warre with thaide of the French king affronted the borders of Englande comprehended in the treatie, and sent aboue two thousand men of warre in to the realme to inuade, who did in ded inuade and spoile and burne and take prisoners, and therefore wold require thempereur according to the treatie to take the French king who hath aided his ennemis for his ennemie, is not thempereur bounde to do it? What say you (quoth I) how do you vnderstande this article. It shuld seme, yes, (quoth Darras) but we will speke with thempereur in it and bring you an aunswer. The woordes be playn (quoth I) and cannot be avoyded. We will speke with thempereur in it (quoth he) and tooke a note of the cace in a payre of tables, wherin also he noted the rest of the thinges afterward moved. Thenne in the seuenth article, where it is said that the prince requiring for his aide, money in stede of men, must, if thinvasion made by thennemy ceasse, restore the money again which remayneth and afterward saith that though thinuasion ceasse, yet if he will folowe thennemy, he shall may use thaide for the tyme appointed in the treatye, saing in generalite (*eo casu subsidiis auxiliaribus &c*) I asked wheder in those general woordes they meane not aswell the money as the men. Wheruppon they seamed to doubt and tooke a note therof to knowe thempereurs opinion in the same. In the (*fo. 159*) ixth article where is treated for the redres of iniuries done by one subgect to another. Ther we fell in to a brawle of half an howre long vpon a question that I moved, *viz*: whenne they tooke justice to be denyed, and their aunswer that we vsed none at all. And here at length I in to their maner of tharrest of our hole nation vpon a knaue mariners complaint, and he what theves our nation was vpon the sea and lawles people, and that they neuer proceded to such extremities but whenne their subgettes had bene in England and justice was denyed. That hath neuer bene seen (quoth I) but if any of your subgetes think himself greved, straight he runneth to Monsieur le Protectour, and he by and by setting a part all the kinges gret affaires must attende to thaffaire of Monsieur le Marinier, orels home runneth he with open cry that he can haue no iustice in England, and you straight beleve, and theruppon cummith all these often brusleries. And do you think it reason (quoth I) that Monsieur de Granuele or you shuld attende to euery priuate mans complaint, you shuld thenne haue a goodly office. No, you sende them straight to thordinary justice and so let that take place and waye as it woll, but you will neuer empeche yourself more with the mater. And reason (quoth he) but the cace is not like with you in Englande for their (quoth he) all thinges cum to the lord protectours hand. There is none other judge nor justice vsed or cared for in the realm. No, and his lettres sumtymes not estemed, and that our poore subgetes feele full often, and therefore must of force resort to Monsieur le Protectour. This is not true (quoth I) but very slaunderous, for I asseure you (quoth I) that Monsieur (*fo. 159*) lambassadeur knowith, turning to Master Hobby, my lord protectour nor none of the pryvey counsaill medle with no priuate mater whose soeuer it be but only with maters of estate, leaving all other thinges to their ordinary course of justice, except that only many tymes to gratefie your ambassadour and to shewe himself glad to nourishe this amite troubleth himself with the complaintes of your subgetes which (by Saint Mary) by myn aduise he shall do no more seing it is so litle consydred but shall referre them to the commyn justice. Wheder is that (quoth he)? To the admiralte (quoth I). Mary, a goodly justice, quoth he, for so shall the poore mans cause be tried before his aduersarye. And why not tryed in our admiralte (quoth I) aswell as in yours. Mary, (quoth he) both be naught. In dede they wer the verye ordinarie courtes at the beginning for redres of maters vpon the see but now they feele the sweete of the gayn such as they care litle for justice. And here aswell for the relief of poore men spoiled and robbed vpon the sea as to avoyde arrestes and such other troublesum procedinges on either side, we fell to deuising and cam to the point

(if the Princes for their partes vpon their aduertisement to thempereur
and we to your grace shall like it) that commission sufficient be giuen
by thempereur to twoo of his priuey counsaill to here and determine
by their discretion summarie and de plano all complaintes by the
kinges subgetes here for criminal causes vpon the sea, and the kinges
maieste to do the like to twoo of his priuey counsaill for the complaintes in like caces of thempereurs subgetes. And this was all we
passed in open conference saving that in the discours for the confirmation of the treatye by the princes and their cuntreis; as they
semed to shew (*fo. 160ʳ*) thempereurs redynes (but yet not so
resolued) that the prince shuld confirme the treatie and that further
any other thing shuld be done that he might reasonnably do to declare his good will to thentretemement and augmentacion of this
amite and affection to the kinges maiestie, so he alledged diuers
reasons why thempereur shuld not seeke to his subgectes to confirme his treaties with foreign princes. We alledged thexample of the
king and the French king in tymes past and what was saide in that
cace at Callai [*torn*] in the presence of himself, De Courieres and
Chapuis wherunto he aunswered that the state of Fraunce was more
restreined thenne thempereur and that the French king could giue no
part of his patrimony nor binde his cuntrey without the consent of
the parliament at Paris and the three estates, but he thought the
kinges of England to haue a gretter prerogatiue, and thempereur he
was sure had a gretter prerogatiue and so had all his auncestours and
therfore woold be lothe to begin nowe to put himself so far in theyr
subgettes daungers. They wer he said xv or xvj parliamentes and if a
thing shuld be proponed vnto them wherof they had never herd the
like before they woold not only muse much at the mater, but they
woold haue also euery one of them the scannyng of it and what wold
cum of it thempereur could not tell, peraduenture dashe the mater
and so preiudice his prerogatiue with them, and that where now he
and his auncestors do and haue alwayes passed treaties with other
princes and binde their subgetes thereby without making them
priuey therto; it wold by this meane cum to passe that from hensforth
the subgetes woold looke to be priuey to euery treaty, which wer not
convenient. Mary, but for the prince that shall succede to confirme
the treaty he thought thempereur could not take it but reasonable
(*fo. 160ᵛ*) and doubted not to bring a good aunswer in the same. So
as we see that for this point it will cum to the confirmacion of the
king and the prince, and vpon any addition or interpretation of the
treatie to thempereur also wherin we entende to go forwarde for so
our instruction beareth vs onles that before the conclusion and shutting
vp of the mater we here from your grace to the contrarye. The thinges

being thus farre passed and our talkes at a point and they redy to depart Monsieur Darras taking occasion (as it seamed) to stay bicaus of the rayne tooke me a syde and asked me wheder I woold commaunde him any other seruice. I aunswered no seruice but frendship and contynuaunce of his good will to the kinges maiestes affaires wherunto he making large offres I began to entre with him how much your grace and all the rest reposed yourselfes in the frendeship of thempereur and the good ministery of his father and him to the furtheraunce of the kinges maiesties affaires; to whom as in that behalf they shewed themselfes gret freendes as did they like good servauntes to their master, for the prosperous succes of thaffaires of thone serued the turne of thother and contrary. Whereupon I discoursed largely asfar as my poore capacite woold extende howe necessary it was for thempereur tayde vs and assiste vs in all thinges so as we wer not oppressed by force or dryven for want of frendeship to take such wayes to kepe vs in quiet as both we ourselfes wold be loth and our freendes shuld afterwardes haue perauenture cause to forthink. I repeted how furst we entred the warre for their sake for the king might haue made his bargain honorably with Fraunce which no man knew better then I how long we haue endured the warre and how long (*fo. 161*) alone howe fauourable they ar to our commun enemies the Scottes, howe vngentle the French be to vs, and by indirect meanes thinke to consume vs to make thempereur the weaker. I recited the practises of the French with the Turk with the pope, with the Germains, with Denmark, his aide of the Scotes, and all vpon entent to empeche thempereur, whenne he seith tyme or at the least attending a good howre vpon hope of thempereurs death to overthrow his sonne if it shall lye in his power, the which the weaker that we be the easelier shall he do it. And if we forgo any of our peces on thisside we must nedes be the weaker, and that so we had rather do, thenne alone to kepe warre against Scotland and Fraunce. Wherefore if they will provide both for their own strength and giue vs courage to kepe still that which we haue, thempereur must be contented to take Boulloyn in to defence aswell as other places comprehended in the treatie; which I sayd we ment not but vpon a reasonable reciprocq. What reciprocq (quoth he) roundely. Therupon aduise you reasonably (quoth I). O, quoth he, I cannot see how thempereur can honorably make a newe treatye for that point without offence of his treatie with Fraunce, and we meane to procede directly and plainly with all men (quoth he). Why (quoth I) we may bring you iustly by and by in with vs if we will aduertise youe as I did euen now put my cace. Yea, if your cace be true (quoth he) but herin will we charge your honours and conscience wheder the fact be so or no. For your grace shall vnderstande that I talked in that mater so suspiciously as though such an inuasion had bene made and that ye woold require commun ennemite. In fine (*fo. 161*ᵛ), Syr, after many motions and persuasions and long discourses vsed on my behalf to induce them to take Boulleyn in to defence and his refuge only that they woold faine lerne how they might honestly aunswer the French albeit I shewed him sum formes of aunswers which he semed not to like, yet in thende I said he was a gret doctor and as he had put the doubt so he was lerned sufficiently (if he listed) to assoyle the same. He said he wold open these maters to thempereur and trusted to bring me such aunswer as I shuld haue reason to be satisfied and so departed. Wherof assone as we haue knoweledge your grace shalbe aduertysed accordingly. And thus we beseche God to sende your grace well to do in all your procedinges. From Bruxelles the last of June in the mornyng 1549.

Your graces most humbly at commaundement

William Paget

Phelyp Hoby

30. *To Somerset. Brussels. 30 June, 1549.*
(*SP 68/3, no. 176, partly in cipher, but deciphered in margins; copies in BM, Cotton MS, Titus B. v, fos. 30ʳ–31ʳ, and Galba B. xii, fo. 41ʳ–41ᵛ; modernized text printed by Strype, ii (ii), pp. 416–18.*)

Sends a separate letter so that Somerset may understand the manner of his proceedings. Reviews the causes of his mission to the emperor. Asks whether the following points should be added to the treaty with Charles V: That he shall be the common enemy that surprises any of the king's and emperor's forts in any places comprehended in the treaty or that shall be added to the treaty. That safe conducts to traffic shall be neither given nor taken either to the common enemy or of their own subjects. Asks whether he should speak of the matter of marriage.

The following is omitted from Galba B. xii, the text printed by Strype:

Sir, themperor growyng now in to age desyreth moche to ryde easely and seekes allwayes he can for that purpose wherfor, Sir, if your grace shall present hym at his cumyng to Graveling by the Lord Cobham whom I think your grace will ordeine to salute themperor on the kinges behalf and your own cumyng so nere your frontiers with vj hackeneys of meane stature goynge easely iiij in the kinges name and ij in your own name it wilbe very kyndly taken and sumtyme such trifles styrve more occasions of frendship then gretter matters or practises do.

> Your graces most humbly and
> hartely at commaundement
> William Paget

31. *To Petre or Smith. Brussels. 30 June, 1549.*
(SP 68/3, no. 175.)

Aftre my most harty commendacions. As I am suer our procedinges here shall appere vnto youe by our commen lettres: So haue I thought good not to molest youe otherwise with the same, only praying youe that I maye here from youe of your occurentes there. Whereby youe shall do me singuler pleasour and therwithall to helpe to procure me aunswere both spedely and certaynly of such thinges as at this present we desire to be answered in from my lordes grace and to retorne my man againe with diligence with the same. And thus I byd you most hartely well to fare from Bruselles the last of June in the morning 1549.

> Your own Paget.

I haue geuen my man money both for his goynge and his retorne. I praye youe to retorne vnto me by this bearer a copie of the lettre I wrote vnto youe with myn own hande of the xxiiijth of this presente. We haue newes here by Andwerpe of gret maystryes that our men haue made in Scotland and out of France that Vervyns[1] is behedd and de Byes[2] cast to be drawen into four quarters but there is hoped for a pardon also that there be descending downe out of Swyzerland into Fraunce xvj^{M} Swyzers. The cyphre wherin I write is Master Hobbyes ciphre.

32. *Paget and Hoby to Somerset. Brussels. 3 July, 1549.*
(SP 68/4, no. 179; a copy in BM, Harl. MS 523, fo. 120^{v}.)

It may lyke your grace to be advertesyd that this gentleman bearer hereof an Italian called Signor Malatesta de Riminye a man as we ar enformed of good estimacion and honnest service and one that hath had the leading of men and excersysed heretofore offices of charge in the warre, being lately put from his lyving and forced to forsake his cuntrie by the bysshop of Rome, intending to present his service in England with sume convenient nombre of men hath byn here with vs to declare his good affection towardes the kinges maieste and the cause of his present repayre in to our cuntrie and therwithall

---

[1] Jacques de Coucy, seigneur de Vervins.   [2] Oudart, seigneur du Biez.

to require our lettres in his commendacion. And albeit after we had gratefied hym with thankes for the good will he semeth to beare towardes the king, we shewed hym that his maieste hath not presently any other thing in hand then suche as we hope his owne subgettes shalbe well enof able to dyscharge without thintrotainment of more straungers then his highnes hath allredy in service and therfore went abowt to perswade hym to stay till better occasion might serve, promesing to cause his gentle offer then to be remembred: yet for that he is cume so farre from home, and so nere England, he will nedes he saith performe his jorney, to thintent that if your grace shall not haue presently wherin to employe his service yet at the least he may se the king and kysse his maiestes hand for which respect he hath required these our lettres which we could not denye hym. Your grace may therfore be pleased if ye mynde not to accept his service to cause hym to be gratefyed with sume gentle woordes for his good will and to dismiss hym. Thus allmightie God preserve your grace with most happie successe in all your affayres. From Brusselles the iij de day of July *anno* 1549.

> Your graces most humbly to commaunde
> William Paget
> Phelyp Hoby

33. *To Somerset. No place. 7 July, 1549*
   (PLB; SP 10/8, no. 4; BM, Cotton MS, Titus F. iii, fos. 274ʳ–276ᵛ; modernized text printed by Strype, ii (ii), pp. 429–37)
Is deeply perplexed by Somerset's policies. Fears for Somerset, the King, and the country. Wishes his earlier advice had been followed. The commons have disregarded the law and have become a king appointing new conditions and laws. Wishes Somerset had acted more vigorously when the rebellions began. Laments war with Scotland and France. Doubts whether enclosures are the cause of popular discontent. Every member of the council was opposed to Somerset's proceedings with the commons. Reminds Somerset how Henry VIII kept his subjects in obedience. Recommends use of military force and firm justice against the rebels. Hopes that Somerset will take his advice graciously.

34. *To Petre. Brussels. 8 July, 1549.*
   (SP 68/4, no. 185; copy BM, Cotton MS, Titus B. v, fos. 33ᵛ–34ʳ.)

(fo. 53ʳ) Master secretary, with my most harty commendacions. Youe shall vnderstande that yesternight Francisco[1] arrived here by

---

[1] An Italian courier in the service of the English.

whom I receaved your lettres amonges the rest, for the which I most hartely thanke youe. Signifying further vnto youe to be aduertised to my lordes grace that I feare I am like to haue here butt a colde iourney for notwithstanding that I haue sent aboue foure tymes for aunswere to our last taulkes, yett I am putt of with fayre woordes and thempereur departed to Lovayn from whens he will retorne to morowe and within a daye or two to Gaunte the highe waye to Englande whether I thinke I maye cum shortly for any greate mattier I haue to do here, butt suche as I thinke wilbe sone concluded.

Viz., the confyrmacion of the treatie, for the other poyntes of myn instruccions ar defalked. The mariage if theye speak not as (I thinke) theye will not is thought good to be no more spoken of, the entre for ioynt invacion is taken awaye, which I like also if they seke it not. And the comprehencion of Bulloyn is taken awaye which I like not, for by vertue of myn instruccions I haue gone so farre as if theye embrace it I se not well how it can be avoyded, and me thinkes it serueth to greate purposse to trye him with all and bring him in. And as for your bownde to defende another place in reciproke therof whenne peraduenture Bulloyn shalbe departed with all is nothing, as who sayth youe maye not do as you haue been done to. Alas, Master secretary, we must not thinke that heven is here, butt that we lyve in a woorld. It is a wonderfull mattier to here what brutes runne abrode here of your thinges at home which killeth my harte to here and (*fo. 53*ᵛ) I wott not what to saye to them because I knowe they be trewe, and theye be aswell knowen here in every mans mowthe as youe knowe them at the courte, and I feare me bettre and that not by Frenche men, butt by these cuntrey men and our own good nacion. If theye conclude vpon the confyrmacion I haue executed my commission as it is nowe restrayned onlesse I shalle talke further of Bulloyn whereof I woolde be gladde to be enformed, and whether I shall vpon the conclucion of this confyrmacion retorne home if theye speake nothing more, or elles remayn here still like a cyphre in algorisme. I haue for the conforte of my poore wief and children sent this bearer my servant expressely to her and appoynted him to saye sumthing to you tooching myn own affayres. I praye youe lett me here from you shortly by my said seruante whom or elles Fletcher[1] I haue willed to retorne to me within two or three dayes and by him if youe or my lordes grace whose pleasour I require youe to knowe in the premisses will any thing to me you may sende me woord and I praye youe do so for it shall cost the king no money. This lettre to my lordes grace we thought good to open leest any thing hadde been in it to haue been done here. Youe write that youe haue sent me the copie

[1] Paget's servant.

of my other lettre which I desired, butt it is not cum. Thus I bidde you most hartely well to fare. From Bruxelles the viijth of July in the morning 1549.

Concernyng the poynt of ordenyng judges of both counsailes for the determynacion of complayntes for matters on the see wherof we wrote in our last lettres and haue non answer, we mynd to follow our instructons onless you send word by the next to the contrary which I pray you to remember.

Your own Paget.

35. *Paget and Hoby to Somerset. Alost.   12 July, 1549.*
   (SP 68/4, no. 187; copies in BM, Cotton MS, Titus B.v, fos. 34ᵛ–37ʳ, Galba B.xii, fos. 101ᵛ–102ᵛ, Harl. MS 523, fos. 68ʳ–69ᵛ, Add. MS 5935, fos. 126ᵛ–130ʳ.)

(*fo. 57ʳ*) It may like your grace after our most humble recommendacions to be aduertised that having sence our last conference with Darras and his company which is now xv dayes passed had none aunswer from thempereur although we haue thre or foure tymes vsed meanes for the same. To thende we woold giue them tunderstand we thought the tyme very long and to knowe (if we could) the cause of the same I, the comptroller, sent yesternight vnto Monsieur de Granuele desyring him bicause I herd saye he went towardes Bourgoyn shortly and I also for any thing me seamed I had to do here might in like maner departe shortly in to Englande to appoint me sum tyme to visite him to knowe if he woold at his being in his cuntrey and I in myn commaunde me in any thing wherin I might do him pleasur or seruice. He returned me woord that if I woold the morowe folowing at viij of the clock take paines to cum to his lodging I shuld be right welcum. And (quoth he) to the messenger ye may see howe I lye (for he was thenne in his bedd) tormented with paines in my legges. But bicaus I my self am not able thereto my son Monsieur Darras doth sollicite the mater to thempereur with whom he is nowe about the same. And let him not think (quoth he) that he is forgotten for I assure youe the mater hath bene all this weke very diligently debated as I shall further declare vnto Monsieur Paget at his cumming hither. According to his appointement we repaired to Monsieur de Granuele this morning to whom I, the comptroller, at my cumming declared that considering his good affection towardes the king my master and hering saye he was minded to depart (*fo. 57ᵛ*) shortly towardes his cuntrey I was now cum both to take my leave of him and to knowe wheder he woold commaund me any service at my cumming in to Englande. He thanked me for my gret offre and after that he had by sundry good woordes set furth thaffection he beareth towardes the kinges maieste and his procedinges. Well, (quoth he) leaving these maters apart, let vs entre in to those that ar of greater emportaunce. And first I promise you (quoth he) that this long staye thempereur hath made to thaunswer of your charge hath not been for any lack of good will on his part or for want of affection towardes the king his good brother, but only bicaus he hath ben letted by other maters of importaunce about the settling of his sonne in these partes by such ordre as hath heretofore bene seldom seen in these partes and therefore hath it bene sumwhat difficult to cumpasse but bicaus he shall not haue conuenient tyme to depeche you hens as his desyre was he prayeth you at your commodite to meet him at Gaunt where he wilbe vpon Sonday at night at the furthest and there the furst thing that he will go about shalbe to despeche youe. Monsieur Granvele, (quoth I) it is now xv dayes as ye knowe sens your son, Monsieur Darras, and I wer last to gidres and considering that in this meane while we haue had neither aunswer nor any motion therof we cannot but think it sumwhat straunge howbeit as ye saye thempereur perhaps hath bene busyed about maters of much importaunce, and esteming those that I am cum for hither but light in respect of thotheres (*fo. 58ʳ*) hath thought best to differe myn aunswer till better leasyr. Nay, (quoth he) I woold be loth ye shuld suspect so for by myn honor and faith that I beare to thempereur my master his maieste fauoureth no les the king his good brother then his naturel son and the furtheraunce of his procedinges as his owne, as whenne tyme requireth shalbe well declared. But (quoth he) his maieste hath differed this aunswer only to gyve the resolution thereof at Gaunt wher he shall be at better leasyr and shall he hopeth dispeche you thene in such sort as you shall haue cause to be contented. I am, Monsieur de Granvele, (quoth I) cum hither as ye see to serve thempereur and to sollicite those thinges that me semeth ar asmuch to his commodite as ours considering that the welth of thone dependeth on thothers surety which besides the particuler affection that I beare and always haue borne to thestablishement of this amite moveth me the rather to desyre the short conclusion herof. Monsieur lambassador, (quoth he) I assure you thempereur my master meaneth non other wayes but vprightly without dissimulation towardes his good brother and if he shuld vse any other termes with you then playn trouth considering he hath no maner occasion therto, I assure you I wold not repute him worthy the name and estimation he beareth. But (quoth he) you may be bold to think he meaneth good faith and tendereth no les the kinges affaires then his owne and be ye sure he will not sei hym (*fo. 58ᵛ*)

C M—E

forgo any small jote of that he hath presently if he may let it as he hath sent plain woord to the French that if the touche the king in never so small point of those thinges that ar comprised within the treatyes with Englande, he will not faile to sei redres therof and the same message hath my sonne, Darras, told thambassador here and biddes them looke for none other but that we will plainly shewe youe all the pleasyr we can. And (quoth he) we knowe aswell by coniecture as by aduertisementes from Fraunce that they will not for thys tyme breake with youe in open ennemite but perhaps procure as their custume is to steale by pollicie sum pece of yours which we vnderstande they minde tattempt shortly. But (quoth he) looke well to your thinges and keepe them out of their handes this yere and doubt ye not but the next yere God will sende you sum assistence that shall help youe and gyve them inough to busy themselfes in as ye shall I trust shortly perceiue. In good faith, Monsieur Granuele, (quoth I) we haue long sence estemed thempereurs procedinges and ours commun and the chiefest cause that might haue moved doubt of his amite which was his aspiration to a monarchie being now of a long while clered out of our stomackes we can not but think his gretnes maketh for vs and do recon our selfes most assured of his freendeship and so do we make accompt of him as our chiefest well willer. Ye nede not (*fo. 59*^{r}) (quoth he) to doubt therof but we must do our thinges with respect temporising them as tyme and occasion serveth but within this viij monethes or ten at the furthest ye shall see what will folowe. And haue an eye (quoth he) to your thinges this yere (which woordes he repeted sundry tymes throughout his talke) and doubt ye not but ye shall afterwarde haue thassistence of your freendes. And here taking occasion to set furth the French vnfrendly procedinges towardes thempereur I shewed him that considering thempereurs prudence and his circumspection it was in vain for me (if I wer of abilite therto as I am not) to go about to perswade them to looke to their thinges in tyme who I knewe did both forsei and provide for all eventes much better then I could conceiue. But yet (quoth I) the desyre I haue to see thempereur and his posterite prosper maketh me wishe that the French wer prevented who as I am sure ye knowe well ynough do gape howrely for thempereurs death (whose lief I wishe to be long) so ceasse they not to practise with sundry princes both of Germanye and other where to be on their syde tabate the prince of Spaines power hoping then to haue a faire tyme to work their feate. And after I had spent sum while in discoursing this mater vnto him touching by the waye in particularites aswell as my wit wold serve me such thinges as for the well setting furth of the mater I (*fo. 59*^{v}) thought metest to be remembred he aunswered me that in dede it was not vnknowen to thempereur that the French vsed these practises which he wold not overpas in silence when he might sei his tyme. But, quoth he, thempereur as ye knowe hath lately ben much troubled with Germanye and albeit he hath thankes be to God brought thestates there to good termes of obedience yet wold he gladly before he procede to any other entreprise put sum surer staye there which after his sonne shalbe settled here he mindeth to go about and hopeth to bring it to passe or it be viij monethes to an ende, and then shall ye perceiue what his meaning is towardes Fraunce. I perceiue Monsieur Granuele, quothe I, that ye wold willingly overpas this yere without stirring towardes the Frenche and in the meane while settle your thinges in Germanie. But yet me semeth (quoth I) seing thempereur hath alredy brought thestate of Germanie to such passe as their bodyes ar holy at his will and commaundement wanting non other thing for their perfit obedience then the consent of their will and hartes which cannot be so soudenly obteyned without sum length of tyme the nerest waye to bringe them herunto is to take awaye the occasion that might encourage their bodyes talienate their mindes and good willes from him amonges which no faile the chiefest is their hope in the French whose practise perhaps might stirre (*fo. 60*) sum innovation if he be not in tyme looked vnto and abated. Ye say true (quoth he) and I promise you[1] their doinges do well declare their good meaning towardes vs but I mistrust not they shall be well ynough prevented. And here tooke he occasion both to set furth the prince of Spaines towardnes and habilitie to guide his thinges whatsoeuer shuld happen of his father and also to dispraise with most biting woordes the French and their double dealing. I wisse (quoth I) the French haue not this opinion of youe for in their discourses they let not taffirme that ye ar much better French then English if for non other respect at the least bicaus ye ar their neighbour in Bourgoyn where if any stirre be betwen thempereur and them they think ye shalle first feele it and therefor wold ye willingly haue them your freendes as long as might be. Ye saye true in dede (quoth he) the good hope I haue of the French freindship and the trust I haue to kepe my thinges in Bourgoyn in quiet haue made me make so small reconyng of them that I haue now lately bought certain possessions here in these quarters where I minde er it be long to settle myself, such is my desyre of their neighbourly frendeship. And as for thempereur my master his maieste when he hath settled his thinges will I doubt not declare thoccasion they haue gyven him to desyre their (*fo. 60*) amite. I wisse when tyme shalbe I haue my slevefuls of querels to breake with

[1] Galba B. xii and Harl. 523 end.

them and in the meane while if they attempt any thing towardes youe be ye sure thempereur tendereth the king his good brothers thinges so much as they shall well perceiue his maieste will not forsake youe as even now I shewed youe he gave them a while sence plainly tunderstande. I touched further in this talke vnto him those pointes that your grace in your last lettre willed vs to put furth *viz.* the restraint of saufconduites, which in dede by the woordes of the treatye aught not to be graunted of any of both parties. The commun ennemite for the surprise of any pece of either partie which I said thempereur having more to looke to then we ought the rather tembrace, and the mater of inuasion with les nombre then is prescribed in the treatye. He aunswered first to the graunting of saufconduites when I demaunded how he vnderstode the woordes of the treatye that said he thought neither part ought to graunte any and therfor graunt you none (quoth he) and for our partes we will not gyve any. As to surprise of any pece of either prince he said that like as thempereur for his parte toke the king my masters thinges to touche him so nere as he wold not faile to haue the same regard to them that he hath to his own, so mistrusted he not but the kinges maieste wold also haue the same respect towardes his maiestes thinges (*fo. 61ʳ*) and considre that the losse of the same cannot but turne to his discommodite. As to the mater of inuasion he said that the same mater was at Vtrecht put furth by our men desyring to haue the nombre of those that shuld invade moderated to vᴹ but God forbid (quoth he) that either you or we shuld at any time be so weke as we might not be able to withstande viij thousand of our enemyes without troubling of our freendes and for my part in respect of both princes honnours I wold be right loth our back freendes shuld perceiue this mater to be put in question. But (quoth he) these thinges shalbe moved to thempereur and aunswered with the rest at thempereurs cumming to the Gaunt where (as I haue shewed youe) he trusteth to dispeche youe to your satisfaction. Herof we haue thought good taduertise your grace bicaus he talked so frankly with vs as semed to vs gret mervaill. And yet for all that it is not woordes can pleas me except I sei sum dedes folowe wherwith if they cum not of very shortly I sei not but this my tarying here now all most a moneth in this sort may serve them to gret purpose els where and peraduenture do no good to your procedinges in other places which I doubte not your grace doth considre and will enforme me of your pleasur therin which I will not faile to folowe accordingly. The bruites dayly do encreace here of your doinges at home more and more. I beseche God to quiete them and put in your (*fo. 61ᵛ*) graces minde to do that which may be the surety of the kinges maieste preservation of the state of the realme and your own honnour which no man desireth more then we do for our partes and wold willingly to that effect spende the best blood in our bodyes. From Allost the xijth of July 1549.

Your graces most humbly at commaundement
William Paget
Phelyp Hoby

36. [*To Petre.*] *Ghent. 13 July, 1549.*
(*SP 68/4, no. 189.*)

(*fo. 71ʳ*) Master secretary, with my most harty commendacions I thanke you lykewise for your gentle lettres of aduertisement praying you though youe shall not haue convenient leisor to write so often to me how thinges go there as you woold yet to cause your clerk to take sum payne therin and your lettres beyng delyuered to Master Mason[1] he will by thordinary post send them to Calles from whens cumyth hither one or other dayly. I long to heare wheder all thinges be appeased well, which wold be moch to my confort. And these men heare I meane the gretist seme to desyre it moche for Granuele at our beyng with hym did sum what toche it uppon occasion of thexcuse for our delay in that themperor for thestablishement of his sonne had sumwhat to do among these people which be sumwhat rude (quoth he) and if themperer had not at the begynnyng drawen his swerde and shewed authorite the thinges he doth with them now woold not haue bene brought to passe and now thankes be to God he hath as obedient subgettes of them as ever prince had. Mary, we here say that your commyns at home font grand barbularye[2] but it is nothing (sayth he) if Monsieur Protector steppe to it betyme and travaile in person as thempereur hymself did with the sworde of justice in his hand. We told hym the mater was at appoynt and made litle of it how hevy so ever our hartes tooke it and so he passed the matter in shewyng how moche (*fo. 71ᵛ*) themperor the kinges prosperite in all his thinges both at home and abrode ar at more length is tooched in our lettre to my lordes grace and therfor I omitt to write any more of it to you but only desyring to be fully answered in euery thing wherof I wrote by my seruant to you. I byd you most hartely well to fare from Gawnt the xiijth of July 1549.

Your own Paget

I pray you let me know how far forth you ar in your enterfore at Aberlady, which I haue had sum tochyng thenemyes eyther haue taken or mynd to take.

---

[1] Sir John Mason, ambassador to France.   [2] Hurly burly.

37. *Paget and Hoby to Somerset. Bruges. 22 July, 1549.*
(*There is no single complete surviving copy of this letter. Cotton MS, Titus B. v, fos. 37ᵛ–38ᵛ is incomplete. The copy in Galba B. xii, fos. 77ʳ–82ᵛ, has the right hand margin torn so that one word is missing on each line; another copy, Galba B. xii, fos. 103ʳ–104ᵛ, is complete but abridged carelessly with names missing. The latter copy and Hoby's letter book, Harl. MS 523, fos. 70ʳ–71ᵛ, which is also abridged, give a different ending.*)

Titus B.v

To my Lord Protectors grace from Master Comptroller and Master Hobby at Burges xxii Julii, 1549

It maye lyke your grace to be aduertised that vpon Mondaye laste cam vnto vs the president St. Maurice wherby remembring aftre there longe delaye to answere vs how Granvela hadde promysed vs we shulde be dispatched ymmediatly vpon the emperors arrivall at Gaunt we loked certaynly to receave even nowe then by the president sum resolucion of themperours mynde in the mattiers proponed by me ye comptroller. And so settling our selfes to gethers and we beynge attentive to here, the president sayd he cam not to trooble vs butt onely to knowe our myndes in two or thre perticuler matters. The fyrst was what we would haue them to do with *hym that had counterfayted the lycence and* begyled the poore marchaunt. The secounde was a request to haue the booke concerning the controuersie betwene the Lady Forman and Petwell to be delivered into the counsayll of Brabantes handes. And the thyrde was in forme of a sute to be good to one Capytayn Buckholte against Thomas Chambrelayn.[1] Touching the counterfayter (we saide) seing we hadde enformed them of the mattier we coulde saye no more butt remitt the rest to thexecucion of there lawes forseying that the poore marchaunt were satisfied. So he shall (quoth the president) and also make amendes honorable to the kinge and further we must requyre you to be meanes where the marchaunt being accused before the counsayll to haue counterfayted the seale didde laye caucion to baulte out the verey counterfayter and cause him to be apprehended, seyng he hath performed the condicion of his caucion that he may be discharged of his caucion which we tooke vpon vs to do. And to the secounde pointe I, Sir Philip Hobby, answered that indede those bokes he required, were in my custodie butt I coulde not (having contrarie commaundment) delyver them furthe of my power. Mary, I said, yf any of the counsaill or other by there appoyntment wold

---

[1] Sir Thomas Chamberlain, ambassador to the regent of the Netherlands.

for ye better expedicion of the mattier haue a sight or pervse any of them, I wold not refuse it, so the passed out[1] furth of my house and custodye, but when I shuld be departed (*fo. 38ʳ*) hence I told him I could not leave the bokes behynde me vnlesse themperour and the Regent wold promysse that yf I lefte them in the gouernance of the marchauntes handes he shuld not at any tyme either by decree, com-maundment, or other wyse be forced to delyuer them out of his handes, but for the shorte conclusion of this controversye to suffre from tyme to tyme such as the counsaill shuld appoynt therto, to haue a syght of the sayd bokes in his house of[2] presence. To Buck-holtes case we answered that the mattier was not Thomas Cham-brelayns butt the kinges whose maieste we knowe hadde been much dysceaved herein, but because his highnes doth not reknoledge any judge and that Buckholte was sumtyme his maiesties seruante we offered (as had been offred to the sayd Buckholte before) to cause him to haue a salve conduicte for his repayre in to England with his bookes and reconynges, where if he could make it appeare yt he had not receaved so much as he ought to haue, we promysed he shuld be payde to the vttermost haulfpeny, so as he also for his parte wolde be bownd if it were proved he had receaved more then is dew vnto hym, to make restitucion therof accordingly. Vnto these answeres ye president made no maner replique but passed furth to other familier talke without tooching any parte of our principall matters wherto we supposed he had brought sum answere, whiche seming vnto vs verey straunge I, the Comptroller, tolde hym that I had well hoped considering the tyme of myne abode here without any consolucion to those thinges I hadde before proponed, that he had now brought ordre to make vs answere therin, but because I harde him speake nothing therof I could not I sayd but marvell much thereat. He answered that he came onely about such mattiers as he had opened vnto vs without any further commission, neverthelesse he was suer that at Monsieur Darras commyng who was gone he sayd as farre as Anwarpe to accompany his father Monsieur Granvela (who is now departed towardes Burgony) and wold be here he supposed the morow folowing we shuld not faile to haue a full resolucion to our contentacion. I replyed that I had been here now a moneth (*fo. 38ᵛ*) or v wekes without having don any thing more then at the firste daye which I could not butt thinke strange. I prayed him yr fore to beseche themperours maieste humbly on my behaulf that it wold please him to cause sum answere to be made vnto me herein, either one waye or other that I might dispatche my self hens, for I was I sayd commaunded by your grace and my lordes of the counsayll to

---

[1] Galba B. xii, fo. 77ᵛ, has 'not'.   [2] Galba B. xii, fo. 78ʳ, has 'and'.

repayre home as shortly as I could, and at the furthest, I tolde him I must nedes be gon the weke folowyng, which he promysed to open to themperour accordingly and so departed. The next morowe the Secretarie Ravas was sent vnto me from themperor to make excuse for this staye that hath been in answering to my charge, prayeng me in his maiestes name not to thinke the tyme longe although his busines about his soones receaving and s[w]earing of these parties hadde occasyoned hym to delaye my dyspatche thus long which he promysed now shuld be gone in hande with all ymmediatly vpon Monsieur Darras cumyng which he sayd wold be yt nyght or the next day by noone and he doubted not but I shuld be dyspatched before his maiestes departure from Gaunt. Yea, so may I be (quoth I) and yet tary a moneth for my dispatche, yf his maieste ramayn so long in this towne. Naye, (quoth he) themperour tarieth not here past Saturday, but you shalbe or at the furthest he wilbe gon on Mondaye, but you shalbe dispatched out of hande as sone as Monsieur Darras commeth. We haue (quoth I) been here so longe [wh]yle and done so lytle that I promesse you I am all togayther verey[1] therof, and to be playn with you I must nedes thinke ye mattier verey straung and though I say lytle I thinke more, butt I pray you beseche his maieste to considre my longe abode and haue in remembraunce the dispatche of my charge in such sorte as it shall please hym, that I consume not any longer tyme here in vayn, he sayed he wolde make reaporte to themperor and doubted not but ere it were longe, I shuld receave such answere as I shuld be satisfied. [*end*]

*Galba B. xii fo. 79*ᵛ

The Thursdaye aftre hering saye that Monsieur Darras was the daye before about dyner tyme cum to town and hauing not till thenne herd any thing from him as was promysed, I sent him woord that his father at our last being with him at Bruxelles promysed that I shulde be dispatched ymediately vpon thempereurs arrivall at Gaunt and because I herd saye that his maieste departed very shortly towardes Bruges I desyred him I might knowe wether he hadde yette resolved vpon any answer to those thinges I had proponed, to thende I might know whereunto I shulde trust. Because (quoth he) to the messenger Monsieur Lambassadeur shall not thinke this delaye so strange & that he maye perceave there lacketh rather leysor thenne good will on my behaulf I praye youe make reaporte vnto him howe I have spent my time sythens my cumyng hether. I arrived here (quoth he) as I am suer youe haue herd on Tewesday at dyner tyme and all that aftre

---

[1] Galba B. xii, fo. 79ʳ, has 'wery'.

none was occupyed in consulting with the heddes of this town for the
maner of the favering of the prince. And the next daye or ever his
highnes hadde taken his (*fol. 80ʳ*) othe and the town sworne to him it
was late in the . . . . . noone and yett not forgetting Monsieur Lambassadeur I th. . . . . to speake with the regent for the sollicita-
cion of his . . . . butt being cum to the courte for this purposse
I fownd . . . . she was walked abrode and therefore coulde I
not speake with her that night and all this morn . . . . . . haue I been
consulting with the state of Heinalte f. . . . . . the maner of the princes
swering there so that . . . . . . trust Monsieur Lambassadeur may
perceave there hath be. . . . . no slacknes on my part hetherto, butt
this aftrenoone will I not faile to procure to speake with the qu. . . . . .
. . that we may wyne to gether and he haue his di. . . . . . tomorrowe
if it be possible which answere whenne . . . . herd I assure your grace
I was not a litle moved. . . . coulde haue well fownd in my harte such
was . . . . . stomack to haue vttered my mynd frankly both to the
. . . . . and his counsaill if theye hadde been present, . . . consydering
the practizes of the woorld I coulde . . . . . me thought iudge that this
there faint excuse w. . . . . any cause of my long staye being a
mattier ov. . . . . playn to be perceaved butt that the chief occasion
depended vpon other handeling and intelligence abrode. . . . my
conceipte wherein I leave to trooble yor grace (*fo. 80ᵛ*) referring the
same to yor prudence which may easely gesse whereunto it tendeth.
The daye following which was Friday thempereur being contrary to
all mens expectacion departed in the fornoone towardes Bruges, in
the aftrenoone Darras accompanyed with president St Maure cam
to my lodging and albeit I was the daye before sum what moved, yett
hoping they hadde brought sum resolucion I quieted my self, and
aftre salutacions and woordes of office I began to geve eare what they
woold saye whenne sodaynly Darras aftre a greate circumstaunce
and many goodly poynted woordes entred thexcuse for my long
abode here with out answere to my charge which he affyrmed was
occasioned by thempereurs busynes about the princes swering in these
townes and prayed me therefore on his maiestes behaulf to take
patience vntill his cumyng to Bruges where without faile he said I
shuld be dispatched, which whenne I harde and perceaving in stede
of the resolucion and answere that I looked for to be only fedde with
fayre woordes I must confesse vnto your grace I could not kepe
patience butt being entred sumwhat into coller answered him that I
was now here at thempereurs will & commandement; he might staye
me as long as it liked him and dispatche me whenne he list, butt
(quoth I) were I ones at home I knowe that nether the kinges maiestie
woolde sende me hether nor I for my (*fo. 81ʳ*) parte to wynne an

hundreth thowsande crownes cum again*[1] about any like mattier consydering how couldly ye have* hitherto proceded and suerly I am sory that either ye shulde iudge me so voide of witt that I coulde not perceave where unto this childishe excuse tendeth or* occasion me to suppose youe so muche without consideratyon* as to thynke I woold be brought to beleve that* the princes swering and receaving into these towns coulde be any delaye to the answering of those thinges* that I am cam hether for. A mattier easy ynough* to be perceaved of such as never hadde any experience* of the woorlde. For who can thinke that thempereur woolde h...... brought his sonne hether to be sworne and receaved of ...... subiectes without having before concluded and determyned th..... hole circumstances thereof with his estates here or can.... occupacion therein be suche and so contynuall as he..... no tyme to answere to iiij or v poyntes proponed to him almost now v wekes past. Hereunto Darras very* coldly answered that in good fayth the cause of my* staye what so ever I thought was only such as* he hadde shewed me and therefore prayed me not* conceave any other opinion for I assure youe (quoth he) thempereur bearith the king his good brother as muche affection as if he (*fo. 81ᵛ*) were his sonne and woold gladly ayde and assiste him in all thinges to the vttermost that he maye convenyently. Butt (quoth he) these mattiers are wayghty and require to be answered vnto with deliberacion. If they semed as waightie vnto you as youe speake (quoth I) I can not iudge butt ye woold or this tyme haue spyed out sum tyme to answere vnto them, and as for thempereurs assistance my master requireth it not any other wayes thenne shall appeare to be requisite and beneficiall for both parties and therefore if thoccasion of this long delaye be vpon any other consideracion thenne ye haue yett declared vs, I woold wishe ye delt like freendes and opened the same franckly; and I knowe (quoth I) that these mattiers were concluded vpon before Monsieur Granvelas departure which maketh me the more to muse why ye shulde so long staye from making reaporte of your answere. Naye, (quoth he) I assure youe there was none answer resolved on at Monsieur Granvelas going nor is not yett, nether is there any other cause I assure youe that hath stayed the same thenne hath been already declared vnto you.[2] At the least (quoth I) in case ye had not resolved vpon the hole, yet ar there certaine generall poyntes which I knowe ye were long sythens determyned how ye woold answere and that ye might in this meane tyme haue declared your myndes and shewed vs which thinges

---

[1] Words inserted from Galba B. xii, fos. 103ʳ–104ᵛ.

[2] Beginning of different ending in Galba B. xii, fo. 104ᵛ and Harl. MS 523, fo. 71ᵛ.

ye hadde resolved vpon and which other ye stayed tanswere vnto thende if any doubtes were moved on yor behaulf we might either haue (*fo. 82*^{r}) clered them or aduertised home of that hadde been s...... withall which woold haue caused vs to haue iudged you to p........ franckly with vs. Butt I having been here about these thinges v wekes and the chiefest parte of my charge been debated at good length with thempereurs ambassad.... England before my comyng over I am now as nere.... I was the furst daye I came hether which maye w....good cause make my lorde protectors grace and lordes .... the counsaill judge a great slacknes and lacke of diligence in me. Monsieur Lambassador (quoth he) we haue .... hetherto answered to any perticuler poynt of your charge because we thought best to make a full answere of the hole to gether, which without faile shalbe at the cumyng to Bruges which wilbe vpon Moundaye .... the meane while his maiestie desyreth youe .... take patience as ye haue don hetherto and then because he turneth another waye youe maye .... suer to be dispatched home. Hereof being the substance .... our discourse hadde with the said Darras haue we thought, ... taduertise your grace, and that also vpon such conclu.... as we shall make here I, the comptroller, ent.... departe home. Thus we besech God send your grace as well to do as we woold wishe .... From Brudges xxij July in the morning.

William Paget
Phelip Hobby

Galba B. xii, fo. 104^r, and Harl. MS 523, fo. 71^v, have the following ending:

The bruites dayly doe increase heare of your doinges at home more and more. I beseche God to quiet them and put in your graces mynde to doe that whiche maye be to the suertye of the kynges maiesties preservascyone of the estate of the realme and your graces owne honore which no men desyreth more then we doe for our partes and wold gladly to that effecte spend the best blude in our bodyes. Sir William Paget, Sir Philipe Hobby to Somerset. Thus we beseche God send your grace aswell to do as we would wishe you.

38. *To Sir William Petre and in his absence to Sir Thomas Smith. Bruges. 22 July, 1549.*
    (SP 68/4, no. 192; modernized text printed in Tytler, i, pp. 190–92.)

Complains about the covetousness of Sir John Thynne. Has not met with the Emperor since his first coming. States that to alter the state of the realm would require ten years' deliberation. Needs to purge himself being well farsed with Rhenish wine. Emperor intends to depart on Friday and Paget as soon as he is dispatched. Received £200, which was worth a scant £150; and that is all spent plus an additional £300.

39. *Paget and Hoby to Somerset. Bruges. 24 July, 1549.*
  (*BM, Cotton MS, Galba B. xii, fos. 83ʳ–89ᵛ, damaged copy; Galba B. xii, fos. 104ᵛ–109ᵛ, Harl. MS 523, fos. 72ʳ–79ʳ, abridged copies; Caligula E. iv, fo. 201ʳ, last page only.*)

(*Galba B. xii, fo. 83ʳ*) It maye like your grace to be aduertised that yesterdaye Monsieur Darras accompanyed with the two presidentes of the counsail Maure and Viglius cam vnto the lodging of me the comptroller*[1] and* aftre sum woordes of office passed on either parte Darras begane* to sett furthe the cause of there cumyng saing that thempereur* having at good length consydered and debated the thinges commyned of betwene vs sence my cumyng hether hadde sente* them to reaporte vnto me his fynall answere and resolucion to* the* same. And furst (quoth he) to your case that at our being* to* gether for the revisitacion of the treatie ye putt furthe upon* the* vjth article for the comyn enmitie in case of invacion his majesty* museth much what ye shuld meane thereby for seing the* cause* is not in vre, he thinketh that doubting of his freendship ye* goe* about by these meanes to grope and fele his mynde which ye* need* not do, he having hitherto shewed him self reedy in all* thinges to shewe the king his good brother pleasure and* to* observe the treaty in all pointes to the vttermost. And yf* this* case shulde happen to cum in vre thenne will he cum* to do what so ever the treaty byndeth him vnto tyll* when* he can make no further answere therein. As to your questyon* moved vpon the vij article of the treaty *viz* whether* money be not ment as well as men by these subsidiis auxiliaribus his maieste taketh the woordes to* be* playn ynoughe and thinketh theye can not be otherwise* interpreted then to be ment as well for money as men,* so doth he vnderstande them. Vnto thordre that was* (*fo. 83ᵛ*) commyned* vpon for thadministracion of iustice on both sydes for matters of spoyle or pyracye vpon the see his maieste having wayed what is best to be done therein, saythe he hath good cause furst to complayn of the over many spoyles that your men haue made on his poore subiectes and the small iustice that hath been hetherto ministred vnto them herein whereof he hath contynualle complayntes and therefore he thinketh it were meter or ever anie further ordre shalbe concluded apon that his subiectes were furst recompenced of

---

[1] Words inserted from Galba B. xii, fos. 104ᵛ–109ᵛ, and Harl. MS 523, fos. 72ʳ–79ʳ, are indicated by asterisks.

those wronges they haue susteyned. And the mattier brought to sum equalitie and his people putt in as muche good case as yours ar, for I assure youe (quoth he) the wronges our men haue susteyned ar many and amonges the rest a poore jeweller having gotten a salve conduicte of the king that dede is to bring in to England certaine jewelles, because aftre he hadde the kinges hande and seale to this licence he hadde not the same sealed also with the greate seale of Englande his jewelles were taken from him, and he being not present (although it were so named in the sentence) condempned to lese them by thordre of your lawes contrary to all equitie and iustice. Which semeth strange, for besydes that the kinges hand and seale shuld appeare to be sufficient for a greater mattier then this, the treaties also provided that the subiectes of thone prince maye frankly without impedyment traffique and occupie in to thother princes cuntrey butt to shadowe the matteir with all one I can not tell (*fo. 84*ʳ) who hath been agreed withall and so the poore man and his heyres putt from there right, which his maieste wisheth to be consydered. And albeit he thinketh that the king your master being vnder age can not him self by thordre of the law* conclude vpon anything now in his minoritie that shalbe* of dewe strength and force able to bynde him and his country* whenne he shall cum to his perfaicte age. Yett taking* that his tutors being auctorized therto by the commen assent* of your parlyament maye go throughe and conclude vpon theis* or like thinges in his name, his maieste thinketh it well* whenne his subiectes shalbe recompensed of the wronges* they haue hetherto susteyned that sum ordre be devised for* thadministracion of justice hereaftre in like cases. As to the confyrmacion of the treaty, consydering that the same* was* furst made betwene thempereur and the King Henry and not ratefyed by the king your master synce his fathers* death, his maieste thinketh that he hath most cause* to* require the same. Wherefore (because as I told you* even now he thinketh that those thinges the king him* self shuld conclude vpon during his minoritie can not be* of* sufficient force) if his tutors shalbe by thauctoritie of* your parlyament abled therto. His maieste is content the treaty be confyrmed by them in the kinges name and* by* the prince of Spayn in suche forme as shalbe thought* (*fo. 84*ᵛ) best* for both parties. As to the comprehension of Bulloyn ye must knowe that we haue a treaty with France aswell as with youe which thempereur can not with out sum touche of his honor breake without iuste grounde. And albeit his maiestie woolde be loth to se the king his good brother forgo either that piece or any other iota of his right, yett can he not entre this defence onlesse he woold breake with France out of hande which in respecte of his other affayres he can not yett doo. Howbeit he will gladly assiste his good brother in any other thinges the best he maye, and will not fayle to shewe him all the pleasur he can with regard to his honor butt with Bulloyn he can not medle at this tyme. And here he staying, is this themperours resolute and full answere Monsieur Darras (quoth I)? Yea, (quoth he) where-with he prayeth the king his good brother to rest satisfied and take it in good parte. Albeit (quoth I) I haue no commission to make any replique therto bycause it was not knowen to your grace what them-pereurs resolucion shoolde be, yett in the way of talke I will be bold to saye my mynde herein. We haue, Monsieur Darras, (quoth I) alwayes estemed thempereurs freendship and desyred thobseruacion of the treaties and thentreteynement of thamitie as a thing necessarie and commode to both the parties for the bettre establishment whereof (*fo. 85*^r) and that nowe and in this tyme sum good fruictes of both might appeare to the woorld to followe of the* same* I was sent hether which was the chiefest cause of my* cumyng. And because that the amitie betwene both* princes might be the fyrmer and that all doubtes being* taken awaye no cause of querell shulde be left, we* thought best to putt youe in mynde of the confirmation* and revisi-tacion of the treaty to thentent that by the one* the woorld might se an establishment of our frendship by* overt dede and that by the other one of vs might* vnderstande another and consydre whether any thing weare* to* be* added for the commoditie of both parties which I suppose standeth* youe as muche vpon to desire as it doth vs. And whear* as* you saye that the kinges maieste because he is vnder age* cannot* conclude or go thorough with any thing that shalbe* of sufficient force, I must nedes tell youe playnly that* ye* tooche his maiestes honner over nere herein for we think* that the maieste of a king is of suche efficacie that* he* hath even the same auctoritie and full power at the first* hower of his byrthe that he hath xxxti years* aftre and what your lawes ar I knowe not but* suer I am that by our lawes whatsoever is done* by* the king in his minoritie or by his ministres in his* name* is of no lesse force and strength thenne if it had* been done in tymes of his full age and yeres* yf* (*fo. 85*^v) once the greate seale of his realme passed there is no remedy butt nedes must he stande therto. Mary, lett the ministres take hede what they do and looke that they maye be hable to discharge them selfes towardes him of there doinges, if he shall require accompte of them whenne he cummeth to age for it is theye must answer him; butt he must nedes stande to what so ever theye haue counsayled him to agree vnto during his minoritie and to prove that our lawes geveth him the same auctoritie nowe that he shall haue whenne he cumeth to his perfaicte age: yf any man, ether for thinstruccion of

lerning or any other cause shulde presume to laye handes or tooche
his maieste in waye of correction he shuld be the lawe be taken for a
traytor. And if the mattier were as ye take it we shuld thenne be in a
straunge and evell case, for nether might we conclude peax, league
or treatie, nor make lawes actes or statutes during the kinges minoritie
that shuld be of sufficient force to bynde him and his to thobservacion
of the same butt ye mistake the mattier muche, and therefore if
thempereur mynde to procede to this confirmacion he may, or
otherwise do as it shall please him. And as toching my case (quoth I)
ye must vnderstand I did not move it without sum iust grownde for
remembring that all yor commissioners and ours being to gethers at
Vtreke for thesclarishement of the treatie, although the woordes of
the treaty were playn ynoughe and coulde receave none other
interpritacion thenne was there playnly written (*fol. 86ʳ*) yett woold
you needes* understand* the* artycles* for common* enmity* in*
case* of* inuasion* aftre your own mynde and whereas by the
woordes of the treaty no* mencion* was* made of any nombre and
therefore with how soever few in nombre of* men* invasion* be
made aught thinvador to be taken for commen enemye, your commissioners did* neverthelesse enterprete the mattier at there pleasure
and woolde nedes a nombre of viijᴹ men vnder which nombre of
invacion were made the treatyes* in* this case shulde not stande to
any force and likeas ye putt a* doute* here where none was to be
fownde so thought I ye might do in other* thinges* were theye never
so playn, and that moved me to putt this case* to* see* whether ye
vnderstode this poynt as ye ought to do aftre the literal* sense and
partly to knowe your myndes therein because perhaps* the* mattier
hath been already in ure. This I saye was thoccasion whie* I* putt
furthe this question and not for any mistrust of themperors frendship*
whom I must confesse we haue alwayes fownde our well willer and
we doubte not he will continewe and therefore I knowe no* nede to
grope his mynd herein nether did I meane any suche* thing* hereby.
As to your answere to thordre of iustice I se not that thempereur
hath so muche cause to complayn of lacke of iustice vnto* ~~whom the
same hath been deyned~~ in his subiectes cases as ye* seme* to sett
furth for hetherto there hath not any man complayned in* our*
countrey and required iustice, vnto whom the same hath byn*
denied* and althoughe sum men abyding thordre of our lawe or
hauing* hadde sum sentence that pleased him not, hath complayned
either* of delaye or lacke of iustice, ye must not therefore by and*
by* iudge that he sayth true or that there is not vprighteousness* or
equitie vsed in our countrey, for we haue there as* ye* have* here
and elles where ministers that ar wise and* well* (*fo. 86ᵛ*) learned*

in the law and are of honesty and good conscience who deale and procede iustly as the ordre of the law leadeth them without respect to favour or freendship of any man. And as for the jewellers case that ye moved ye must vnderstande that as ye haue lawes here in your countrey for the dyrection of your commenwealth so haue we also in ours, whereby amonges the rest we do forbidde for good respecte the bringing in or transporting furthe of certaine thinges without the kinges salve counduicte and lycence and although as ye alleaged byfore the treaty geveth liberty to the subiectes of either prince to traffique in to thothers countrey it is not for all that ment hereby that theye shall not be bownde to observe the lawe and ordre of the countrey whereunto they traffique for this liberty is onely graunted for the securitie of there persones to go and cum without empechement and maketh them not for althat lawelesse and whereas further it is provided by our lawe that in certaine thinges to be graunted by the king the same graunt must passe vndre the greate seale thenne if any of those thinges passe vnder any other seale theye be not of dew force vntill they haue also passed the greate seale of England wherefore if the jeweller either by negligence or covetousnes of him self or those he putt in trust did not observe this ordre butt therto contrary for sparing a litle cost did presume to bring in his jewelles before his licence cam to the greate seale me thinketh nether he nor any other can have iust cause to saye that he was wronged if according to our lawes he were sentenced to lose the same and yett aftre he was thus condempned more to gratefye thempereur* thenne for that I tooke it to be so reasonable I my (*fo. 87ʳ*) self was* a* suitor* to my lord protectors grace for some* recompense* to* be* made* to* the jewellers wief whome we knewe and none other to be party* for she followed the sute, she presented the peticion in her name made and fynally she and none others was by thempereurs ambassador* commended unto vs. I haue seen the sentence (quoth he) and do myslyke* nothing so muche there in as that the man is condempned and named* to haue been present at the tyme of his condempnacion whenne in dede he* was* dede a good while before. He was present (quoth I) in the person of* his wief who was his procurator and represented him and* I* knowe that those before whom this mattier passed ar men both learned* and of good conscience and suche as woolde not haue done hearin* any thing against right and ordre of the lawe. The sentences that ar geuen in our countrey by the iustice and ministres there are* just* and trewe, and therefore nether can we nor will we revoque them* for* any mans pleasure aftre theye haue ons passed the high court* from whence there is no further appellation no more then you* will here call backe suche fynall ordre as hath ben in any* case taken by your highe courte of Brabant, and the cause* why we for our parte misliked not this ordre of iustice was for the* bettre establishment of thamitie and to avoyde the contynuall arrestes that* ar made on our poore men to thende also that this sorte of suitors* be the soner dispatched without troobling either my lorde protector in England* or youe here whenne ye ar busyed in other affaires of more importance.* And as concerning the comprehencion of Bulloyn in good fayth bycause we thought that if the same shulde happen to be taken from the kinges maiestie by force as I trust it shall not, the losse should be commune, and touche (*fo. 87ᵛ*) thempereur almost as nere as vs, we thought good for the better suerty thereof to move this comprehencion, which we take to be as necessary for thempereur as us, and althoughe we ar not so wise and well seen in your thinges as your selfes ar, yett do we looke towardes youe and gesse of your affayres a farre of and perhappes do sumwhat vnderstande the state of the same whereof I coulde saye more thenne I now entende. Butt ye saye this is thempereurs resolucion herein. We take it for an answere and shall do accordingly. Mary, where as ye sticke so muche vpon your honnore in breaking your treaties with the Frenche, I remembre Monsieur Granvela your father at my being with him did not lett to saye that he hadde his sleve full of querelles against the Frenche whenne ever thempereur list to breake with them. Yea, so haue we in dede (quoth he) butt the tyme is not yett cum. We must temporise our thinges in this case as the rest of our affayres ledeth vs. Ye saye well (quoth I) ye haue reason to regarde chiefly the well guyding of your own thinges, and yett me thinketh sum respecte ought to be geven to freendes. Butt seing this is your answere I will replye no more thereto. Yett one thing, Monsieur Darras, (quoth I) I moved to your father which ye make no mencion of and I wolde gladly knowe your mynde in, which is the graunting of salve conduictes to the commen enemye, which the treaty by playn and expresse woordes forbyddeth either prince to doo. In dede Monsieur Lambassador (quoth he) the woordes of the (*fo. 88ʳ*) treatie ar as ye saye playn ynough and yett the matter* were very straight if it shulde be taken in suche extremity,* for here aftre in tyme of warre ye might happen to haue nede of woode canvas or wyne and we of the other necessaries and if in such cases the prince shold not haue prerogative to graunt salve conduictes it shold* be* a great inconvenience and a thing not hereaftre seen* howbeit* thempereur for his parte will not I think* stycke* muche herevpon butt obserue the playn meaning of the* treaty. Neverthelesse I cannot saye any thing* expressely on his behaulf herein by cause Monsieur de Granvela spake nothing thereof. And yett didde

C M—F

we* move him of it (quoth I) and he badde vs graunt* none and thempereur for his parte woolde not graunt* any. No more hath he done (quoth he) sythens his coming* in to this countrey nor entendeth not hereaftre. He* nedeth not (quoth I) for those that haue byn geven out* before ar sufficient for a great while. Naye, then* ar they not (quoth he) for the lengest was graunted for* a yere and now ar they expired and whereas a while* sythens one presumyng vpon his salve conduicte cam into this countrey to traffique, because the tyme thereof was expired* he was taken and emprysoned. The sayd Darras aftre* this talke touched further vnto me two poyntes which thempereur he sayd desyreth maye be reformed. The furst was* that* our* (*fo. 88*v*) marchauntes, contrary to thordre of thentrecourse do enhaunce the price of there woolles and wool not sell at such prises as they ar bound by thentrecourse wherewith there merchauntes here do fynde them selfes agreved and therefore thempereur desyreth sum ordre may be taken herein. Whereunto I answered that I vnderstode not the mattier and yett I supposed our men didde not this butt vpon sum groundes and iust occasion by reason of other breache of ordre on their partes here. Howbeit I shewed him I woold enforme your grace thereof and doubted not butt if anything were amis on our partes it shuld be reaformed accordingly, looking for the sembable on there behaulf. The other he sayd was that our men haue lately be gonne to buylde a bullwark which standeth haulf on the kinges maiesties grounde and haulf on thempereurs territory, and althoughe Monsieur de ..... Rue haue veued the same and perceaving thempereur to be wronged thereby hath requyred our folkes to procede no further therein yett cease they not to buylde still which thempereur marveleth muche at, and thinketh we woolde not take it well that he shulde attempt the like fortification vpon the kinges territory, and therefore requireth that sum redresse maye be geven in tyme there. I answered that I knewe not of this thing howbeit as I went homeward I woold enforme my self of the case and make reaporte thereof to your grace whom I doubted not woolde take suche ordre therein as should stande with reason. And here Monsieur Darras sette (*fo. 89*r*) furthe with many good woordes thempereurs amities to wardes the* king and readines to shewe his maiestie pleasur in all thinges that he conveniently maye that in case we proceded to any treaty with Fraunce he doubted nott butt we woold haue regarde* to them according to our treaties and that also if we grew to* any* peace with the Scottes seing that his maiesties is entered in to enmite* with theim chiefly for our sake whereby his subiectes* haue* ben* sundry wayes endamagied, he trustethe we will haue consideracion* to se that convenient recompence be made to them by the Scottes or ever we go thorough with any conclusion, the rather because the Scottes haue and cease not to offre besides a lardge recompence very great condissyons* his maieste woold fall to any peax with them which chiefly for our sakes he hathe and will refuce to do. We* answered hereunto generally that the kinges maieste in* such case we doubted not woold haue due respect to* thempereurs amite and procede herein as apperteigneth. This was the substance of there coulde answer as your grace maye se of smalle effecte although entred laced* with plenty of good woordes which we also thought best* to vse towardes them and requite them with the like.* And thus aftre I hadde required of Darras a tyme to take my leave if thempereur and his promesse to procure the same as shortly as he might, we departed. (*fo. 89v*) Thus we beseche God to send your grace as well to do as we do wishe. From Bruges the xxiiijth of July 1549.

Wm Paget
Phelip Hobby.

40. *To Somerset. My chamber. 6 August, 1549.*
  (PLB; another copy Anglesey MSS, Vol. ii, fo. 5r.)

Sir, because I se your grace so muche troubled with these melancoly matters whereby memory is sometyme empeched, I haue thought it my duetie to put your grace in remembraunce to refresh your selfe and your spyrites as muche as youe can devise, and then to laye before your eyes the state which youe stand in at this present. And what will by all lykelihode folowe the same which for my knovledge ys this. Youe haue to maintayne contynually during the warres great nombers of men against Scotland, great garrison against Fraunce both by land and sea, and no small power thorough your realme, for the reducynge of the same to the kinges obedience. All which can not be furnished with out great sommes of money wherof what store your grace hath I knowe litle, but if youe haue sufficient thankes be to God all shalbe well. But if youe want (which I feare) then for Goddes sake caste your charges aforehand and take suche wayes vpon depe consideration of the matter as if youe shall see that youe shall not be able to go throughe with the maintenaunce of all that youe haue begonne, yet then that maye be lefte of which we maye beste spare, and aboue all thinges regard the kepinge safe of the state at home, how soeuer for necessitie youe do with thinges abrode. Whereof I doubt not but your grace will haue consideracion, and throughly debate with yourselfe or otherwise, as youe shall thincke beste the matter accordingly. Almightie God sende youe his grace and power in all your doinges *et cetera*.[1]

W.P.

41. *To Somerset and Council. No place. 28 August, 1549.*
  (*PLB*)

A Discourse to the Duke of Somerset and Counsaill xxviij th of August, 1549

Albeit I knowe that with out myne advise your grace and the rest of my lordes can determyne the matter proponed by youe the last daye furst apart to me and then in counsaill concerninge your procedinges for Scotland: yet for discharge both of my dewtie of conscience and also bond of service to my soveraigne and countrey, I haue thought good with humble submission of my judgement to the wisedome of your grace and the rest of my lordes and others of the kinges majesties counsaill to saye myne opinion as foloweth. And furst I thincke that the suertie and honour of the kinges maistiee and the realme is to be preferred above all other thinges which surtiee and honour is not to be measured by any one present acte, as to take this or that place, oneles there be also a foresight of a certayne habilitie and power to kepe it stille and to defend throughly all other inconveniences which may grow by occasion of the same, for elles to seke honour by getting of a place, and afterward for lacke to be enforced to lose or leave the same againe, or ells to lose in the meane time some other thinge that shall countervaile two suche as yow thincke to get ys rather a reproche and a dishonour in the world, by whose judgement in meane thinges honour dishonour better and worse is determyned. When Bulloyne was wonne the victory semed honourable at the furste and so dyd our entrey into warre after the death of the kinge vpon Scotlande. But now having felt the charges of bothe to have bene so great and the inconvenience of them suche as we are not (for any thinge that I knowe) able to avoyde. The moste part of men forthincke the takinge of Bulloygne, and diverse wise men wishe that we had lived in the surceance of warre with Scotlande. When Bulloigne was wonne yt was saide we shuld never haue good peace with Fraunce tille yt were restored. And when we beganne warre firste with Scotlande the French kinge said he wolde rather lose his realme then leave them. And when saide he so? Mary, when he was already in warre with thempereur (which I touche to declare his greatnes) and so (to confyrme his sayenges)

---

[1] Anglesey MS ends 'From my chambre 6 August 1549'.

he wolde never agre to any peace without there speciall comprehension. Wherfore without peace with Scotlande I beleve that the
French kinge will neuer be at peace with Englande. Then yf warre
with Scotlande bringe warre with Fraunce, yt is good to consider
whider we be hable to maintayne warre with Fraunce so many
yeres as we shall make them wery to take parte with Scotlande. And
yf we be, then maye we be the bolder to contynewe our conquest
and fortifications in Scotlande. But if we be not (as vnder correction)
I thincke we are not then to take more and fortefie more and in
thende to be enforced to leave it over to your enemie, albeit the first
parte *viz.* takinge, hath a visage of honor: yet the other parte *viz.*
after waste of much tyme, spence of much money, losse of your
people, to leave to your enemie, that which youe haue gotton, and
to the kinge, his owne realme in mysery and beggerye when he shall
enter him selfe to governement, ys a certayne and inevitable dishonour in the judgement of the worlde. Wherof (not to seke farre)
youe haue had nowe profe by Newehaven, I feare youe shal haue
like experience by Bulloygne. Youe do consider I am suer, how great
a prince the French kinge ys, for we haue sene it in our dayes by no
small experience of his contynuall warres with themperour and vs
almost xxv yeres, whereof iiij were but as playenges with vs to speake
of. So as nowe he is somewhat refreshed and moreover the multitude
of his owne subiectes is growen to be souldiers and so they haue not
bene here to fore. And on the other side how we are exhausted and
worne to the bones with these eight yeres warres both of men money
and all other thinges for the warres your grace and my lordes knowe
better then I, what credyt youe haue to borowe abrode, youe haue
very lately experimented, fearing greatly any amendement yet, how
muche money youe owe abrode, and more at home, and howe like
we are to haue any helpe of your subiectes yow se presently before
your eyes. As for the abandoninge of Hadington ys no dishonour
but rather a wisedome and so reputed throughe the worlde. Yea
and the Scottes themselfes can not thincke the contrary, amonge
whom for this matter youe nede not feare your credyte, for youe
have none with them lenger then youe are stronger. The king that
deade is being a prince with longe continuaunce of great fame &
reputacion, vpon consideracion of his estate and condition at home
could fynde in his herte to forbeare the warres with Scotlande havinge
the same querell that we pretende nowe, and yet was yt no dishonour
to him at all. All I suppose (vnder correction) that if we who haue
renewed the warres and wonne by them forbeare now further invasion for a tyme and stand to the defence of so muche of that
which we haue wonne of Scotlande as our power will serve to, in

respecte of our scarcitie, nother the Scottes nor any other prynce hath cause to thincke dishonour in vs, and thoughe they dyd for want of knowledge of our estate: yet must we do that we maye and are able to do, which me thincketh is very litle, and not so much as will suffice to preserve the kinges maiestie and the realme from civile spoile and ravyn. The disobedience of the people is so great, and the event of yt so incertaine and fearefull. Wherfore myne opinion (which I declare simplie without entent to contende with your grace or my lordes therein submittinge the same to your consideracions and wisedomes) is to abandone Hadington as sone as youe can, onelesse youe shalbe able to kepe yt all ye wynter, and by some practise in the meane tyme to falle to some agrement, and with suche numbres as youe haue already in the northe overrunne and waste the contrey of your enemyes, victuall and perfaicte the fortifications of your owne, laye your straungiers this wynter in garrison vpon your furthest frontier towarde your enemy, send out of hand more victualles to Bulloigne, and transpose all the rest of your care, studie, travaile and expences this wynter ceason to the conservacion of the state of the realme here at home, for what availeth yt to seke to wynne foreyne realmes, and to lose your owne wherein youe dwell, or to seke to be conquerours of other dominions abrode, and to be made slaves and bonde in your owne contrey of your owne subiects. Bringe the subiectes into the obedience wherin youe founde them and that must be done by force and terrour, and then may youe commaunde them, then may youe consider what is expedient for the comyn wealth, and do yt honorably, then may youe vse them as youe shall thincke convenient, and then may youe ask of them suche ayde, as wherwith youe maye the better be able to mayntaine the warre, or elles making peace this winter season by practise, though somewhat to your disadvauntage for the time in respecte of a greater commoditie to folowe, youe may establish in perfection your pollicie, paye your debtes, growe in riches and wealth, wherby yow shall encrease the kinges honour and estimacion, furnishe the kinges younge age with riches for such enterprises as he may peradventure desire to assaye, and wynne to your selfe throughe the worlde great credite with the reputacion of wysedome for your good procedinges. And thus havinge saide my conscience and myne opinion I besech your grace, and the rest of my lordes to take the same in good parte.

W.P.

42. *To Lord Cobham. Hampton Court. 3 October, 1549.*
(BM, Harl. MS 284, fo. 44ʳ.)

My Lorde. With my right harty commendacions. I haue receaved your sundry lettres by one ~~whereof~~ of the which I perceave your desire for licence to repayre over for a tyme to ordre your own thinges. My mynde wherein I haue tolde to Wylkyns who I doubte not will reaporte the same vnto youe and I thinke good that your Lordship abyde tyll Alhalowetyde[1] at which tyme without any further troobling or writing to my lord protectors grace youe maye vse the benefite of his graces lettres, which he writes vnto youe and take the same for a licence for so it is. So that ~~after~~ against that tyme youe may come over and nede not tary [*two words deleted and illegible*] for any further leave. Tooching your soonnes sute I vnderstande it not otherwise, thenne to be discharged from Bulloyn, in which parte I will do as shalbe convenyent, and because he hath a good while syrued an evell master, and one that could not do so muche for him as his desire was, I haue putt him to a bettre that is to the kinges maieste, who hath accepted him, and is sworne squyer for the body. I praye God sende him as well to do as I woolde myn own soonne, and as for God will to do him good, there shall not want in me whereof he maye be assured. Thus hartely I bidde your Lordship fare well from Hamptoncourte the iiird of Octobre 1549.

> Your lordships most assured
> to my power
> William Paget

43. *Archbishop Cranmer, Paget, and Sir Thomas Smith to the Lords and others of the Council at London. Windsor. 8 October, 1549.*
(SP 10/9, no. 26; modernized text printed in Tytler, i, pp. 223–7.)

Have received the council's letter explaining why they have assembled and detailing charges against the protector. Believe that rumours of the intended destruction of the protector induced him to organize the defence that he has assembled and that similar rumours moved the lords to act as they have done. There has been a lack of good understanding of each other's right meaning. Plead for the lords to take pity on the king and the realm. Affirm that they are true men to God, king, and realm. The protector cares little for the place he now has but thinks it unreasonable to be thrust out violently against his will. The protector fears that if he surrenders to the lords without knowing

---

[1] Feast of All Saints, 1 November.

*the conditions they may seek his blood and death. Remind the lords
that the protector was never cruel to any of them. Hope the lords will
make a quiet end of these terrible tumults.*

44. *To the Earls of Warwick and Southampton. Windsor. 10 October,
1549.*
(*PLB.*)

After my moste humble and hartie commendacons to your good
lordeshipps I haue by my servaunt, Master Bedell, perceaved at the
full to my great comeforthe the favour ye haue shewed me in this
myne absence, for the which as I haue always borne youe my good
will: So beinge the same encreased by this I shall contynewe yt
durynge my liefe. Besechinge youe to bere with me hauinge my
hedde full thoughe I wryte not this with myne owne hand. Thus
trustinge to see youe shortely to my great comforte, I shall forbeare
tenlarge this lettre, and praye God send youe prosperous health in
honor. From Wyndsore, *et cetera.*

W.P.

45. *Cranmer, Paget, and Smith to the Lords and others of the Council
at London. Windsor. 10 October, 1549.*
(*BM, Cotton MS, Caligula B. vii, fo. 412ʳ, a copy in PLB; modernized text printed in Ellis, ii, pp. 171–3.*)

*Have received the council's letter to the king. Will be able to account
to the lords for their actions in such a manner as they doubt not that
the lords will be satisfied. The bearer of this letter, Sir Philip Hoby,
will inform the lords of the whole discourse of all things. Ask whether
the king should remain at Windsor or come forth immediately. Paget
will cause three of the best chambers to be prepared for the lords who
will come for the king.*

46. *Cranmer, Paget, and Sir Anthony Wingfield to the Lords and
others of the Council at London. Windsor. 11 October, 1549.*
(*SP 10/9, no. 42, also a copy no. 43; modernized text printed in
Tytler, i, pp. 241–3.*)

*Wingfield arrived this morning and has the Duke of Somerset in his
keeping. Somerset has been removed from the chamber adjoining the
king and placed under strong watch in the Lieutenant's Tower. The rest
of his followers are also forthcoming except for Richard Whalley who
was sent to comfort the duchess at Bedington. With Somerset are his*

*son the earl and his brother. Have ordered them conveyed to Somerset's
house. The king is much troubled with a great rheum. Paget has spoken
for provision to be made at Richmond for the king, but his physician
prefers Hampton or London. The king is in good health and after
breakfast today saw Wingfield and the rest of the gentlemen.*

47. [*Paget, John Russell, Earl of Bedford, Sir William Petre, and
Sir John Mason*] *to the Council. Calais. 30 January, 1549–50.
(BM, Cotton MS, Caligula E. iv, fos. 203ʳ–204ʳ.)*

After our most hartie commendacions vnto your good lordships
. . . . .
day we arrived at Callys, and towardes nyght th. . . . .
Guidot[1] returned backe agayn from Monsieur de Rochepo[2]. . . . .
French commyssioners bringing with his lettres from the sa. . . . .
the copie wherof your lordships shall receyve herwith. . . . .
both by those lettres and more fully by Gudottes declaracio[n]. . . . . . .
appeareth that they were not mynded to come to Ardres. . . . .
after advised consideracion of the matter thought good to. . . . .
Guidot backe agayn with other lettres wryten by me the lo. . . . .
seale by consent of vs all because the said Rochepot. . . . .
alone. And for that we wold Guidot shuld the better. . . . .
the consideracions moving vs, not tassent to this meting. . . . .
Bulloyn we haue caused a breve memoriall to be deliuer. . . . .
him for his own instruccion the copies of the said lettres and mem. . . .
your lordeships shall also receyve herwith. And where in thende. . . .
of this memoriall mention is made of other matters committed to
his credit the same was to declare that seing we shuld mete to talke
of the rendring of Bulloyn, that place was not mete for this treatie
aswell for thonor of the kinges maiestie

fo. 203ᵛ

. . . . go to Bulloyn. . . . .
. . . . shuld breake of vpon this occasion. . . . .
. . . . the honor of the kinges maiestie myght. . . . .
. . . . hed yf we agre to mete in that place we my. . . . .
stay from the full appoyncting therof vntill we shall heare from
your lordships agayn, and as your lordships shall thinke mete we
will not faile texecute without respect to any inconveniences that
might fall to our selfes. Wherof we haue some cause to thinke for
suche mater as we remembre to haue byn advertised from the Lord

---

[1] Anthony Guidotti, Florentine merchant acting as English diplomatic agent.
[2] Francois de Montmorency, seigneur de Rochepot, French commissioner.

Clinton[1] in the tyme of the late protector, the lyke whereof we partely vndrestand by a lettre from Captayn Lytton to Master Awdley which we send vnto you herwith. This day we receyved by Frauncys the currour your lordships lettres of the xxviij th of this instant, and according to your pleasure signified by the same will not fayle to gyve my lorde of Huntingdon[2] our pore advise aswell as we can in all such matters as he shall requi[re]. Wherin as we must beseche your lordships to take our good willes in good parte so must we referre vnto your Lordships such matters as we shall thinke of importance to be considered and aunswered as your great wisedoms shall thinke bes[t]. As for the forbearing of attemptates we toke your lordships meanyng to be yt my lord of Huntingdon shuld forbeare to lay siedge to any place or to attempt any great enterprise with his whole power. But for cutting of of victualles eskirmisshing or doing of such small annoyaunces you ment not to restrayn him and so haue we both tolde and advised him the rather bycause the Frenchmen yesterday bothe at Bulloyn and Guysnes

fo. 204[r]

.... your lordships to signifie your p[lea]sur ....
... tingdon, how many, at what tym............................
you will haue them discharged in our..........................
also verey necessary to consider before.........................
will do with our own soldiars incase the pe.....................

Here is moch talke that some others of........................
and other ministers also be sequestered from....................
sithens our comyng thens. And because........................
able to say any thing therin we be ask..........................
be glad tunderstand some pece of the matters....................
shall so seme good to your Lordships.

We do lykewyse here bruted here that ther....................
now of verye late byn many conspiracies atte....................
sondry partes of the realme. Wherin albeit we....................
not but your lordships doth give spedy ordre without dele........
can we not but signifie that our opinions yt ..... necessarye you make
    an ende of the parliament an....
away the noble men and gentlemen to their countrey.............
suche instruccions and ample commission as you shall............
good. Whervnto we beseche your lordships for Goddes passion.....
a vigilant and earnest regard.

We haue conferred with my lord of Huntingdon and others..

---

[1] Edward Fiennes, Lord Clinton.
[2] Francis Hastings, earl of Huntingdon.

touching the state of the kinges maiestes affaires here, from whom we doubte not your lordships shall haue within a day or two a perfect declaracon of the state of all thinges. And yf your lordships shall mynd the discharges of any parte of thalmain..............
shortly yt most be considred out of hand and money sent before the next pay day, which day shall appeare by this certificat to be sent to your lordships, from Callys the xxx th of January, 1549.

48. [*Paget, Bedford, Petre, and Mason to the Council*] *No place, probably Calais. No date* [*probably February, 1549–50*].
(*BM, Cotton MS, Caligula E. iv, fo. 208ʳ—208ᵛ. Incomplete.*)

..........were sent vnto yo...................................
....we rendre vnto your good lordships our most...............
therin we dyd that which to our poore o.......................
pedient for the service of the kinges m.......................
are most bounden) travell from tyme to tym....................
of our powers, to satisfie his maieste and your..................
expectacions in the rest of our doynges and pro.................
within two hours or lytle more after that we..................
Lordships said lettres Guidot returned from the fr...............
with such lettres from them to me the Lord Pryvie[1]..............
Lordships may perceyve by the copye wich we send he...........
lettres and the reaport of the F messynger it appeare.............
that the French commyssioners remayn wilfully bent.............
to Ardres but to stycke to haue the metyng be...................
when we asked Guidot what reason moved them.................
precise, his answere was bycause Rochepot was so si.............
was not able to travayll bycause he was governor................
And Chastilion[2] hath charge of Nuehaven and there.............
And besydes the allege there shuld be moch losse of t.............
we shuld be at Guisnes and they at Ardres. An.................
by their cheif and in effect onely causes why the...............
not come to Ardres.

Whiche when we had harde and after some consideracion.....
parte therof, consulted to gaythers we could not but moch........
aswell for the wylfulnes of their partes, as also for that...........
left seyng they stycke thus in a matter of no importance..........
they begynyng and that also without any good ground of reason....

[1] John Russell, earl of Bedford.
[2] Gaspard de Coligny, duke of Châtillon, French commissioner.

they will shew lesse conformytie herafter in thother thinges of importance then hath byn loked for.

And suerly we do so moche myslyke their wylfull bravery in this poynt as for our own dispositions we could haue byn well contented to shew our selfes as froward as they yf our instructions had not willed vs not to stycke so moche at any ceremonye of they plac.....

fo. 208^v

.........vpon the French gr................................

.........your Lordeships we may............................

........then we dyd by your last......for....................

........of such sort as ther can no more be wayed of............

........then there....for they be matters to be wayed and iudg....

........the eye of they mynd and not of such nature as the out....

..ward eye can judge of them, O no doubt the same shall be more throughly and better considered by your lordships there beyng a greater nombre of wyse heddes then by vs so smale a nombre here. And so shall his maieste be moch better served a great deale then yf your lordships vpon any trust of our simple wittes shuld remytt the determynacion of thinges to vs. The small successe that we feare shall ensue of our meting forseth vs to remember your Lordships that no lesse diligence may be vsed in sending victualls to Bulloyn providing of money and all other neces................

ries for the warres then shuld be yf you loked for continua.........

of the warres, wherin the better you shalbe furnyshed the more tractable shall theis men be and the lesse cause shall there be to feare then yf they will refuse to grow............................

to honorable condicions of peax. By Master Wallops[1] lettres herin closed your lordships shall perceyve that they French haue made a full pay to all their garrisons vpon their frontiers. We wold to God we had done the lyke. And we assure your lordships the kynges maiestes debt of this syde ys greater then you wold thinke of, for we haue....

tryed yt that there ys dew in master treasorors charge here for the crewes onely puttyng my Lorde Hontingdons nombers apa[rt] and shalbe the xxiij of this present about xiiij^m *li*. The said crewes beyng in thole nombre m^l and vnpayd almost xij monthes.

[1] Sir John Wallop.

49. [*Paget, Bedford, Petre, and Mason*] *To the Council. No place, probably Calais. 8 February, 1549–50.*
(*BM, Cotton MS, Caligula E. iv, fos. 209ᵛ–210ʳ*.)

After oure harty commendacions vnto your good lordships we haue receyved youre lettres of the vij th of this instant by the which we vndrestand your pleasures for our meting with the French commyssioners at Bulloyn, before the recept of which lettres we had dispatched Guidott agayn to Bulloyn and from thence to the French commyssioners with other lettres to the same effect yt your lordships hath appoynted as may more fully appeare by the copie therof which your lordships shall atteyne herwith

fo. 210ʳ

.... to th..
....ch diligence as we may...................................
This mornyng we receyved lettres and.........................
from the Lord Clynton addressed vs...........................
the Lord Pagett wherunto we haue made........................
appeare by the copye of our lettres which.....................
also herwith.

And wheras my lord of Huntingdon doth....................
bearer Lucas Fringar with a declaracion of....................
here, except your lordships do without delaye gy...............
for payment therof we verely thinke that.....................
spoyle and wast of the countrey which is hea..................
ned of, ther shall lytle service be done to th...............
besyde other inconveniences that chance to....................
Here is also moch complaynt made for the.....................
specially for the beare, and not without cau..................
victuallores them selfes that be here do confesse.............
arresteth of the outras of the bernars on th..................
for in every tonne that is sent them ther.....................
lviij gallons, wherin ye may lyke your lordships...............
gyve ordre.

50. [*Paget, Bedford, Petre, and Mason.*] *To Lord Clinton. No place, probably Calais. 8 February, 1549–50.*
(*BM, Cotton MS, Caligula E. iv, fo. 210ʳ–210ᵛ*.)

My Lorde we haue receyved your lettres and other wry............
by this bearer tochyng the buylding of a house by................
Frenchmen whervpon considering that yf they shuld..............
make a house vpon pretence to serue for our meting and..........

then eyther not meting or meting and not agreyng they............
shuld in a nyght eyther by fylling and massyng yt or otherwyse
fortifieng therof make such a pece as myght take our haven from vs
or otherwyse anoye

fo. 210ᵛ

..........shalbe there at....................................
..........And in case vpon....................................
....the place which they appoynt mete to.....................
....why you thinke yt not mete to thintent....................
....avoyded, and to say further that but for their...............
...eis the buylding of a house is to small purpose..............
..yf they intend to make a peax it is not by solempne
...tinges and assemblyes that they thinges whilbe done as some in
their company haue heretofore had experience. And yet neuerthelesse yf they will nedes haue a house in Goddes name so they sett out
of all suspicion if doyng hurte to the kinges peces, or haven wherein
they will not sticke yf they meane playnly, we pray your lordship
to send vs word whether you haue any tent or noo? because els we
may otherwyse furnyshe vs a meane one will serue well ynoughe.

51. [*Paget, Bedford, Petre, and Mason to the Council*] *No place,
    probably Calais. 10 February, 1549–50.*
    (*BM, Cotton MS, Caligula E. iv, fos. 210ᵛ–211ᵛ.*)

After our most harty commendacions vnto your good lordships we
haue receyved your lettres of the vii th of this instant by Francisco
the currour, and according to your pleasures signified by the same
as sone as we may receyue our saulconduct mynd to goo to Bulloyn
where we will not fayle to travayll by all the wayes and menes we
may possible, and to thutter most of our poore wyttes to bryng
thinges to such good conclusion as your lordships desyreth. We wold
haue byn there before this tyme saving that by sending to and fro
for thagreyng vppon the forme of our saulveconduct some more
tyme hath byn spent then we wold haue wished notwithstanding that
on our behalfes as moch hath byn done to take away all occasions
of delaye as their myght for with our last lettres to them which were
sent vppon Wednesday last the copyes wherof we haue sent to your
lordships. We dyd send vnto them the copye of a

fo. 211ʳ

...their lettres which we send vnto...........................
send any copie of their commyssion...........................
Monsieur de la Rochpott offered to s..........................

for the which we have now agayn sent.........................

Touching the money dew here wherof we.......................

in our former lettres to your lordships we assure.................

estimate you make there what myght suffice....................

that true which we haue wryten to your lordships................

for notwithstanding the sommes sent allready...................

tyme, the numbers and both the treasorars.....................

vewed and throughly considred wherupon th...................

declaracions were also made, which we doubt not...............

receyved before tharrivall of these our lettres, yt.................

lyke you to gyve ordre in that matter accord....................

the myserye, wantes, and exclamacions espetially...............

ordinarye vues about Guisnes and the lowe.....................

verey greatt, And as touching thextraordinary..................

your lordships make reckenyng to haue them in the..............

Clere, indede Master Clere medleth not with them...............

my lord of Huntingdon had gon to the feeld then.................

taken them into his charge of payment and.....................

you from thence appoynted them to remayn in...................

pay. Howbeyt you may appoynt them now......................

you will, for any money eyther of them hath....................

the same crewes beyng as appeareth by the byll.................

you aboue m^l vi^c and my lorde of Huntingdons foo.............

Englishe about xiij^c and thenglish horsemen about...............

besydes, and the dyettes of thofficers we thinke your lordships w....

consider that accompting vj^m *li* for a month for the hole..........

nombers both Englishe and strangers will be a great de...........

shorte, when that Germayns band of horsemen cometh..........

to be the monthe lytle lackyng of viij^c *li* and thalma..............

pay by the moneth at mmmm *li* and aboue thoughe they take the guld after the rate of iij s ij d, but yf they

fo. 211^v

..........haue wrytten to be................................

..........we haue wrytten to be due to.......................

..........your lordships are due aboue the prestes for as bef......

......d there hath byn travayll taken to bult the th.............

......and in Master Denys[1] handes remayneth not c *li* and in.....

......Cleres hand besydes your money which is to come over and hath taryed at Dover these v dayes for want of wasting) there remeaneth about viij^c *li* as we suppose he hath hym self aduertised lately. Post script we here that thempereur prepareth a great army

[1] Maurice Dennis, treasurer of Calais.

by sees. And that the same is in great towardnes, we heare also that he hath gyven commandment to all his men at armes to furnyshe them selfes of vaunt bardes of buff lether or other bardes to what ende this is done we knowe not. We haue lykewyse harde from Bulloyn that there is great want of beare in so moch as the great nombre of them are forced to drynke eyther wyne or water.

52. [*Paget, Bedford, Petre, and Mason*] *To Sir Anthony Aucher. Calais. 11 February, 1549–50.*
(*BM, Cotton MS, Caligula E. iv, fo. 211ᵛ.*)

After most harty commendacions we haue byn this mornyng aduertised from Bulloyn by a messynger expressely sent to vs for that purpose that their is not within that towne one drope of bere neyther yet bread or bread corne for vj dayes. What inconvenience may come yr of aswell towching the daunger of the towne, as the hynderance of such good purpose as we are sent over for we referre to your consideracion. In the reuerence of God loke hereupon with all diligence and se not onely this present necessitie to be furnyshed out of hand but that the lyke extremytie may be forseen for the tyme to come. Thus fare you hartely well from Callays the xj th of February 1549.

Your assured loving frendes.

53. [*Paget, John Russell, Earl of Bedford, Sir William Petre, and Sir John Mason to the Council*] *Calais. 12 February,* [*1549–50*].
(*BM, Cotton MS, Caligula E. iv, fos. 212ᵣ–213ᵣ. Incomplete.*)

........the said count h...................................
....was abought to leuye men...............................
sayd Lorde Clynton and prayed hym of........................
bande myght be comytted vnto his charge......................
my Lorde Clynton beying verey gladde for.....................
myght herby some honest meane be deuised....................
a tyme from the company of Spinola..........................
wordes of hope in the matter that he shuld d.................
vnto vs. At whose handes he douteth not......................
a reasonable answere according to his aduise.................
day vnto vs so when we haue made answere.....................
the truth is that the kinges highnes myndeth for.............
renforce the nombre that his maiestie presently hath.........
we that be here no kynd of commyssion therin.................
wold goo into England and open his suite to yo...............

haue our lettres to you in his favor, wherof he th................
promised that he wold so do. Your lordships doth..............
the meanyng of my Lord Clynton which we haue..............
consulting to his goyng over, to thintent you...................
entreteyn him with good wordes vntyll such tyme..............
lykeliodde of our procedinges may minister occasion............
determinacion in the matter. By the credyt of th................
messinger we vndrestand also much to our sor..................
they haue not one droppe of bere in Bulloyn,..................
nother of bread or breadde corne they haue the.................
for ij dayes. In so much as they souldiours are e................
into their proporcion, and my lord for exemple sake.............
him self to one lofe a day. What a courage the Fre..............
shall conceyve by the knoledge herof your lordships can well.......
And surely yf that matter be not spedely and earnestly loked vnto
not for this tyme onely but for the tyme to com.................
such inconvenience is lyke to grow therof as we wold............
loth to lyve the seyng of ytt. We haue wrytten therin to Master
Auchar trusting that your lordships will not forgett to do the lyke.

fo. 212ᵛ

.... conveyng ....
..... his former liberty, and.................................
[maiesties] subiectes though he be taken a....................
..... of ryght prysoner to his seconde takers this...............
..... Master Hall[1] hath and is therfore fre from all matters
..... may be layed vnto his charge towching any cryme
... mytted within the realme before his escape. The lyke sentence
wherof your lordships haue geven lately by your lettres in this
towne of Callaye, which was that where a French man beyng here
condempned of fellonye and to dye therfore chaunced to brayke the
pryson and so to escape was sythen taken agayn as a prysoner in
the warre by certayn Jermaynes bande, and brought agayne into
this towne. Your lordships beyng aduertised of the case thought not
reson that he should be answerably to the felony but to be permytted to remayne vnto his takers as a prisoner taken in the warre.
These cases beyng lyke and thexperience of them both in one place,
it were mete in our opynions vnder reformacion that one kynd of
iustice were vsed in the one as was in thother. Neuerthelesse Master
Hall hath promysed to send for him agayn into Flaunders where he
is at this present and within iij or iiij dayes as he saith he shall be
here at your lordeships commaundment, he was spoyled by such as

---

[1] Francis Hall, comptroller at Calais.

take him at St. Omers of all that ever he had so that at this present
he is not worth a grote. And when the matters shalbe thorowly
wayed the kinges pardon helpeth though he were his maiesties mere
subiect

fo. 213ʳ

.......fyrst some releif shuld...............................
them and he saith that yf ther ha...............................
small pynnasses keping about that............................
intercepted aboue fourtye French vi...........................
to move your lordships my lorde of W.........................
of the kinges shippes myght some tymes.......................
as he saith and so do we that they be.........................
pere tyll this mornyng that two of...........................
with the kinges money. And we most also......................
that some of the passingers and bottes of.....................
commaunded to resorte to Bulloyn for els......................
no meanes to send our lettres when we be th...................
Clynton saith it is now xxj dayes sithens.....................
lettres oute of England, vpon Saturday at my..................
mynde neuertheles to be at Bulloyn trustin....................
meane tyme that some good help will com.......................
England which myschance of lacke cometh ill t.................
for the matter we haue in hande. Thus we......................
leaves etc from Callays the xij th of Februa..................

54. [*Paget, Bedford, Petre, and Mason.*] *To the Council. No place,
probably Calais. 20 February, 1549–50.*
   (*BM, Cotton MS, Caligula E. iv, fos. 214ʳ–216ʳ.*)

After our most harty commendacions vnto your good.............
shalbe tadvertise you that on Saturday last...................
Callys to this towne and Monsieur Chastillon arriv............
day at the French forte, on Sonday thyther came...............
and the rest vpon Tewesday last before none we................
lytle house which they had caused to be made vpon.............
syde of the water in maner haulf wayes betw...................
and their forte, other place then this we could not h.........
mete at. And therfore according to your lordships lettres.....
to mete there. At our meting after some good wordes...........
and sight of the commyssions Monsieur de Mortier[1] made a....
of the cause of their meting, declaring in the same that......
his master had vpon iust groundes entred theis warres f.......

   [1] Andre Guillart, seigneur de Mortier.

that which was his and defence of his own right and.............
yet was he contented and verey well mynded to come............
apoyntment and an honorable peax, so as these thinges...........
this warre beganne may be reasonable provided for. And.........
hering of the lyke good disposicion in the kinges maieste our master
        and......
councell he had sent the rest and hym to treate and conclude......
perfect and sincere peax. Nothing doubteting but that the kinges
maieste and your lordships wold accorde to the restitucion of
Bulloyn and all other peaces of this nue conquest, the which.......

fo. 214ᵛ

....posicion after conference to githers I the lorde................
........the common assent of vs all made a short answer.........
........the causes of they commencement of theis warres
..them and also with their allies whom we thought to be theyr
......causes beyng as they were indede just and honorable and
......d by the kinges maieste our late master moch agaynst his will
....this town and all other peeces conquered by his maieste or the
....ge our master that now is vpon them or their said allies be his
....by just tytle of conquest in the keping and defence wherof
....iniurye was done eyther to they kyng their master or to the
...Scottes as at our next metyng shuld more playnely appeare
....yng wherof at more lenght we were then forced to differe
bycause bothe the tyme was spent and they tyde so requyred that we
most departe. As for they good inclinacion of ye kyng their master
to an honorable peax it was tolde them that they kinges maieste and
your lordeships had the lyke. And for declaracion therof had sent vs
thyther in whome they shuld fynd such conformytie as yf good
successe folowed not in this metyng they faulte shuld be in them,
which we trusted shulde not be. And this at that tyme we ended
talke of this matter with verey good wordes of bothe sydes. At this
metyng was agreed vpon betwene vs and them a surceance of armes
by land for xv dayes to begyn this day and the same yesternyght
sealed and delyuered on both sydes the copye wherof we do send
vnto you herwith. And yesternyght we signified this agrement to our
verey good lorde therle of Huntingdon to whome we sent an other
copye therof with request to his lordship to cause they same to be
proclaymed and obsyrued accordingly.

of. 215ʳ

........ting no wordes.......................................
...ey contrary in the end they...............................
that to cut the disputacion of theis............................

a good peax he wold [*blot*] two................................

that for all theis old [*blot*] ers we s............................

Whyte Bokes, and for [*blot*] yn sett a..........................

which he said shuld be payed, or elles sa.......................

respect of the minoritie of your kinge o........................

respect thinke not good to make whyte b........................

those olde querelles remayn as they be so as....................

be reserved to clayme and ours to defend.......................

this present. And lett vs frankly speake of......................

recompence for Bulloyn. As for the Scot......................

that mattier is determyned, and so hath answe..................

to Senior Guidotti that they kinge our master...................

her for his sonne, and therefore we pray you....................

no more of that matter but reson to what.......................

will grow so as we may grow to a shorte ende..................

answered that we were as desyrous to grow to...................

ende as they. Mary, thinges of such importa....................

be required to be considered. And for the deb..................

they kinges maieste you may (said we) make doubtes............

as you will, but yf this be not a ~~just~~ pl........................

and just debte which is confessed sworne judged................

many treaties confirmed we can not tell what...................

be sertayn. They lyke was said for that matter of................

Scottyshe quene and justices of our warres aswell...............

that matter, and for their breaches of treaties, as for th...........

contrary to the comprehencion in the last treatie with Fraunce.....

they had invaded England. But whatsoever was or could be said if
in these or any other matter now in variance wherin we trust your
lordships will thinke we dyd omytt nothing that our poore wittes
could devise all

fo. 215ᵛ

........bycause they haue in this...........................

........for they Scottisshe quene two of the first...............

......tioned in our instrucions be taken away yf they s..........

......any of thothers, which may appeare vnto youe in a scedule
h......

......y shall refuse to conclude any peax onlesse all thinges taken
from the...

....maye also be restored wherof they speake as they dyd for their
own

...lbe at a staye to say any further to them onlesse it may please
your

...eships to signifie vnto vs the kinges maiestes further pleasure
therin.

...he shew them selfes so precise and so imperious in their talkes
and so

..sting still for an aunswere, that we doubte moche whether they
will

...ary our sending to and fro into England. It may therfore please
your

lordships to resolue whyther youe will haue vs sticke precisely to
thinstruccions deliuered vs at our departing, or elles whether youe
will in any parte enlarge the same, wherin we besche youe we maye
know your pleasures perticulerly and certaynly with as moch spede
as youe maye. In the meane tyme we will not faile to traveyll to the
best of our powers to temper this their prescise talkes, and to wyne
the tyme we maye till we here from your lordships agayne trusting
that whatsoeuer the successe shalbe your good lordships will take
our poore good willes in good parte. Guidotti notwithstanding that
by private talke with vs he myght well perceyve that we thought for
sondry causes parte wherof we declared vnto him that it was not
expedient for vs to treate of any mariage betwene the kynges maiestie
and the French kynges eldest daughter yet doth he continually call
vpon vs for that matter, saynge still that it shalbe harde to make a
good and durable peax, if it be but a drye peax for so he called yt
yf it be without this mariage, the French comyssioners hytherto haue
spoken no worde of this mariage, yf they shall say any thinge therof
we shall answere as we be appoynted. Two dayes past Guidot beyng
earnestly in talke with vs of this treatie said he was hable to shew
vs xvij great causes for the which it was necessarye, for vs to conclude a peax. Which causes because we tolde hym we wold be glade
to see he put in wryting the copie wherof turned into Englyshe we
do send vnto your lordships herewith. When he

fo. 216[r]

..........we must say to your lordships......................
...nges tolde him by vs, and hadde credit with.................
prepare and ripe thinges betwene vs, and them..................
service to the kinges maieste then he yet hath don...............
able to do. And yet haue we no grounde......................
he dothe the best he can, Mary, we thinke he hath...............
with them in overtures specially touching the mariage...........
speake for vs so largly as he myght els haue done...............
advertise your lordships of the notable good service th...........
Clinton dothe to the kinges maiestie here, who besides his........

and travelles vseth all his doynges with such a ~~dexter~~............
and good dexteritie as he hath not onely therby obteyned.........
but also loved of all the souldiers, whom he hath in.............
and obedience as we wold not haue loked for in this............
that hath full well appeared in this tyme of scarcitie............
parte of the souldears haue dronken nothing but water, and.......
smale proporcion of bread, and yet remayned quyet.............
exclamacion or open grudgyng. The rest of thofficers............
doth their partes lykewyse verey well. Yesterday came into this porte
      xiij seales with wood and v...............................
but three of the kynges maiestes provision which will helpe........
but not longe.

55. *To John Dudley, Earl of Warwick. Boulogne. 22 February, 1549–50.*
    (BM, Lansdowne MS 2, fos. 81ʳ–83ᵛ; another copy, damaged, Cotton MS, Caligula E. iv, fos. 232ʳ–237ʳ; modernized text printed in Strype, ii (ii), pp. 437–42.)

The French will have Boulogne by fair means or foul and be tributaries to England no longer. They will acknowledge no debt, but will consider making a reasonable payment after Boulogne has been handed over to them. Has failed to achieve anything through private talks. Believes peace must be made regardless of terms. Thinks Boulogne should be surrendered rather than risk its loss in further war. The French say they are not bound to continue the pension granted to Henry VIII. Asks Warwick to discuss with the rest of the council what sum of money they would accept and then to inform him of the decision in a common letter.

56. *[Paget, Bedford, Petre, and Mason to the Council.] No place (probably Calais). No date (probably February, 1549–50).*
    (BM, Cotton MS, Caligula E. iv, fos. 216ᵛ–218ʳ.)

..........offers sundry consideracion........................
........ld in reason assent to these condicions wh...............
........the behalf of the kinges maieste our master. And of th....
........ed suche vnreasonablenes dishonor and inequalitie to be in t....
........ys proponed by them. In the setting furth of bothe which partes..
......sed as many persuacions and alleged also as many consideracions as we

....e devise to serve for this purpose wherin beyng by vs a good
     tyme spent

....Frenche commyssioners after a lytle consultacion to gaythers
     made vs a shorte

....a resolute answere that the wold in no case assent to any of the
     overtures

....vs proponed. And yf quoth they youe lyke, none of these yt were
..pened by vs then is our negotiacion ended for other commyssion
haue we nott. Here stayed we a whyle some tymes bearing them
in hande that we must then breyke of. Sometymes that we were
sorye ther came no better successe of this metinge. And yf none
other conformitie hadde byn loked for this travayll had byn saved,
and suche lyke seyking herby to sucke out of them whether they
wold discende to any other overtures or not but all prevealed nothing.
They stucke styll to their furst condicions and shewed there selves
redye to breake. Wherupon (as yt was before agreed amonges vs)
seyng none other remedy we told them that for asmoche as we had
taken the paynes to come hyther we wold be sory to departe without
some fruct of our meting and therfore wold we propone to them
two other overtures so reasonable as yf they ment to conclude a
peax indede they wold not in our opinion refuse. The first that the
king their master shall haue Bulloyn payng to the kinges maieste all
maner debtes and arerages due by any former treaties, continuyng
     the payment of the pensio...........................
and razing the fortes mentioned in our instruction. The seconde that
yf yt overture pleased them not lett the pension be payed quoth we,
and for thincrease and interest we wold be contented to abate and
aske no more but the debt due before the commencement of the
last warres so as in that case the kinges maieste may cause all such
fortificacions as he hath made here about the peeces now in his
maiestes possession to be razed seing that he shall haue nothing
toward the making of them.

fo. 217ʳ

........furth by waye..
....saw, we told them we could..............................
of proceding verye strange we told th.........................
brought your lordships from the kinge ther.....................
much more conformitie then now appearred.....................
the said Guidott enformed your lordships th.....................
said to the king their master that without pay...................
which is due to Bulloyn wold never be restored..................
said master aunswered agayne, that so as the kin................

render Bulloyn he wold that was due to be......................
thing Guidot beyng present affirmed And......................
denye all debtes and without any grounde of reson..............
as both be most manifestly due and we thought.................
never haue denyed we know well ynough nothing...............
true nor playn but pretenses of reason and argument............
made against yt. Well, said they, we haue told yo................
And what the king our master told Senior Guidott..............
not, but to vs he neyther said nor other comm..................
we haue tould youe which as we haue said we ney...............
nor will excede. In thende we proponed the last.................
our instructions which is tassent to rendre Bulloyn so a..........
will continue the payment of the pension and....................
debtes due before the begynnyng if the king our late.............
warres, wherunto they answered as before saying think............
youe that the king our master will be tributary to youe............
no no and as for the debtes we haue told youe th.................
because youe haue gyven thoccasion of theis warres wasted his
cuntrey and therby caused him to expende more money then that
debt amounted vnto, he taketh himself acquyted, he may take yt as
yt shall please him

fo. 217

........gentle one nor other co...............................
......their furst overtures. We told them......................
......do well yet that reporte were made to....................
....des of all such overtures as haue byn made so as th..........
....s known we may grow to such an ende as they shall
....be. We know (quoth they) our masters pleasure throughly, and
....fore to send to him we nede not, and yf we shuld having
....playnly told before he wold and myght well thinke vs of
....le discrecion, and hervpon wold yet agayn as it semed haue
broken saving that we told them we wold aduertise the kinges
maieste and your lordships and as shortly as we shuld haue aunswere
grow to a fynall end with them. Thus haue we repeted to your
lordships theffect of our doyng this daye by the which theis mens
disposicions appeareth. Pension they will pay none, debtes none, nor
reason will they heare none, they haue prescribed as yt were two
lawes which they call overtures the fyrst that we shuld make white
and relinquishe old matters as well pension, debtes, arrerages and
other querelles, for the which and for Bulloyn they will (saye they)
gyve a reasonable recompence in money. The second yf your lordships will not relinquishe all these rightes which they call olde

querelles then do they offer to haue them remayne in suspence reserving to eche parte his right, and for Bulloyn they will gyve a
recompence in money and make a peax. They pressed vs moch to
hast thanswere so as they may not be forced to tary longe here for
that said they shall profit neyther partie but rather profitt the thirde
which seketh advantage against bothe. It may therfore please your
lordships to resolue and signifie your pleasures vnto vs what we shall
saye or do further with them they be so a lofte that we verely thinke
they will

fo. 218ʳ

........semeth they will pro................................
....les which thinges considred your lordships maye.............
whyther we shall finally sticke to euery........................
instructions touching Scotland or not..........................
we shall endevour our selfes according to our most..............
to sett it furth in all thinges as may be mo.....................
maiestes honor and profytt to the best of our poss...............
Post scripta. This evening late Guidott came v..................
deliuered vs this lettres inclosed addressed from him.............
vs which because it soundeth to these thinges we................
written we haue thought good to send the same..................

57. *Paget and Bedford to Lord Cobham. Boulogne. 10 March, 1549–50.
(BM, Harl. MS 284, fo. 75ʳ.)*

After our most hartye commendations vnto your lordshipp. We haue
receiued your lettres wherrby we perceiue you make difficultye to
place thalbanoys their alledging the scarcite of horsmen. My lord,
albeit we know that you haue the[m] we grie[v] plentye yet we
suppose that the scarcite cannot be such but these men may be
placed their for a tyme which shalbe not long. Wherin we pray your
lordship to take ordre thinking that though you haue sent your own
horses in to Englande yet it was not for the lack but rather to haue
them kept their better cheaper then at Callays. And thus praing your
lordship eftsones to take ordre herin we bidde your lordship most
hartly well to fare from Boulloyn this x th of March, 1549.

> Your good lordships
> assured loving friendes
> J Bedford   William Paget

58. *To Warwick. Boulogne. 15 March, 1549–50.*
   (*Anglesey MSS, vol. ii, fo. 6ʳ–6ᵛ; endorsed 16 March, 1549.*)

My lord, we haue agreed uppon a peax although not with so good
condicions as we could haue wished yet within the lymittes of our
instructons and sumwhat better in sum thing and myht peraventure
haue bene moche better in many thinges if peax and warre had bene
so indifferent to vs[1] as we myght haue aventured sumtyme ~~to have
broken off~~ or to haue staunden in thinges aboue our instructons
therby to haue cum to the best in our instructons but this men haue
feared to do doubting the worst. And therfor haue, folowyng our
instructons taken what we may, seyng we can not haue that we woold
contenting our selfs till God send better, wherof by his grace for my
part I doubt nothing vtterly perswading to my self that peax is the
furst degre to it. And as for the other degrees if your lordship and the
rest of my lordes shall please to steppe, there is no doubt but you
may shortly get up to the highest steppe, I meane the commyn
welth & estate of the realme may be browght to a perfait & happy
estate. And the rather if the begynning the progresse & end of euery
thing be depely forseen considered and provided for bycause ~~we haue
in our commyn lettres specially toched the poyntes of our agrement
and also haue determined to depeche[2] to your lor the kinges
majeste and your lordships mr mason~~ Master Mason is a sufficient
messanger to declare everything of our procedinges[3] at more length.
I forbeare to molest your lordship lenger but with myn humble
comendacions to the same and to my good lady I pray God send
you and al yours aswel to do as I wish to my self. From Bullen the
xvth of March 1549. Your lordships most assured to commaunde
during lief.

William Paget

Post script (*fo. 6ᵛ*). I cannot tel wheder I shall now please or dis-
please Master Mason, but for the service of the king I think (vnder
correcton) that if you haue not otherwise determined he shall do
well for a yere in the place of thambassador in Fraunce.

59. *Advice to the King's Council. No place. 23 March, 1549–50.*
   (*BM, Egerton MS 2603, fos. 33ʳ–34ʳ.*)

In the name of God the father
the soonne and the holly goost.

Furst, the counsaille to love one another as brethern or deere

---

[1] The treaty of Boulogne was signed 24 March, 1549–50.
[2] Followed by an interpolation, struck through and illegible.
[3] Interpolated.

freendes and one to honor another in theyre degrees whereby will cum to passe that others shall honor them and haue them in great estymacion.

Item, that none of them be contented to here ill spoken one of an other and if he do heare any ill thenne to bring the mattier and reaporter to the counsaill boorde to be harde to the reproche and punishment of the reporter, if his reaporte be fownde woorthie.

Item, that six at the least of the prevey counsaill be contynually attendant in the courte whereof the lorde chauncelor, or lorde treasorer, or lorde great master or lorde prevey seale or lorde great chambrelayn or lorde chambrelayn to be two, and one of the secretaries to be a thirde, and that the six in thabsence of the rest maye passe thaffaires occurrent and shall haue theyre procedinges ratefyed by the rest whenne theye cum.

Item, that the counsaill attendant in the courte shall assemble them selfes three dayes in the weeke at the leest for the kinges affaires *viz.* Tewesdaye, Thursdaye, and Satordaye and oftener if the kinges affaires so require and shall mete in the counsaill chambre in the morning at viii of the clocke and sitt till dyner and aftre noone at two of the clocke, and sitt till foure, and for private sutes theye shall assemble vpon the Sonndaye aftre dyner at two of the clocke, and sitt till foure.

Item, that all lettres shalbe receaved by the secretarie and brought to the counsaill boorde at the howers of meting onlesse he shall se theye require a very hasty expedicion in which case he shall reasorte to the highest of the counsaill thenne attendant and he the saide highest if he shall thinke so nedefull to assemble the counsaill at what tyme so ever it shalbe.

(*fo. 33*ᵛ) Item, that euery man do speake in convenable answer his opinion and conscience frankly in mattiers opened at the counsaill boorde without reproufe, checke, or displeasyr for the same of any parson.

Item, that all billes of supplicacion to the kinges maieste or the counsaill shalbe delyvered to the master of the requestes and he to delyver to the lorde presydent all suche that conteign mattier that can not be determyned butt by the king or his prevey counsaill and the lorde presydent to exhibite them to the counsaill vpon the Sonndaye to be ordred as shall apperteign and the partie to receave his answere at the lorde presydentes handes or suche other ministre as the lorde presydent will appoint on his behaulf, saving that all billes of sutes shalbe delyuered to the hed officer of the sutor and billes of complaint remitted to the law or courtes of conscience as the case shall requyre.

Item, all offices and benefices of the kinges gifts to be preferred to the king to be disposed by the more voyces of the counsaill present vpon the Sonndaye at the counsaill boorde the more voyces to be tryed by two balles a white and a blacke to be putt by euery of the counsaill in two seuerall pottes, vpon the one of which pottes the suters name shall be sett and the counsailor to putt one balle at his pleasour in to that pott, and thother balle in to thother pott, the sute to take place if th[eyr] shalbe putt mo white thenne blacke balles in to the pott with his name. But if two sewe for one thing thenne either pott to haue a name, and the most white to obteign. If theye be founde equall white balles in either pott, thenne the lord presydent to preferre the sute and so likewise if mo thenne two do sewe for one thing.

Item, that no sute of any the kinges syruantes be preferred for them of the prevey chambre butt by one of the sixe lordes having charge of the kinges parson and by the lorde chambrelayn or vice-chambrelayn for them of the outwarde chambres, closett and chapell, by the lorde great master, treasorer or comptroller for them of housholde. By the capitayn for the pensyoners, by the master of thorses for them of the stable. By the lorde presydent for the rest.

(*fo. 34*ʳ) Item, that the clearke having charge of the counsaill booke shall dayly entre all ordres and determynacions by the counsaill, all warrantes for money, the substance of all lettres, requiring answere and the next daye following at the furst meting presenting the same by the secretary (who shall furst consydre wether the entrey be made accordingly) to the boorde the counsaill shall the furst thing theye do signe the book of entrees, leaving space for the counsailors absent to entre theyre names whenne they cum, and the clerke which kepeth the booke shall attende thereunto only, and be burthened with no other charge.

Item the secretarie shall se to the keping of all lettres, minutes of lettres, to and from the king for the counsaill, instruccions and suche other writinges as shalbe treated vpon by the counsaill.

Item, that none of the kinges prevey counsaill shall in no wise speake or write for his freende in any mattier of justice betwene party and party, nor in any other mattier aboue one tyme for that the request of a counsailor is in a maner a commaundement.

60. *To Cardinal du Bellay. Greenwich. 26 December, 1550.*
   (*Anglesey MSS, vol. ii, fo. 8*ʳ.)

Monsieur, les lettres que mauez escriptes en faueur de Messire Loys Regina mont bien asseure que incessament maymez et me tener au nombre de voz amys, dont vous remercie bien humblement et de bon coeur. Et comme ne seray jamais suffisant assez pour vous en faictzy recompensa encores ne me fauldra oncques le desir de le faire, et seray on occasion se presenter commode. Quant a ce gentil-homme je le troeuue tel que le mauez recommende et pour ce lay mis au calendaire de mes amys. Luy na eu nulle grande opportunite de m'employer ny moy nay sceu pource remonstrer la grandeur de mon affection de vous seruir en son endroict. Toutesfois vous me pouuez commander en aultres choses encores plusgrandes, et moy, je reste prest a vous obeyr. Comme scait le Createur qui vous ait (Monsieur) tousjours en sa saincte garde. De Grenewich le jour de Sainct Estienne 1550.

61. *To William Cecil. Drayton. 31 July, 1551.*
   (*Anglesey MSS, vol ii, fo. 12ʳ.*)

Master secretarye, I commende me hartely vnto youe and havinge the bringer herof Master Chamberlains man brought lettres from his master vnto my lordes of the cownsaill beinge desirous to retorne againe, he wolde be gladde to haue (if nothinge ells) but three wordes to his master with hym, to declare that he hathe made the deliuerye of theim, wherin methinkes youe shulde do well to helpe hym to his expedicion. I am glad of your amendement and do desyre to here how Master Peter doth. Wherof you may do me pleasyr to aduertise me if you know ought of his estate. And as for myn it hath bene troublous inowgh by reason of this new sicknes wherof thankes be to God I haue bene clere these ij weekes but yet dare not resort to the courte aswel for that at my departing I was appoynted to absent my self til I wer sent for, as also bycause yesterday one of my servauntes swet (he sayth it was vppon a surfett) and two others also in this village swete yesterday so as I mynd vppon Monday to remove to my soone Lees[1] house there to take clene ayer for a sevenyght or x dayes trustyng that myn absence welbe taken in better parte then my boldnes to cum to the courte shuld be, except I wer otherwise appoynted by my lordes wherin, bycause I wer lothe to offend, I pray you know sumthing & let me here from you. I woold haue written also to the master of thorse[2] herin but that I here him to be absent thens. Thus I byd you hartely wel to fare from Drayton the last of July 1551.

                                        Your own assured frend
                                        William Paget

---

[1] Sir Henry Lee, married to Paget's daughter, Ann.
[2] William Herbert, earl of Pembroke, master of the horse.

62. *To William Cecil. Drayton. 28 August, 1551.*
  (Anglesey MSS, vol. ii, fo. 13ʳ.)

Master Secretary, I thank you with all my hart for your aduertisement this daye and pray you to helpe myn excuse to my lordes
which is vnfayned, for otherwise I wold not willingly be so long from
seyng of my master his maieste beyng so nere within v myles of my
house. This berar my servaunt Litle is sent from me of purpose to
declare the cause of myn absence, albeit you haue partly sum knowledge therof before. And so I byd you most hartely well to fare,
praying you to let me knowe my lordes pleasyr for my cumyng or
taryng. The matter wherof you write might haue bene done better
vppon the furst proclamacion of the money then now and then
shuld two kynd of men haue bene only touched with it. From
Drayton the xxviijth of August 1551.

Your vnfayned frende to my power
William Paget

There can not be wel one prise of thinges in all shyres. And the
people which ar in money matters (as in all others) to wise and know
the just valew of your money look to haue them full to the old
fynes. And besides other incommodities which they fynde they want
that pece of money which is most currant within the realme *viz* a
grote, and they fare now as a boye that looks to be jerked never
quyet til they be past theyr payne.

63. *To William Cecil. Drayton. 3 September 1551.*
  (Anglesey MSS, vol. ii, fo. 14ʳ.)

Master Secretarye, I commende me moste hartelye vnto youe. And
because I sent youe vpon Sondaie by Sir Edward Warner a lettre
with an other to Master Cheeke and since do here nothinge eyther
of the deliverie of thone or thother, I have thoughte goode to write
vnto youe these few woordes and therby do praye youe to let me
know whider youe have received the same or not, and if youe have, to
aduertise me what answere Master Cheeke made vnto my lettre,
wherby youe shall do me pleasure. I wrote to Master Cheke for his
lettre to the baylif of Rislip to sell me forty or fifty tymbre trees
out of the wooddes belonging to the Kinges College in Cambridge
which may be spared very well and prayd you to further my sute
and to send me answer therof. And thus I byd you hartely well to
fare from Drayton the iijrde of Septembre 1551. Your harty frend
most assuredly.

William Paget

64. *To Sir William Cecil. My house. 23 October, 1552.*
   (*Anglesey MSS, vol. ii, fo. 19ʳ.*)

Master Secretary, your frendshippe hath bene and is such towardes
me as I am therby encouraged to pray you to tak occasion (if youe may
conveniently) this night to shew ~~exhibit~~ on my behaulf to my lord
chamberlayn this my submission and supplicacion conteyned togidre
in one in this scedule herinclosed for that knowyng hys lordship to
be specially fauorable vnto me I wold not willingly do any thing
that shuld myslyke his iudgement. I woold haue come my self to
hym therwithall but that I am evill at ease prayng hym to take my
vnfayned excuse in good parte. And I am so importune vppon you
for the shewyng of my sayd writing to my lord chamberlayn this
night bycause I woold willingly present the same to morow before
dynner to the lordes of the counsail. And thus good Master Secretary
assuryng my self of your frendship for movyng of my lord chamberlayn to further such one of my sutes in (*torn*) bill as he and you shall
thynk best. I pray God send you aswell to do as I woold myself.
From my howse this present xxiij th of Octobre 1552. To morrow
mornyng I wilbe bold to cum to you myself and afterward visit my
lord chamberlayn.

Your own assured to commaunde
William Paget

65. *Offers of Lord Paget to the King. No place.* [*November, 1552.*]
   (*SP 10/15, no. 58.*)

(*fo. 123ʳ*) Wheras being taxed to paie in the name of a fyne to
the kinges maieste viijᵐ pounde it hathe pleased his maieste, of his
great goodnes, to mitigate the same, and to remit the moyte, requyring of me for the payment therof cc *li* lande: I moost humbly
thanke his maieste prostrate at his feete, for his great clemency vsed
towardes me in this behalf: But speially aboue all thinges, I thanke
his maieste for that he is pleased to forget his displeasure against me,
and to begynne the world new againe with me, and vpon the vsage
of my self like a good subiect to continew my good and my gracious
lorde. For thaccomplishment of his maiestes ordre tooching my
said fyne I am contented, willingly to deliuer vnto his maiestes vse,
the parcells of lande following.

Middlesex
The manor of Harmondesworthe is in rent of assise by yere....
cj *li* xj *d.*

The perquisites of courtes *communibus annis*. . . . .

iiij *li* xiij *s*. iiij *d*.

The wooddes worthe to be sold c *li* estemed *communibus annis*. . c *s*.

Summa. . . cx *li* xiiij *s* iij *d*

Wherof

Diducted for the tenthes paid to the kinges maiestie. . . . .

ix *li* x *s* x *d ob*

The rent of Hatton staid by my Lord Windsore. . . . . ix *s*

Summa. . . . ix *li* xix *s* x *d ob*

And so remaynethe clere. . . . . c *li* xiij *s* iiij *d ob*

Certaine tenementis in the parishe of St Clementes without Temple Barre in the tenure of Rauf Jackson and Eustace Ripeley by Indenture by yere xvj *li* vj *s* viij *d*

A tenement in the same parishe in the tenure of William Neale by yere. . . . . xxvj *s* viij *d*

Summa. . . . xvij *li* xiij *s* iiij *d*

Leicestershire

The manor of Appulby in rent of assise by yere. . . . . . xvij *li* x *s* iiij *d*

The perquisites of courtes *communibus annis*. . . . . . xiij s iiij *d*

Warwickshire

The manor of Aldestre in rent of assise by yere. . . . . lii *li* x *s* iiij *d ob*

The perquisites of courtes *communibus annis*. . . . . . . xxvj *s* viij *d*

(*fo. 123ᵛ*) Derbyshire

The manor of Ilum in rent of assise by yere. . . . . . xj *li* iiij *s* x *d*

Summa. . . . . iiijˣˣ iij *li* v *s* vi *d ob*

Wherof

Diducted for a perpetuall pencion payde yerely out of Aldestre. . . .

xx *s*

And so rentes cleare. . . . . iiijˣˣ ij *li* v *s* vj *d ob*

Summa total of they cleare valewe. . . . . cc *li* xij *s* iii *d*

Neuertheles forasmochas it hathe pleased his maieste to call me mooste unworthy of all men to the degree of a baron, and that this land being deliuered from me, I shall not be hable neither my self nor myne heires after me, to live in sorte as that place requyrethe, onles his maieste be my good and my gracious lorde: I shall moost humbly beseche his maieste, that the said land might remaine with me still, and that in lieu therof, it wolde please his maieste, to take fowre thousand poundes wherof one *m* to be paid at Christmas, and a thousand pound every yere, till the other *mmm li* be paide: Or if his maieste like not this offre, that then it may please him to take c *li* lande with a m *li* to be paide at Christmas and an other m *li* that tyme twelmonethe: I know how moche I am bounde to his maieste, and yet if it shall please his maieste to take one of these my two offres, I shall thinke my self more bounden if more maie be where mooste is already, and if his maiestes pleasure be determinatly to haue cc *li* lande, then how poorely soever I shall live herafter, yet do I willingly and humbly submit my self vnto his maieste that I may be admitted to his presence, and (thoughe mooste vnworthy) to kisse his maiestes fete, whiche shalbe more comforte vnto me, then the remission of the one half, of that I haue to pay, shuld be without it.

66. *To Simon Renard. Richmond. 23 December, 1553. French.*
(*Brussels, Archives du Royaume de Belgique, Etat et Audience, 384; printed in L. P. Gachard,* Collection des Voyages de Souverains des Pays-Bas (*Brussels, 1876*), *iv, appendix; calendared and translated by Royall Tyler in* C.S.P. Spanish, *xi, pp. 451–53.*)

The French ambassador had an audience with the queen on the previous day. The proposed marriage with Philip of Spain was discussed. The ambassador feared that peace would be endangered by the marriage, but the queen said that she intended to observe all treaties.

67. *To Simon Renard. No place. No date, enclosed with Renard's letter of 29 December, 1553. French.*
(*Vienna Imperial Archives, E. 20; calendared and translated by Royall Tyler in* C.S.P. Spanish, *xi, pp. 474–5.*)

The French ambassador has asked how France would be able to live in peace with England inasmuch as the queen was taking France's greatest enemy as her husband. The ambassador was informed that nothing in the marriage treaty obliged England to go to war.

68. *To Simon Renard. No place. No date, headed April, 1554. French.*
(*Brussels, Archives du Royaume de Belgique, Relations avec l'Angleterre, Classement Provisoire; printed in Tytler, ii, pp. 381–383; calendared and translated by Royall Tyler in* C.S.P. Spanish, *xii, pp. 229–30.*)

Suggests that Renard asks the queen for a list of names of those persons appointed to serve his highness. Believes affairs are going all awry.

69. *To Simon Renard.   No place. No date, probably 19 April, 1554. French.*
(*Brussels, Archives du Royaume de Belgique, Relations avec*

C M—H

l'Angleterre, Classement Provisoire; calendared and translated by Royall Tyler in C.S.P. Spanish, xii, pp. 219–20.)

Will not consent to a bill disinheriting Princess Elizabeth. Asks Renard to persuade the queen to dissolve parliament and to urge his highness to come to England.

70. *Paget and Sir Edward Hastings to Philip and Mary. Brussels. 13 November, 1554.*
(SP 69/5, no. 293; modernized text printed in Tytler, ii, pp. 457–61.)

Have had an audience with the emperor, who thanked God not only for the great miracles showered upon the queen to make her His apt minister for restoring the kingdom to its ancient dignity, but also for giving her so soon a certain hope of succession. After leaving the emperor, met with the lord cardinal. Believe the country will benefit when the cardinal comes to England. The cardinal left the emperor yesterday as did they. The cardinal will not arrive at Calais until Monday because his weak body cannot make long journeys. Have written to the lord deputy of Calais to arrange the cardinal's transport.

71. *Anonymous Diary of Negotiations at Marcq.[1] May to June, 1555.*
(BM, Cotton MS, Caligula E. v, fos. 21ʳ–29ʳ; damaged and incomplete.)

[upper part missing]

9 May   after he had taken his leave of the king he departed from thens the same night and in the way visited my lord cardinall tyme at Richmonde.

10 May   My lord remained all day at London. And received for his dietes cc markes.

11 May   At vj of the clocke in the morning he....Gravesend, and from thence rode to....to diner, and so to Sittingbourne..

12 May   From Sittingbourne to Cantorbu....ymediatly after diner, was newes brought..from Rome of Marcellus the new pope..having bene chosen not longe be..his election not paste. From thence to Dover to bed, where..Medina Celi, and his brother to passe.

---

[1] There is a detailed account of these negotiations in E. H. Harbison, *Rival Ambassadors at the Court of Queen Mary* (Princeton, 1940), pp. 244–50, but the author apparently did not examine this diary.

fo. 21ᵛ

.... Treasord
....................................poincted for
...................................is backe againe.
...................................they dined with
Lord Gray capitaine there. Whither at diner tyme came
Monsieur de Lansack one of the Frenche kinges pryvy
chamber who after some talke had with my Lord Paget
aswell of tyme and place of meting, as of the way thither
for the Frenche departed to Ardres.

[15 May] The same night arrived Don Antonio de Toledo, and Doy
at Calais from the themperors court. Newes was brought
of the lord chauncelors and lord of Arondelles being at
Cantorbury the same day.

[16 May] My lord received a lettre from Monsieur de Lansacke. He
rode in the afternone to Marke. Don Antonio de Toledo
with the other gentleman departed from Calais towardes
Englande about ix of the clocke in the fornone. And at
night about vj of the clocke arrived my lord chauncelor....
Calais. And about half an houre after him therle of
Arund

[17 May] Monsieur de Lansack came from Ardres to visit the commissioners at Calais. And declared vnto them, that he had
certaine lettres of credit to the lord chauncelor from the
conestable.

fo. 22ʳ

18 May [*missing*]
The imperialles....came to Gravelins....Secretary to my
lord. Jaques Wingf....Darras. A gentleman sent to my
lord..of Savoy.

19 May [*blank*]

20 May Wheras the Imperiall commissioners des....vnto them
from vs the mediators to vnd....and mande with the
circumstaunces of our meting..appoincted for that purpose and this 20..Gavelins to diner, where at his comyng
..Darras, conte de Lalaine, Monsieur Benny..president
of Mechlin, the duke de Med..Viglius the other two commissioners, were..thither. After that my lord had bene..
of them, Monsieur Darras beganne to ent..said vnto him,
that he was desirous to..sort we for our partes ment to
procede,..by what meanes, we had deuised to....

fo. 22ᵛ

....said he)
.... And
....was first
....pages shuld
....all arrivalles
....self, as they
....................................to say in this
...........so is making reap...other party. We might
.....likewise their desires that after this visitacion of them
they should go to the lord legates house to visit him, and
from thence to the counsaill house together, and for the
first day to passe it over with ceremonies and shewing
onely of commissions which Monsieur Darras semed to
like well ynoughe, and send againe that they had no commission but to here and aduertise. Mary (quoth he) I
moche mervaill, that a mater of such importaunce as this
is, such personages being called together, as there be,
thinges be so rawe, and so smally treated of before.

[21 May] The Frenche commissioners being at Arde and vnder-
standing of my lordes being yesterday at Gravelins with
the Imperialles, sent likewise to haue him come vnto them:
And this day, my lorde rode to Guisnes to diner, and after
diner to Ardres to visit the French commissioners, who
having declared vnto him that they were fully determined
at their first entre in to the matter to fall to disputacions
and reasoning of titles, which he altogether misliked as an
vnmete thing for such a purpose, and the Frenche to be
contented to talke first aparte, with vs which they wold not
consent vnto they said but desired to talke fare

fo. 23ʳ

[*upper part missing*]

22 May [*damaged*]

23 May T.........scencion daye....appointment altogether at
Marke wh....were prepared and set vp for vs v small
sparres, and covered all over....with portalles for
entry in to them, one was....legate by him self, and for
Thimperialles....vs the mediators ech a house apart,
b....and 24 fote wide a pece having in them 4....of 40
one of 20 one of 12 and....8 fote long conteining in hight
....to the eaves 10 fote and in the....a house for the
comyn assembly of 30....and 24 fote wide without any

partie. . . .with the rest, and loking thendes therof. . . .
frontes of Thimperiall and Frenche h. . . .of canvas stretch-
ing on the out side. . . .therof from the lord legates house
. . . .deuyding Thimperiall and French s. . . .house loking
towardes that part of the. . . .whence eche of the commissioners arri. . . .placed vpon a rounde circle were com-
passed. . . .about with a ditche and a wall of sodde. . . .

*fo. 23*ᵛ

. . . . .st received
. . . . .to their houses
. . . . .d to visite
. . . . .house till. . .

thimperiall. . . . .ers had bene with. . . .from whence the
. . . . .the house of Consultacion. After verey curtoise
and gentlemaner meting the Imperialles and Frenche im-
bracing one an other we sate all down, at a table prepared
and set in good order for vs *viz* my lord legates grace at
the tables ende Thimperialles on the right side, the
French on the left, and we placed on eche side the legate,
who seing vs before placed declared openly in the Italien
tongue an exhortacion to the. . .odite of peace, declaring
certaine causes which at this moved the same, which ended
the Duke de Medina spake a few wordes to the same
effect, and consequently Monsieur Darras prosecuted the
mater, sumwhat more at large, and semblably the cardinall of Loreine, whom the constable of Fraunce followed
said sumthing likewise. . .their partes. This done we shewed
our commissions. . .to an other, and after a few wordes
passed betwixt . . .rose vp, appoincting to mete againe the
next day. And ymediately was brought in a banket prepared by vs the mediators, caryed in the handes of iiijˣˣ
gentlemen which was presented and distributed to the
noble men and others. . .Thimperiall and French traines as
they stode

*fo. 24*ʳ   [*upper part missing*]
. . . . .misliked the bringing. . . . . .question, for (quoth he)
it is a thing w. . . .rather for a pike or querell, then a. . . .
they pretended. And then the conestab. . . .thinges to prove,
that the French king. . . .for non other respect then to
defende h. . . .eftsones the cardinall toke by thende a. . . .
to the declaracion of the French kinges rig. . . .whose talke

being such in extremites.... to breake of, and so they
departed. The Imperialles assone as the French.... likewise conducted to my lord legates.... was declared our
hooll discourse.... commissioners, and their talke to vs
.... with the cause of their entre into the.... by the conestable in sort as by.... their comyng was opened vnto
vs.... Monsieur Darras answered, and said.... allegacions
were of small force,.... hable to confute the same, and
to ch.... entre into the warres I haue (quoth he.... scedule
(which he, shewed vnto vs....

fo. 24

.... by
....cell or pike
.... to discide
......................................will do what
....................................do wishe some
....................................the. Heruppon
..................................of a demaund
...restitucion of all th.... taken by the Frenche since these
laste warres, with recompence to be made for interest and
damage, which overture being altogether misliked... we
said that we thought the same farre vnmete... this purpose
we went aboute, and exhorted them to avoid these kind of
extremites, and to deuise some other more quiet meanes.
We haue not (quoth Monsieur Darras any commission to
deuise any meanes, but to here what was said and to
aduertise the same. And here after a few wordes passed
we staid our commvnicacion... they resorted againe to
their house. We then revisited... Frenche, and opened
vnto them suche thinges and maters as had passed betwene
Thimperialles and vs... here when they had consulted a
while together, they answered vs by the cardinall of
Loreine, who not... standing our mislikinges of question-
ing of titles,... toched Milaine with vtter deniall of the
scedule... dged by Monsieur Darras against them, and so
... brake of appoincting to mete againe on Sonday... the
xxvj th of this monethe. In this meane tyme

fo. 25^r [*upper part missing*]
to......... to their de.... Quenis maiestes behaulf as
otherwise.... answer was made, but rested for.... next
meting. And then we dep.... night.

25 May [*no entry*]

26 May We met eftsones at Marke, and bec....away all conten-
cion, we went to the....oners who arrive first, and brake
....and amongst other thinges deuised by....them our
deuise for a mariage to....the kinges sonne the infant of
S....doughter of Fraunce with such pe....honest condicions as we could deuise....to agre therunto, to which
they....misliked not the overture proceding fr....they)
we thinke it to parciall for th....yet notwithstanding
desired vs they might....

fo. 25ᵛ [*upper part missing*]

....vs to
....to do, and
.... forasmochas
.... mencioned
....................................and that now
..................................Themperor hath
....whome he des......to your doughter with condicion
to give the remaindre of Milaine to the second sonne to
be borne of them and to their heires males, he to take her
with a convenient dote, and to appoinct her a dower out
of that state, me thinkes (quoth we) this overture is
reasonable and not to be refused, and therfore we mynde
the rather to persuade youe and them therunto, for the
other treaty (quoth we) is a thing paste, and not to be
...oqued and renewed. Having thus farre entered in this
mater with them, we repaired to the Imperialles and
[de]clared vnto them aswell our overture and discourse
therupon [h]ad with the Frenche, as also the overture
proponed by [t]hem vnto vs as before mencioned. They
liked our [ove]rture well, but refused to talke at all of the
Frenche and thus the day being spent without any certaine..icte we departed every one home.

fo. 26ʳ [*upper part missing*]

.............the Frenche comm....for which purpose
one was from th....who moved the French therin, which
....(they said) to let the mater passe....in it as Monsieur Bennyngcourt....execucion of ponishment vpon
thoffendors....mater rested pacified. The Frenche....
alighted and in their house, were h....where at the first
they beganne to....vs this overture. If Themperor (quoth
they)....contented to mary sum nepce of his to....that
nowe is, in such sort, and with such....a treaty hertofore

of like overture was....condiscende therunto, and herin
(quoth they)....with Thimperialles. But as for any resti
....without restitucion of Milaine vnto vs, we....for
(quoth they) Thimperialles may asu....Parrise their
owne, as Piemont restor....old inheritaunce, and therfore
let th....without Milaine for any restitucion. As....vnto
vs we mislike not, but are contente....

*fo. 26*ᵛ   [*upper part missing*]

.... the
.... conducted
....red vnto
...................................acion with vs
...................................for the maner
..that if........that which we..they wold.........
which being..mande the some of Thimperialles talke with
vs ...declared to the Frenche, who desired (for before
that tyme they never talked together, but were commyned
withall apart at my lord legates and their owne houses) to
haue private talke with them, saying and protesting vnto
vs, that they wold not make any mencion of any thing,
which might move them to disputacions, but to tell them
quietly what they wold do eyther of or on, eyther for treaty
or for a dissolucion of the hooll. . .nd so without any thing
done further, appoincted to mete againe the day following
at one of the clocke and so departed home.
[*space*]
Arriving and meting alltogether at the house of consultacion the verey same mater, which were proponed and commyned of yesterday, were eftsones proponed and talked of
this day, without addicion or any good done at all, saving
that my lord legate tolde them that it was a straunge thing
in these cases of titles

*fo. 27*ʳ   *vltimo* May [*upper part missing*]

Viglius...at my lord legates house....first commyned
with all aparte, and to....diuerse overtures for the con-
ducing of....bushop was generall talke ministred....of
condicions. In thend in [*sic*] was agred th....shuld be
proponed onely at their next m....to be the next day
wherof the first....a mariage to be made betwene the....
thinfant of Spaine, and theldest dou....her dote to be in
money, and her dow....vpon the Duchy of Milaine. The
seco....mariage of the Duke of Savoy to a....without

dote and restitucion of him in Sav....iij fortes to be
reserved to the Frenche, and....Imperiall. The last was
that the co....them for the titles of Milaine and Burg....
be diffined by the next generall co....there condicions the
Imperialles desired....be proponed without addicion of
any....tyme as they might perceive how....the same.

fo. 27^v   [*upper part missing*]

....the king
....their allies
.....................................disputacion eche
.....................................and not with
.....................................that mater at
..................................to their first tale
...opinion..........trariete betwixe them in suche extremites we....to say that we wold break vp, and yet after
thought better to move a delay of further commvnicacion,
till the Imperialles might here again from their master,
which the Frenche on all handes refused to do, but in
thende graunted to it with condicion that in the next
meting vpon Friday following they shuld bring with them
perfect and full instruccions..other unto they might accord
eyther of or on. When these talkes were almost ended,
Marrillac the bushop of Orleanne deuised together with
my Lorde Paget, who asked him to what poinct we shuld
come, there are only two endes (quoth he) themperor and
the French king, if themperor will loke for restitucion for
his confederates, the king must do the like for his what if
the emperor wold say nothing of the confederates (said the
Lorde Paget) will the king make restitucion of those
thinges which haue bene taken in these last warres. Yes
(quoth he) if themperor will in like case do so, mary
otherwise he will not

fo. 28^r   [*upper part missing*]

leave......curtoise w....that day and appoincted to....
following being the vij th of June....
[*space*]
In this meane tyme we the mediators....at Calice and
deuised toching the....caused new plattes to be drawen
for....

7 Junij   According to thappoinctment the commis....met at
Marke, where ymediately after....assembled in the house
of consultacion....with sum circumstaunce of speche,

declare....contentment with thouerture which we ha....
proponed tochyng Milaine, Burgo....of Savoy with the
mariage of the....et cetera and the mariage of the king our
....with the French kinges doughter to wh....did
slightly answer, and in conclusion....to their former
arrest, for (quoth they)....nothing to any themperors
frendes or all....will for his part do the reciproque to
o....

*fo. 28*ᵛ   [*upper part missing*]

.... ady
....of Charlois
....sion, let vs
.................................and our doughter
.................................that which he hath
...refering the.......right to the same to the generall
counsaill and...other poincte then this the Frenche wold
not come to, and as for the mariage of their suster they
refusid vtterly, onles the Duke (they said) wold come in
to Fraunce to wooe her, for she is (quoth they) of age to
mary her self, and the king our master will not otherwise
move her. In which poinct as in the rest we vsed many
persuasions vnto them, first openly that the Imperialles
myght here vs and then aparte to themselfes, but in thende
no other persuasion wold serve then that they of them
selfes had deuised, not to any other poinct wold they be
dryven. And so finally they desired vs to do vnto them so
moche grace (for so they termed it) as they might take
their leave for this tyme foi that thinges they said were not
yet ripe. Wherunto seing their disposicions both the
Imperialles and French so farre dissonant we shortly
accorded. And thus the Imperialles protesting their good
disposicion to contynew still for all tymes herafter, when
any occasion shuld

*fo. 29*ʳ   [*upper part missing*]
8 Junij

wherby...........n to send a....on the...behaulf of
the Italion amba....bene promised vnto vs, to be disch...
....to Calice were still kept at Ard....or stay at Calais
was onely for their....

9 Junij   The ambassadors of Italie were sent to....10 and 11 Junij
the wind was still co....

12 Junij   We toke shippe at Calais about vj of....the morning,

　　　　having the wind verey....vs, which contynued not, for or
　　　　ever....the scales there rose a suddein storm....con-
　　　　tynued for the space of [blank] the wind not onely decayed,
　　　　but tor....so as or ever we could atteine to Dov....half
　　　　an houre past two of the clock....all night at Dover.
13 Junij　My lord with the rest rode to Canterbury to di....diner
　　　　leaving my lord cardinall, the L....therle of Arundell at
　　　　Canterbury, rode to....where he lay the same night and
　　　　in th....
14 Junij　toke barge to London, and from thence....ton to diner.

72. *To Sir Thomas Carden. The Star Chamber. Tuesday, 11 February,*
155[5–6].[1]
(*Folger Shakespeare Library, L.b. 296; modernized text printed in*
A. J. Kempe, The Loseley Manuscripts (*London, 1835*), *p. 56.*)

Requests a loan of 'masking' apparel remaining in Carden's custody for
the use of the Venetian ambassador.

73. *A Note of the Demands of Lord Paget for his Diet. No place.*
April, 1556.
(*BM, Cotton MS, Galba B. xi, fo. 29*[r].)

The Lord Paget asketh allowaunce for his dietes at iiij *li* by the day
in his journey to the emperor begynnyng the vj th of Aprill and ending
the xvij th of May being in all xliiij daies.................clxxv　*li*
Item he asketh allowaunce for posting charges for myself and a guyde
with xxv[t] servauntes outward and homwarde........cxxvj *li* xj *s* x *d*
Item more for sending of lettres twise, ones to the quenis maieste,
ones to certaine lordes of the counsaill..............xv *li* viij *s* viij *d*
　　　Some of the hooll allowance...... cccxviij *li* vj *d*
　　　　　　　　　　　　　　　　　William P[aget]

74. *To Mary. Brussels. 25 April, 1556.*
(*BM, Stowe MS 147, fos. 178*[r]*–180*[r].)

It may please your maiestie to bee advertised that arriving here upon
Munday before dinner, and having accesse to the (*fo. 178*[v]) kinges
maiestie in the afternoone I delivered to him your maiesties letters
and ringes with such commendacions on your maiesties behalfe as
appertayned; which his maiestie received very gladly and cheare-
fully, not a little glad to heare of your good estate, much inquisitiue

[1] Kempe gives the year as 155–.

how your maiestie did, how you had your health, and whither you
were well againe in such sort as it seemed vnto mee that hee had bin
advertized that you had bin lately sicke. I answered that your maiestie
was now meetly well againe; marry the newes I thought which your
maiesty had of the king of Bohems[1] comming hither had troubled
you beeing before in a certaine expectation to haue seene his maiestie
shortly, and here I tooke occasion to say what mee thought for that
time convenient touching his long absence out of England; wherevnto his maiestie said, that hee was not a little sorry to haue had such
occasion to tarry here as had chanced, trusting (hee said) that your
maiestie had well vnderstood, and by your wisedome waighed and
considered the same. The next day his maiestie of his great benignity
takeing the paine to haue mee through the parke to the emperour,
and to present mee to his maiestie I delivered to him your maiesties
letters and ringes with (*fo. 179ʳ*) such commendations and other
good wordes as is between your maiesties convenient, which hee
tooke in most thankefull manner, desiring also much to vnderstand
of your good estate, wherevnto after I had on your maiesties behalfe
declared the cause of my comming vnto him, likewise congratulated
with him his truce with such words as the matter required. I answered
that your maiestie did indifferently well as one might doe yt wanted
of that you loved aboue all earthly things; I haue heard (said hee) that
shee hath bin lately sicke, and named the sicknes to mee, it was then
(quoth I) sir, vpon advertisement of some new occasion of delay of
the kinges comming over. It is true you say (quoth hee) and turning
his speech to them who sate by and might heare our communication
said, I thinke it was the newes of the king of Boheme and my
daughters comming downe. Shee writes to mee (quoth the king) to
bring them over with mee; that cannot well bee (quoth the emperour)
(and turned his speech to mee againe) for besides many other great
respects it would bee some occasion of delay of my sons arrival in
England. Wee feare (quoth I) that if busines may bee let of (*fo. 179ᵛ*)
his maiesties returne, that wee shall not haue him there shortly, but
that after the king of Bohems dispatch, there may arise some other
new occasion of delay. And there I was so bold though your maiestie
gaue mee no commission to say as much as seemed to mee good, like
as I haue done and will doe to some others about the kinges maiestie
for the necessary beeing of his maiesty in England, not onely for the
contentment and satisfaction of your maiestie which I and every one
of your honest servantes and naturall subiectes ought to desire what
is in him to that effect, but also for that I am not ignorant how
necessary his beeing in England is aswell for that thing which should

---

[1] Ferdinand I, Holy Roman Emperor, 1556–64.

bee comfort to all your good subiectes, and for the benefit of your realme, as also for his owne affayres here and in other places, trusting as his maiestie hath graciously heard, so your maiestie will likewise interpret my doeinges in this behalfe. The emperour said which the king confirmed that no new matter should stay his son here. And the king coming homewardes told mee by the way, that, out of doubt, hee would bee with you in the beginning of June: and (*fo. 180*^r) would come to you in post, leaving his traine to come after; and I beleiue verily that no new matter shall now stay him, his will is such to bee with you. And I was so bold in most humble wise to beseech his maiestie, because diverse dayes had bin appointed before, not to appoint any more except his maiestie might bee sure (God willing) to keepe the appointment I trust within two or three dayes you shall heare from himselfe the certaine time of his returne. In the meane time I haue thought it my most bounden dutie to write thus much to your maiestie, most humbly beseeching you to accept my meaning in gracious part, which is none other then to serue your maiestie truely to the best of my poore power as knoweth our Lorde, who send your maiestie long to raigne over us in all honour and prosperitie.

From Brussels the 25 th of

Aprill in the morning

1556

Postscript

I haue delivered your maiesties lettres and ringes to the queene dowager of France and Hungary[1] and also to the duchess of Lorraine[2] with your highnes most harty commendations.

75. *To James Bassett. Temple Bar. 15 December, 1556*[3].
   (*Anglesey MSS, vol. ii, fo. 41*^r*-41*^v*; endorsed 'minute to Master Bassett 1559'.*)

(*fo. 41*^r) Master Basset,[4] I thanke youe for your paines taken in shewing my lettres to the qwenis maieste and according to her maiestes pleasure my lettre to the kinges maieste shalbe ordred. It is sufficient that her maieste findeth the fault, for a fault it is wheresoever it be that those three thinges be not done, and as for the iiijth I wolde to God it were done and better tyme shall their never be to do it then now and by other meanes then hathe bene now talked of I dare boldely say it can never be done, the determinacion wherof

---

[1] Eleanor, sister of Charles V.
[2] Christina, daughter of Christian II of Denmark.
[3] See the letter from Bassett to Paget of the same date in Appendix H.
[4] Private secretary to Queen Mary.

resteth onely in her maieste—our lord put that into her hart that
shalbe for the best—but in mans iudgement neither shall the prince
of this realme nor the clergie nor the noblemen nor gentlemen nor all
other suche as lives vpon certainties as all kinde of servauntes &c be
hable to live according to their estates nor the prince stand by his
frendes nor shew his face to thenemy til this bedone, and I wold to
Goddes passion that I were bounde to eate no fleshe this xij monethes
that the other three were done, and, alas, why shulde they not be
done? I can survey my lande and so can every other man and by
making of leases, sales of wooddes, making of copies, grauntes of
fermes and otherwise raise honest sommes of money towardes my
relief and haue my revenew brought home to my house with a small
charge. Why shuld the qwenis maieste not haue the like toching the
order of hir house &c? I wolde not haue any one man that might be
for hir maiestes honor or other necessary service toched. Mary, I
wolde haue that beggery mangery in corners and typling like ale-
houses taken away and that rablement of raskalles that be in and
resort to the house avoided. I wold haue hir maieste furnished of
wood and coles of hir owne wooddes and vnderwooddes. Other men,
if their fathers haue let out any fermes or pasture groundes that were
necessary for the finding of their houses, can be contented, ye, and
will travaill, to redeme the same again into their owne hands thoughe
they pay more for them then they be presently worthe. Why shulde
not the quenis maieste redeme with liberall recompence (as other
men wolde in like cases) the grauntes of herbages of necessary parkes
and therehens furnishe hir self of befes, muttons, lambes and veales
and the like of warrens for conies, and as for whete for ready mony
she might be furnished for a noble a quarter and malt of a reasonable
price and for the rest of thinges good husbandry vsed. I dare saye
(and I am sure their be of hir maiestes counsaill whiche know this is
to be proved) that there is more drink [?] spent in a day in hir house,
then taking out the tappe of a vessell and letting it ronne still till it be
ronne out and so out of one vessell after an other all the day long I
say more dronke in a day then can ronne out. This semis straunge
and yet it is trewe, and my lorde of Winchestre[1] decessed (*fo. 41*ᵛ)
(God haue his soule) proved it to be trew in the presence of some
whiche liked him ever after the worse for it (and as for thimprove-
ment of her custumes by one meanes or other I beleve might, if men
wolde goo about, be brought to some good point. But what a fole am
I to trouble youe with these maters and my self bothe whiche are to
be lefte to the consideracion of suche as of these thinges bothe haue
the speciall charge and better meanes and credit to furder the

[1] Stephen Gardiner, bishop of Winchester, died 12 November, 1555.

accomplishement of them then I haue and therfor I make an end with my harty commendacions bydding youe aswell to fare as I wolde myself. From my house by Temple Barre this xvth of Decembre 1556. I send youe my lettre because youe shall see I will conclude in it.

76. *To James Bassett. My house. No date [probably 1556]*[1]
   (Anglesey MSS, vol. ii, fo. 43ʳ–43ᵛ.)

(*fo. 43ʳ*) Master Bassett, I thanke youe for shewing my lettre to the qwenis maieste whiche I write to the duke of Savoye, Mary, so do I not for shewing of my lettre to Sir Ruy Gomes,[2] for it was no part of my meaning to haue her maieste troubled withall, as it semes by your lettre to me that her maieste is presupposing that I shuld not thinke the kinges maieste wold comme if he might, whiche is no pece of my thought, nor my lettre purporth no such thing, nor he to whome the lettre shulde haue bene writen wold (I am sure) so haue conceived by the contynew of the lettre. Thoughe I be not the wisest man, yet do I sumwhat vnderstande the state of that countrey having aswell bene ambassador there in my dayes half a dozen times as also otherwise both bene there and (by all meanes I coulde) travailed tunderstand the nature of the people and the conduict of the state of the countrey. He to whome I wolde haue writen knoweth where I laye the fault and wolde, I dare say, helpe the best he coulde to amend it. In the kinges maieste I thinke no fault for I beleve (as veryly as God is God) that the king is as good a husband as any man living. But as it is no fault but one of the chiefest virtues in a king and one of the pillers of his most assuraunce to followe thaduise of his counsail, so durst I (with the gracious suport and vndre the correction I speke it of bothe their maiestes) take vpon me to prove against any one counsaillor his maieste hathe that it were more expedient for his maiestes affaires that he were now rather present here then there. Mary, I thinke his maieste being not so persuaded and knowing the goodnes of his good wiefe to be suche that in respect of his affaires she can be contented to forbeare his presence, differethe his coming to thintent to come with his affaires well determined, wherfore I forbeare to write the laste parte of my lettre and will amend the first part toching the Darcyes according to your wryting and so I pray youe to shew hir maieste and to beseche her to take my meaning in gracious part which is suche to her maieste to that good king hir (*fo. 43ᵛ*) husbande and to this realme as I wold to Goddes passion she coulde see into

---

[1] See the letter from Bassett to Paget in Appendix G.
[2] Ruy Gomez da Silva, personal adviser to Philip.

the botome of my hart where my care and my meaning liethe. I pray
youe let me know hir maiestes pleasyr how long I shall forbeare the
court and procure as moche as youe can the depeche of Quarre who
(because he was specially recommended to me by the duke of Savoye)
sendethe to me every houre crying out for his dispatche and even now
one tellethe me he is here to speke with me for the same purpose.
Thus I leave to trouble youe and byd youe hartely well to fare. From
my house this Saturday.

77. *To Margaret, Countess of Bath.*[1] *London. 30 January, 1556–7.*
(*Cambridge University Library, Hengrave Collection, vol. i, no.
57.*)

After my right harty commendacions to your good ladishippe. I am
veray sory that it was not my chaunce to see your ladiship at your
late beyng here by reason of your short abode for that I was mynded
to haue moved a matter vnto you such as wherby my good will
towardes you, and yours myght haue appered and bene vnto bothe
pleasur and commodite if the same had taken effect.[2] Lykeas it may
do yet if it so shall lyke your ladiship for on my behaulf it is still
desyred ernestly lykeas this berar my servant Master Bedel your
tenant will by my appoyntement open presently vnto you praying
your ladiship to credit hym and in effect to shew yourself as desyrous
of my poore frendship as I am desyrous to be bownde to you. And so
I tak my leave of your ladiship wishing you aswell to so as I wold
myself. From London the xxx th of January 1556.

Your ladiship assured to commaunde,
William Pagett

78. *To Margaret, Countess of Bath. London. 25 June, 1557.*
(*Cambridge University Library, Hengrave Collection, vol. i, no.
91; modernized text printed in John Gage,* The History and Anti-
quities of Hengrave (*London, 1822*), *pp. 174–5.*)

*Because of occasion to be still at London, he has not seen Master
Kitson at Drayton. Did not ask him to come to London because her
ladyship would not like it. Would like more conversation with Kitson.
Her short letter has given Paget a large commission over Kitson, but
Paget will not use it except according to her ladyship's special appoint-
ment.*

[1] Third wife of John Bourchier, Earl of Bath; died 1561.
[2] Reference to the proposed marriage between Jane Paget and Sir Thomas
Kitson, son of the Countess of Bath by a previous marriage.

79. *To the Privy Council. Drayton. 28 July, 1557.*
   (Cecil MSS, vol. 152, fo. 11ʳ.)

It may lyk your lordships to vnderstand that I haue receyved your lettre with the complaynt therinclosed of Tylman Odenstell. Wherby I perceyve the partye hath distinctly in articles set furth his cause to your lordships with the most advantage to perswade as moch as one partye beyng only herd may be perswaded. But to enforme your lordships briefly of the matter it is playnly confessed that the half of the salt was Frenchmens gooddes (as is redy to be shewed to your lordships) wherby the shippe caryng the same is by the Frenchmens and the Englishmens law of the warre vsed euen amonges them in our tyme (as by diuerse presidentes I am able to shew) a good prise, but to enforce the matter the more this Tylman (as will appere by the deposicions of diuerse witnes which I can shew) is a denyzen in Fraunce. Nevertheles to avoyd your lordships of trouble and myself also sekyng now specilly quyetenes and for charytes sak towardes the poore man I haue wrytten an ernest lettre to my man at Plymowth to restore to this berar his ship with thappertenance as by the same may appere to you which if your lyk it may please you to delyuer to the berar to be conveyed to my ser[uant] as toching the mysdemeanors with the maiors of Plymowth and Saltashe it grew vppon between the two maiors for the libertyes. Thus I take my leave of your lordships from Drayton this 28 th July, 1557.

Your lordships most hable to command
William Paget

80. *To Thomas Thirlby, Bishop of Ely, and Sir Francis Englefield.*
   Bindston. 28 August, 1557.
   (Anglesey MSS, vol. ii, fo. 48ʳ; endorsed, 'Toching the coyne'.)

After my right harty commendacions I haue received your lettres which were deliuered to me in the way hitherwarde, and for answer to the same these may be to signify vnto youe that likeas I am and wilbe ready to the best of my power to do all thinges for thavaunce-ment of the qwenis maiestes service, so I trust I shalbe excused though I give not so sodenly advise in the mater wherof youe write, for surely I nother dare presume being ignorant how the qwenis maieste is disposed to or fro the same nor yet am I now hable to do it con-sidering the weight of the mater, and that I myself these vj wekes haue thought nothing of the mater nor bene with youe and others of the counsaill to heare what might haue bene said to or fro the setting forwarde of the same. But this I thinke (vnder correction) that this

C M—I

tyme of the yere is the best tyme to do the thing if thinges mete for
the purpose had bene put in arredines before hande, and then some
of those courses which by your lettres seme to be lettes wold haue
furthered the mater moche, and saving reformacion I thinke not
those courses to be courses of let, and if they be then will the thing
that youe write to be so necessary never be brought to passe for those
causes or such like are and wilbe ever to be alledged &c. Youe two
and I were named commissioners toching that mater, but hitherto
yet had we nother commission vnder the great seale nor instructions
signed by her maieste nor other declaracion by mowthe how farforthe
we shuld procede sufficient for our discharge. And we either to haue
sued for a commission or to haue presented one of our owne making
had not bene wisdome in suche a case. I trust to see youe ere it be
long at London, for now I am enforced to remaine here for a while
for sum rest, being as evill in all the partes of my body at this present
(saving the swelling in my legges is not so moche) as I was at my going
to the baines. Suche as haue experience of those waters haue tolde
me of two properties in their operacion, the one that strait after the
leving to resort to them the persone greved shall for a tyme fele himself very ill and the other that after a monethe he shall finde great
ease and benefite by them, and if he returne againe to the vse of them
in the spring parfaict healthe. The first propertie I am sure I fele; I
pray God I may finde the other. And thus being my fingers so lame
with wryting that I can no longer hold the penne I take my leave of
youe, wishing youe aswell to do as I wolde my self. From Bindston
the xxviijth of August 1557.

81. *To Margaret, Countess of Bath. Paget Place, London. 24 June,
1558.*
*(Cambridge University Library, Hengrave Collection, vol. i,
no. 115.)*

With my verey harty commendacions vnto your good ladishippe. It
may like the same to vnderstand that vpon the good happe of my
doughter Kitsons comyng hither, my doughter Lee the next morning
after was brought to bed of a goodly boye God save her, and was
therwithall moche weakened, but now thankes be to God doth fele
her self moche amended.[1] My doughter Kytson hathe made in-
staunce vnto me for her retorne downe vnto your ladishippe, and
notwithstanding forasmoche as she is still troubled as she was before
her going thither with the greine sicknes,[2] I am bould to kepe her

---

[1] This child died in infancy.
[2] Jane Kitson died not long after this letter was written.

still with me here, where there is the best remedy to be had therfore, for which purpose I do vse the advise of the best learned in Englande, not doubting but that she shall be remedied therof, and that done which I truste shall not be long vnto, I will send her downe vnto youe, oneles my sonne Kitson will like to come for her himself. In the meane tyme I beseche your ladiship to be contented to beare with her absence and to desire my sonne Kitson to do the like, and if your ladiship will licence him to come hither he shall be hartely wellcome and haue such grosse chere, as he knoweth. And thus with my verey harty commendacions vnto my good lorde and the like from my wief vnto your good ladyship and him, I take my leave. From Paget Place the xxiiij th of June 1558.

Your good ladiships most
assured to commaund.
William Pagett

82. *To the Privy Council. Drayton. 26 September, 1558.*
(SP 69/13, no. 827.)

(*fo.* 179ʳ) It maye like your lordships to vnderstande that this night last past abowt ix of the clocke I receyvid your lettre whereby I doe perceyve your wise and deepe considerations of such thinges as are to be movid for the queenes behaulfe in this treatie of peace now in hand.[1] And forasmichas your pleasures is I shulde write my opinion vnto you both towchinge thesame thinges and also what I thought els were to be movid, me thinketh the queenes maiestie hathe made good choise of the commissioners and devised well for the sendinge over of the commission to Master Woutton[2] who beinge him selfe a wise man and shall have there what healpe he will of advice and cowncell of the kinges maiesties commissioners maye if the matter require such hast as may not tary the cominge over of the rest of the queenes commissioners procede accordinge to his commission now to be sent over vnto him. Your lordships have reason to require the restitution of Caleyse of Guinesnes and the marches with the furniture of the artillerye and municion left therein and that for avoydinge of contention hereafter the lymites maye be made certayne and therefore I thinke in any wise that the arrerages of your debts and pencions be askid and earnestly steeke vnto to thintent that if we have that agayne wich we never lokid for *viz.* Caleys etc. we maye forgoe in recompence (if a better bargayne can not be made) that that we never

---

[1] Refers to the negotiations after the loss of Calais, ultimately leading to the treaty of Cateau Cambrésis in 1559.
[2] Dr Nicholas Wotton, ambassador to France.

hopid for: The arrerages of debts and pencions which as I maye now remember comes to xv or xvj hundred thousand crownes besides greater somes covenanted by Kynge Frauncis then was payd by the kynge that now is for the restitution of Boulen. I dowbte not but the French will loke for some recompence eyther at the kynges hande or the queenes hand if Caleyce be restorid for restitution (I beleve) is made on both sides with recompence reciproque as for any other demaundes to be made besides those which commonly be insertid in all treaties I remembre not els what can be required of the French except there shalbe demaunded the crowne of Fraunce the duchies of Acquitaine and Normandie, which demandes whither it shalbe better to passe over now with scilence vntill another tyme or els to move now presently, I dowbte not but your wisdomes can considre and to demaunde that this peace extend to the Scotes vnder your corrections I thinke it not convenient but to leave that demaunde to the French for the queenes maiestie (I dowbte not) shalbe in this bargayne a principall contrahent with the French kinge and if he lyst to move that the Skottish queene maye be a comprehent (as I dowbte not but he will and will not otherwise conclude with yow) then it shalbe meete in place to move that your articles for your Irish Ilelanders and the racinge of Aymouth and Rexborough to as farre as I remember the treatie then made can certaynly declare. Thus have I troubled yow and my selfe to with my *(fo. 179ᵛ)* folishnesse trustynge your lordships will take it in good parte accordinge to my meaninge and thus I praye God to preserve yow all in good health. From Drayton the xxvj th of September in the morning abowte seventh of the clocke 1558.

> Your lordships humblie at commandement,
> William Pagett

83. *Note touching the Hanse. No place. No date.*
(SP 69/8, no. 492.)

(fo. 124ʳ) Sythens the commyng of thambassadors of the confederate cyteys of the Hanze the queenes maieste considering that they came recommendyd from your maieste willed vs to cause ther causes to be considered with diligence.

And for the bettar debating of those matters wee the Lord Paget, ye Bishop of Ely and Secretary Petre war commawnd to conferre with them. In the begynnyng of which conference the sayd ambassadors prayed to be restored to thatt libertie of traffique which they say they haue allwayes vsed of hertofore in the seuerall tymes of many kinges of this realme, which libertie they sayd was to bring in to this your maiestes realme all kyndes of merchandizes as well of ther own cowntreys as of all other nations, and to cary forth the merchandizes of this realme to all other cowntreys att ther pleasures payng only such small customes as (*fo. 124*) they haue accustomed our awnswar was thatt many yeres after the fyrst grawnt of ther sayd liberties they used to cary owt of this realme butt small quantites of merchandizes and the same only for ther own cowntres bringing in only ye commodites of ther own cowntreys, butt now of lat ther trafficque is so generall and so excedingly increased as if ther be nott a moderation they shall not only tak away the traffique of all the merchauntes of this realme butt doo ouer (*illegible*) preiudice to your maiestes crown of this realme in yor customes for they pay for the most part in fyve partes fowr lesse then other marchauntes strangers doo pay. It hath byn alleged also thatt for many causes particularly and att good length declared vnto them ther pryvileges doo nott bear thatt they may vse this generall traffique. Besides it hath byn sayd to them thatt by the lawes of this realme they may cary no white clothes above the price of iiij *li* the peece. And therfor the last moderation permitting them to cary one white cloth for (*fo. 125*) every iij colored clothes, and permitting also thatt bringing in ther own merchandizes for three partes they might for the iiijth bring in any foreyn wares paying only ther wonted small customes, this moderation (we sayd) hath in it moch more fauor towardes them they may by ther liberties right expownded iustly clayme.

And wher in ther talk of this matter they seme to pretend thatt certayn cyteys within yor maiestes dominions of Gelderland, Frise land and Hollande, shuld tak preiudice by this moderation and restraynt of ther excessiue carying owt of clothes, wee uppon further examination do fynd thatt if they shuld be suffred to carry owt as they desire, it wold nott only be a very greatt decay of your and the queenes maiestes customes of this realme, and a greatt hinderaunce to all the merchantes of this realme, butt wold be also very preiudiciall to yor cowntreys of Flannders of Brabant, for thatt thies clothes being now for the greatter part sold colored and dressed ther and from thens conveyed (*fo. 125*) into Allmayne the same if thes men might haue ther requeste wold be caryed strayght from hens to Hamborough wher they haue prepared dyvers fullers and other artificers for that cowntrey and so from ther upp into Allmayn and by thes meanes of long contynued traffique in those yor maiestes hereditary dominions wold be allmost holly taken away. For thies and many other causes we haue in thend in gentle sort awnswered them thatt this forsayd moderation last mad, is both fauourable for you and such as may nott be presently broken and if bicause thees men hadd no commission to conclude any thing if ther citeys shall agree to send and stand hither any commissionars suffisiently authorized your maiestes will be pleased thatt here shall be holden a diett and in the same such further order may be taken as may be agreable to iustice and tak away all occasions of furthar contention, and some reasonable moderation commodious for them withowt ouer moch preiudice to yor and the queens maiestes crown and subiectes of this realme may be agreed uppon and in the mean tyme thorder last taken to contynue.

(*fo. 126ʳ*) The kinges and queenes maiestes our most gracious soveraigne lord and ladie being fully informed by vs from tyme to tyme of all such matters as haue byn proponed by yow on the behalf of thonorable societye of the confederatt cyteys of the Hanz hath willed vs for awnswar to declare vn to yow.

Fyrst, thatt ther maiestes well remembring the awncient and long contynued amitie between ther realmes and the confederatt cyteys aforsayd be as desyrous to contynue and by all good offices enterteyn the same as any of their progenitours kinges of Englond haue byn and will bee gladd to haue the same awncient league frindyshipp by some reasonable meanes strengthened, yea, and increased rather then enpayred in any poynt.

And for a manifest declaration of ther sayd good affections ther maiestes of ther speciall favour haue hertofore licenced them to cary owt of this ther realme clothes on dressed and onwrought nothwithstanding the lawes and statutes doo forbydd the same, (*fo. 126ᵛ*) butt toching thatt absolut libertie claymed to cary owt and bring in all sortes of wares and of all cowntreys and for the caring owt of wares into the cowntreys of Neythar Germanye.

Ther maiestes bee informed thatt in for sondry partes of this generall clayme ther haue in tymes past in the reignes of seuerall ther progenitors kinges of this realme, many contrauersies, disputes, interruptions and some ordres also made contrary to thatt yor lordships doo now pretend to be dun by your privileges.

They doo consider also thatt the privileges aforsayd long after the fyrst grawnt of them was vsed with suche a moderation as was commodious to the confederatt cyteys and not ouer preiudiciall to the king and crown of this realme, but now of late thexportation and importation of wares is so moch increased and the sayd privileges otherwayes so moch abused by sondry men pretending them selfes merchauntes of thatt societye thatt the same may nott withowt ouer greatt preiudice both to their maiestes rightes and customes and to all ther merchantes be longer suffred in such sort as hath of lat tyme byn claymed.

(*fo. 127*ʳ) ~~Ther be many other just considerations that we the lordes and gouerners can of them~~ soo besides this many abuses haue of late crept in both of reason ought and for the bettar enterteynment of thamitie bee necessary to be reformed and made mor certayn. For reformation wherof ther maiestes bee well pleased thatt ther may be our dyett holden in this ther citey of London att any such tyme within one yere next as the sayd confederatt cyteys shall think good in which some good men well chosen may tak a fynall order and agree vppon some such reasonable and equall moderation in this traffique as may be commodious both for the Hanze and the merchantes of this realme and wher considerations may be hadd also thatt ther maiestes ther rates and customes susteyn no greatter losse then by the fyrst grawnters of those pryvileges was ment and by the vse of them xx or xl yeres after the fyrst grawnt wolle ~~was~~ declared by theis meanes wher reasonable consideration is hadde to ech partye and equalite vsed all occasions of furthar contentions may be well taken away wherin ther maiestes offer ther good fauours.

(*fol. 127*ᵛ) And for the meane tyme ther maiestes be pleased att the request of your lordships to enlarge the last moderation made here and to grawnt thatt wher it was permitted to carye owt only the iiijth cloth whit thatt now ther merchauntes of thatt societye may for the space of one hole yere next (by which tyme the diett may be hadd and finisshed) carye owt for euery twoo colored clothes one white and so the iijrd part in whit clothes.

84. *Acts to be Repealed. No place. No date.*
    (*Anglesey MSS, Misc. Box, no. 7.*)

21 Henry VIII	First two braunches toching the dispensacion of pluralites of benefices and of non residence
24	*Item* the acte restrayning appeles to Rome to be repelled
25	*Item* two actes restrayning the payment of anates and first frutes to the sea of Rome and elected consecrating of bushops within the realme
25	*Item* one act intituled the submission of the clergy to King Henry the viij th
25	*Item* one act intituled the act of exoneracion of exaccions paid to the see of Rome and for obteyning of dispensacions without sute to Rome
26	*Item* one act toching and declaring the king to be supreme head of the churche of England and to reforme abuses

26 Henry VIII	*Item* one acte for nominacion and consecracion of suffraganes within this realme
28	*Item* one act for thextinguishing the auctorite of the bushop of Rome
28	*Item* one act toching releasing of suche as haue obtained pretended licences from the sea of Rome
31	*Item* one other act auctorising the king to make bushops by lettres patentes
32	*Item* one other acte concerning precontractes of mariages and toching degrees of consanguinite
35	*Item* one other act toching the kinges stile for the supremacye
35	*Item* one braunche in the act toching the succession of the imperiall crowne for one othe to be made against the bushop of Rome
37	*Item* one acte toching doctors of civill lawe being maryed to exercise ecclesiasticall iurisdiccion
1 Edward VI	*Item* one braunche in the acte of repele of treasons and felonies against such as do extolle the authoritie and supremacy of the bushop of Rome
2 et 3	*Item* one acte made for abstinence from fleshe
	Item one acte toching nominacion of xxxij persones anno 27 Henry VIII remayning yet against the see of Rome
	Item all that parte of one act made in the 28 yere of Henry VIII intitled an act for thestablishment of the succession of the imperiall crowne asmoche therof as concerneth a prohibition to mariage within the degrees

85. *Proposal Touching Wine. No place. No date.*
(Anglesey MSS, Misc. Box, no. 10; endorsed, 'Medley[1] *toching wine.')*

Yf it wold please the kynge and quens magystyes with theire honorable councell to make a restrent by parlament or otherwyse that no wyne shalbe browght in to this realme of England for the space of [*blank*] yeres butt only by theire specyall lysens.

And that it wold please theire magysties to gyve to me and to

---

[1] George Medley was related to the Willoughby family and acted for them. He came into contact with Paget because Paget had the wardship of the Willoughby heir, Thomas, who was married to Paget's daughter Dorothy. Cf. *Hist. Mss. Commission Reports, Middleton.*

myne assyngnis lysens to bryng in wyne and none other for the terme of yeres a fore sayd.

And that I may haue lysens in the tyme of warre to bryng in as well woad, salt, canvis and other comodyties owte of Fraunce as wyne, and to convey suche comodyties owt of England in to Fraunce as is to be ventyd, not beyng restrenyd by any specyall lawe.

And that I may lade any of the sayd merchandyse as well in any strangers shipes as in Englyshe shipes.

I wilbe bounde to serve the quens magystye [*blank*] tonne of Gascon wyne att vj *li* the tonne.

And also I wilbe bounde to sett no ~~Gascone~~ wyne a bove the price that it is nowe sold onleste the scassytye of wynes where they be made be the cawse therof.

And for to haue this before requiryd I will gyve the quens magystye euery yere for so long as I or myne assyngnis maye inioye the same tene thowsande markes corrant money of England ouer and above the ordenary custome and to pay the same x thowsande markes within iiij mounthes after thend of euery yere and for the performans therof to be bounde in suche bondes as shalbe thowght requesett.

86. *To the Queen of Navarre. No place. No date.*
   (Anglesey MSS, Misc. Box, no. 25.)

Madame, La grace et faueur quil a pleu a vostre excellence den user enuers moy en France auecques la chrestienne charite que Jay tousjours congneue en Icelle mont donne hardiesse de vous escripre ceste en faueur dung paoure gentilhomme Anglois nomme Mre Wingfield prisonnier aseurs en France Il a este La longuement detenu. Et combiens quil ne soit grand heritier mais asseurement ung simple homme darmes toutes fois son possesseur ne le veult changer pour aulter prisonnier ny le remecter prisonnier sans rancon des raisonnable. Parquoy suplie treshumblement a votre excellence de faire que sondit possesseur veulle relaxer quelque peu de sa rigeur et extremitie car la votre excellence scait tresbien que nulle chose est plus execrable que lextremitie, et pleust a dieu que les aultres puissent auoir este enduictes aultresfois a Lindifferencie et a le bon moyen lesquels Jay tousjours congneues destre en votre excellence. Certes les choses outre les deux Roys ne foussent Jamais este en les termes ou nous les voyons maintenant ny le grand dissimulateur et hipocrite qui a tousjours trompe et trompera le monde (de qui votre excellence ma parle et moi a elle bien souuent) pouvroit auoir monte la ou il est presentement. Lexperience monstre bien cler questions et votre Excellence et moy tous deux vrayes Cassandras. Nous prophetisones la verite qui depuis est advenue mais pour lors Lon ne nous a voullu croire. Neantmoins (Dieu mercy) ung aduantage nous y est encore demeure qui a failly a Cassandre car dommaige certain et perte Irrecuperable suiuoit son vaticine La ou la consequence du nostre nest encore venue a telle extremite qui ne peust rabille si ung de lung coste veult faire la raison come Laultor de laultor couste la veulte entendre et que lon tenue bonne main en saison oeuure qui me semble digne de votre excellence Princesse bonne chretiene vray religieuse, et (pour la quelle chose vous vous devuez recongnoistre en plusgrand obligation deuers Dieu) prudente singulerement oultor Lentendement de sexe feminin. De moy tout ce que je pouvray adjouster sans toucher mon honneur et loyaultie vous vous pourrez promector asseurement. Ainsi Treshault et tresexcellente Princesse vous faisant de rechief souuenaunce audit paoure prisonnier Laffaire duquel vous scaura dire plus amplement ce porteur. Auquel vous plaira donner audience et me recommendant treshumblement a la bonne grace de votre excellence Je prie adieu vous avoir en sa saincte garde et de vous donner La grace dauancer sa parolle.

87. *Benefits done to the Lord Admiral.*[1] *No place. 1559.*
   (*Anglesey MSS, vol. ii, fos. 67ʳ–68ʳ.*)

That I was against him for having of his office againe, it cometh of his suspicious nature for that I being in credit then with the quene, and he thinking that I might do what I wolde & thought also because I gatt him not his office againe I was against him in yt saing the quene that dead is told him so, which I dare sweare she did not for I knowe by other men that this suspicion he had of me before he was much in the quenes favor againe.

That I was his enemye at Wyattes coming in.[2] I dare say he speaketh against his own knowlege and his conscience.

He might as well lay to my charge ~~that I was his eneme fore his goinge to Bulloine~~

That I was his enemye when he was first sent to Boilloine.

That I wrote against him from thence when I was there with the old erle of Bedford and others.[3]

That I was his enemye at Framynham.[4]

That I dyd what I could that he might haue byn sent into Ireland.

That I was against his calling againe to councell.

---

[1] Lord Clinton.   [2] Wyatt's Rebellion, 1554.
[3] Refers to negotiations at Boulogne in February and March, 1549–50.
[4] Framlingham, Suffolk, where Queen Mary raised her standard in July, 1553.

That I was against him for having his office last in Quene Maries tyme.

That I was against him for keping of his office now at this tyme.

As for the fyrst poynt my lorde of Arundell and Master Petre who be men alyve know what I dyd in yt with others ioyntly. ~~who that be men~~

(*fo. 67*) As for the seconde: I knowe no frende that opened his lippes for him but I, and by my meanes, the matter was kept secret from me both toching him and an other man also till it was almost to late and as sone as ever I knewe yt what I dyd in it the late bushope of Winchestre yf he were alive could tell and so (I thinke) can my Lord Wentworth, Sir Thomas Cornewallis, and some others that were then of the quenes pryvy counsaill. And he him self can tell what comfort I gave him when he came to my house at Drayton.

As toching the thirde, I suppose Master Secretarye hath harde that I was the meanes to my lorde of Somersett att the request of my lorde of Warwicke for his going to Bulloine.

Toching the iiijth, he himself sawe and hard what lettres I wrote in his commendacion and how from tyme to tyme I dyd set him furth.

As toching the vth, indede my lorde of Arundell was his very good lorde and in what stede I stode him there my Lorde Wentworth, Master Cornewallis, Master Garnyngham, Master Ingelfeld, and others of the quenes councell then can tell, and how well the quene was affected vnto him at Framyngham at that tyme and also after her comyng to London.

As toching the vjth, he him self saw lettres that I dyd wryte to the king for his stay at home.

As toching the vjith and the viijth, the king of Spayne and (I thinke) some others too, knowe what I dyd for him when I knew that the quene wold nedes haue my lorde chamberlaine that now is out of the office. Yea, and what I dyd for my lorde chamberlayne too at that same tyme, besides the king that then was there be others that knowe how so ever it cometh to passe now that neither my lord admirall, nor (*fo. 68*) the other, now, can geve me agood worde.

As toching the ixth, Master Secretarye can be a wytnesse what I spake on the behalf of my lord admirall at the quenes comyng in.

Now you se the good natures of men in these dayes. Let my lord admirall take vpon him to prove or disprove eyther the affirmative or the negative of any of my ix articles and prove them or disprove them indede and I will make him what amendes the quene or her counsaille will esteme. Or yf he will I will take vpon me eyther the prove or disprove of the affirmative or the negative as he will, in every poynt by witnesses yet alive and by apparent circumstances.

What amendes then will he make to me? I aske none other amendes but that which shalbe to his own honor and benefite, that is to say to change his nature which wilbe brought to passe by custome if he will from hencefurth vse yt. Na, na, the matter is none of all these: my licence my licence[1] is the matter. Hereof cometh all this busines. But now me thinketh that my licence taketh not effect, these displesures and sklanderous talkes shuld cease for by them they dishonest not me, but dishonor them selves. With what countenaunce or conscience can any of them come to Goddes borde, well, I say no more but God helpe vs and pardon vs all of our evill dedes. We had nede to pray for I feare God will scourge vs, all one with an other, our charitie is so cold and so great is our malice, envye, flatterie, discimulacion and other iniquities and specially among such of vs who as best example shuld be given. Let vs all amend and then yet I trust God will hold his handes, and so for my parte I do intend to do and daylye pray to God of his grace for yt.

88. *To Sir Thomas Parry and Sir William Cecil. My house. 3 February, 1558–9.*
    (*Cecil MSS, vol. 152, fo. 30ʳ–30ᵛ; modernized text printed in Haynes, pp. 207–8.*)

Sends two devises for the amendment of the monies. Recommends that only the queen and four or five councillors be informed of this matter. Will declare at next meeting that they of the mint have warning to coin little silver and much gold and to keep the gold in their hands. Prays his suits will be remembered.

89. *To Sir Thomas Parry and Sir William Cecil. My house. 20 February, 1558–9.*
    (*Cecil MSS, vol. 152, fo. 31ʳ–31ᵛ; modernized text printed in Haynes, pp. 208–9.*)

Laments that his health prevents his coming to court. Reminds them of necessity of friendship with Burgundy and natural enmity between England and France. Urges them to move the queen to put her sword into her hand.

90. *To Sir William Cecil. My house. 5 March, 1558–9.*
    (*SP 12/3, no. 11.*)

Master Secretary. Forasmochas there is a bruit that it is like to be peace, I thought good herby to put youe in remembraunce, that

[1] Refers to Paget's licence for wines.

wheras in every traictie there is a commun article making mencion of free *commercium* and passage *per maria et per aquas dulces.* Incase the quenis maiestes pleasure be to contynue thincrease of her custume vpon wine and clothe, according to the order already taken, it shall not be amisse (in myne opinion) that these wordes *Saluis tamen vnicuique principium suis legibus aedictis et priuilegiis quibuscunque* be inserted to the traictie, wherby there may bothe commodite arise to her maieste in sort aforesaid, and otherwise. And so I take my leave of youe. From my house this v th of Marche 1558.

Your verey frende
William Pagett

91. *To Sir William Cecil. My house. 17 March, 1558–9.*
  (*SP 12/3, no. 34.*)

Master Secretary. After my very harty commendacions. I haue forborne to trouble youe with my writing, for that I know youe are otherwise busied and likeas I haue alwayes bene bould of your frendship, so I am now occasioned to pray youe of the same: My Lord Williams of Tame[1] is very sicke and not like to recover, for whose office of presidentship in Wales, I shall pray youe to ioyne with Master Treasurer[2] on my behalfe, to whom I haue writen to that effect, nothing doubting your furtheraunces to the perfection of the sute. And thene ceassing to clog youe with wordes, I haue prayed Master Waade[3] briefly to breake my mynd vnto youe. From my house this Friday the xvij th of Marche 1558.

Your very frende
William Pagett

92. *To Sir Thomas Parry. My house. 23 April, 1559.*
  (*Cecil MSS, vol. 152, fo. 78; modernized text printed in Haynes, p. 210.*)

Inquires whether his licence for wines will be granted. Complains that the lord admiral and Lord Hastings of Loughborough have raised false tales against him. If the queen thinks him unworthy to continue in his place, he will seek a writ of dotage whereby he will have the liberty to absent himself from all parliaments. States that Lord Sussex and he are not all one, but hopes matter may be compounded by friendship. Asks that this letter be communicated to Mr Secretary.

[1] John, Lord Williams of Thame. [2] Sir Thomas Parry.
[3] Armigill Waad, clerk of the privy council.

93. *To Sir Thomas Parry. No place. No date.*
  (*SP 12/5, no. 35.*)

(*fo. 55ʳ*) Sir, I send you hereinclosed a note of my debtes. And pray youe to helpe me to asmuche favor for the stallement of the same as youe can. I haue sent the like to Master Secretary.

Your own
William Paget

(*fol. 56ʳ*) A Note of the Lord Pagettes Debtes to the Quenes Maiestie
Item the Courte of Wardes . . . . . . viijᶜ xxiij *li.* vj *s.* iij *d.*
Item Thexchequier for the last subsidie in Quene Maryes tyme. . . . . . cxx *li.*
Item Thexchequier for the first payment of the subsidie in the Quenes maiestes tyme. . . . . .iiijˣˣ *li.*
Sum total. . . . . . m xxiij *li.* vj *s.* iij *d.*

94. *To Matthew Parker, Archbishop of Canterbury. Temple Bar. 13 March, 1562–3.*
  (*Cambridge, Corpus Christi College, MS 114, no. 96.*)

Sir, I beseach your grace to pardon my boldenes determyned to make sewte vnto youe for the presentacion of an honest man vnto a benyfice nowe voyde, and of your graces gyfte in Kente, I am hereunto encouraged by your graces old good will and favor vnto me, renewed nowe of late and confyrmed by your gentle vsage of me: The benefice wherof I desire to have the presentacion is called Ivie,[1] the partie whome I desire to have presented is the mynister of Itham, in Kente called John Hooper a learned and honest man, and so taken amongest his neighbours. If yt shall please your grace to satysfie my desire, youe maie accompt the obligacion of my good will vnto youe muche encreased and me readie to discharge and paie the same at your own apoinctement yf occasion shall so serve me. And thus I take my leave of your grace. From my poore howse besides Temple Barre this xiij th of Marche 1562.

Your graces most
assured at commaundement
William Paget

[1] According to Parker's register, Andrew Peerson, a clerk of the archbishop's chapel, was presented to Ivychurch on 31 March, 1563. *Registrum Matthei Parker Diocesis Cantuariensis AD 1559–1575*, ed. W. H. Frere (Oxford, 1928), ii, p. 801.

APPENDICES

A. *The Duchess of Somerset to Paget. No place. 8 October, 1549.*
   (PLB.)

Good Master Comptroller, I have receaved commendacons from
yow by my brother, for which I geve yow thankes from a sorrowfull
hart as ever woman had. Ah, good lorde, what a miserable vnnaturall
tyme is this? What hath my lorde done to any of these noble men? or
others? that they shulde thus rage and seke thextremitie to him and his
that never had thought in the like towardes any of them. Ha, Master
Comptroller, I have ever loved and trusted youe, for that I have
seine in yow a perfyte honest frende to my lord who hath always
made the same accompt and assuredly bare yow his good will and
frendship as yow your selfe hath had best tryall. God hath geven
yow a great wisdome and a frendly nature. A, good Master Comptroller, for Christes bloodes sake spare not for payne study and
wryting as I here yow do, the lyvinge God will prosper yow and yours
the better. I knowe yow maye do muche good in these matters beinge
a wiseman. Howe can God be content with this disorder to daungier
the king and all the realme in sekinge extremities. God must
nedes of his rightuousnes sore plage those that seketh these matters.
Oh, that I could bere this as I ought to do with patience and quietnes,
but it passeth all fraile fleshe to do. For knowynge so well my lordes
innocency in all these maters that they charge him with all, they be so
vntrewe and most vnfriendly credyt that surely it hath bene some
wicked persone or persones that furst sought this great vprore. I saye
againe yf I could bere the tyme, I know well and assure my selfe that
God will kepe and defende him from all his enemies, as he hath
alwais done hitherto. Good Master Comptroller, comefort my lorde
as I trust yow do, both with counsaile and otherwise, for I muche
feare he is sore greved at the hart, furst for the kinge and the realme,
and as greatly to se these lordes frendeshippes so sclender to him as it
doth appear and specially of some, albeit he hath pleasured them all.
Alas, that ever any Christian realme shulde be so sclaundered. Thus
to ende with all I crie to yow eftesones shewe youe, shewe your selfe
like a wurthie counsailour and a servaunt to God and the kinge that
these tumultes might cease.

                                                      Anne Somerset

B. *Sir Thomas Smith to Paget. No place. No date, [October, 1549].*
(*PLB.*)

Sir, I furste commend me unto youe as humbly and hartely as I possibly maye. And whereas I had thought that ye had taken, that already I had opened all my harte unto youe, I perceive by a worde caste owt to my wiefe that ye do not even fully take it so; furste that I euer conspired your deathe, or herde of any suche thinge in my presence I do fully denye yt, and renounce God if euer I dyd, who nowe at this tyme hath moste nede to helpe me. I do not deny that on the Sundaye in the morninge I trowe it was or Saturdaie late at night when my lordes grace fyrste opened this broile unto me (for ye knowe before I was away) I told him if it were so that youe did knowe what it was there was no doubte. Then he told me that he had sente youe and Master Petres awaye, to that I sayd, alas, Sir, then haue youe done evill for there is no man so able to helpe it in the world as he is and could better do yt, and if youe had had more of the counsaill about youe it had bene better, for the love of God staye him aboute youe, and I wold wishe Master Petres to. And herein vse their aduise, all that remaynethe here ells hathe no experience. And ye shall be suer they will lesse attempte violence againste youe havinge them here. No, saithe he, I thincke he be as evill as the beste of them; thoughe he be, Sir, quoth I, yet I am sure he will invent somethinge for youe. Well, sayth my lorde, go your wayes and helpe Cicill to make some more of those lettres whiche he is a makinge, and if he be not gone already, I will have him tary here. This is the moste that euer I spake of eny suche matter which I did then because I thought it trewe. Eny conspiringe or mocion to kille youe or any other, or that youe shuld be commytted to Master Cotton, or any other I knowe not, and suerly yt was not my deuyse, nor I was not made previe. But as youe knowe in this trepidacion tumulte and broyle many wordes might be spoken, and no man knoweth better then youe many moste fonde and false rumours and tales be brought and spred to all parties. I euer said (I can not denye) that youe knewe the lordes hole intente and to what extremities yt wold come and what could be already done. The which I dyd gesse of your naturall wisedome, longe experience, and great familiaritie that ye haue had with them all, who I thought wold not hide so great a thinge from youe. This I praye youe persuade your selfe fully vpon me that I never sought, nor could well to be sought the deathe of any persone. And if vpon this suspicion, ye haue borne any grudge vnto me, I praye youe forgeve yt me, and nowe extende your clemency and favour vnto me, the which God shall rewarde and whiles I lyve ye shall haue me yours with my contynuall prayer and no vnkind nor unnaturall man; alas, it were small pleasure unto youe to caste me awaye, and to save me and helpe me in these extremities a perpetuall benefite to bynde me to youe and all my power and wytte. The which I praye youe let me feale, as my trust is and as youe haue promysed unto my wife, whom with my selfe and all that I haue I holly commend and commyt vnto youe to dispose of at your pleasure, and so take I my leave of youe for this tyme, tyll it shall please youe to vouchesafe to speake with me. This Frydaye.

T. Smythe

C. *John Dudley, Earl of Warwick, to [Paget]. London. 1 February, 1549–50.*

(BM, Cotton MS, Caligula E. iv, fo. 206.^r*)*

...tremely and vndre my lyste ....
and good digestion I was rather lyke to ....
yf I had not entred the new dyet the which ....
eased me thorroly of my payne, and where....................
xxx ti and xl ti dayes, I kept yt but xiiij and ....
my self with good and holsome meates agayn ....
thes x dayes to be able to do my dewtie an...................
ding vpon my master. This haue I declared ....
present estate, with thankes according that youe wo............
to heare of yt, the parliament prorogeth this day ....
of Maye. To morow the Lorde Ferres,[1] who ys a..............
of the pryvie councell shalbe created viscount ....
Therle of Wiltsher receiutes to morro the staff of ....
saurership. The marques of Northampton thoffice of ....
chamberleyn and as I am advertised the kinges maieste ....
wold I shulde be great master of his highnes house the ....
of Dorsett justice of the forrestes, the Lord Wenforde[2] ....
to be lord chamberleyn of the house, the erle marsha............
and the presydentship of the councell remayneth sty.............
kinges handes vndetermyned or disposed the rest of our ....
they haue in the commen lettre, and so I leave with a wea.........
faynt hande requyring that I may be commended hart............
my verey good lord therle of Bedforde and to the rest ....
coleges and to my lord of Huntyngdon, and my lord deputy ......
all other noble men and gentlemen as yf I rehearsed ....

---

[1] Walter Devereux, Lord Ferrers, was created Viscount Hereford.

[2] Thomas, Lord Wentworth.

names not forgetting me to myne olde acquayntaunce Sir ....
Wallop[1] with my most harty thanckes for his gentle and fr........
aduertisementes which I wyll requyte with as often sending to h....
assone as I shalbe able to sytt in councell as knoweth God who
graunte you to fynishe the worke you haue in hand to thonor of the
kinges maieste, your owne, and the welth of the realme. At London
this fyrst of February 1549.

> Your lordeshippes assured frende
> J Warwycke

D. *Edward Seymour, Duke of Somerset; William Paulet, Earl of
Wiltshire; John Russell, Earl of Bedford; Edward Lord Clinton;
Thomas Lord Wentworth; Sir Thomas Cheyney; Sir William
Cecil; Sir Ralph Sadler to Paget. Westminster. 27 November, 1550.
(DL 12/14.)*

After our right hartye commendacions to your lordship. Whereas our
verey good ladye the Duchesse of Suffolke hath made humble sute to
the kinges maiestie for to porchasse the colledge of Spylsbye in the
countie of Lincoln to thuse of her seconde sonne the Lord Charles,
his maiestie was pleased for dyvers considerations, the same shuld be
freely geven, as heretofore your lordship hath ben aduertised.
Neuertheles the booke hath ben so drawen, that she hauyng therin
but estate for terme of lyffe and her soonne the fee simple, that if it
shuld so passe, she might rather take losse being here after accompt-
able to him at his full age. Wherefore to the amendyng therof, the
kinges maiestie is pleased that the same booke shalbe newly corrected
in this pointe only, that is to saye that the estate of the fee symple be
conveyed ioyntlye to the said ladye and her sonne which thing we
pray your lordship to cause to be put in effect and then the boke
signed by your lordship and the counsell of your corte may be furder
accomplisshed as the cace requireth. So we bid your lordship farre
well from Westminster the xxvij th of November 1550.

> Your lordships loving frendes
> E. Somerset
> W. Wilteshyre
> J. Bedford
> E. Clynton
> T. Wentworth
> T. Cheyne
> W. Cecyll
> R. Sadlyr

[1] Sir John Wallop.

E. *Anne Paget to the Council. No place. [1552].*
   (Anglesey MSS, vol. ii, fo. 20ʳ.)

In mooste humble wise besechethe youre good lordships, youre
dayly oratrice Anne Paget to be good and gratious lordes vnto her
husbande. And wheras her saide husbande hathe submitted hym self
to the clemencie of the kinges maieste that it wolde please youe to be
mediators vnto his highenes to haue pity vpon hym and me and our
poore childerne, and to determyn a gratious & mercifull ende of our
trouble having consideracion of the poore state wherin we stande as
by a schedule herinclosed maye appeare vnto youe. And we and our
childerne with all ours shall as we be alredy moost[e] bownden dayly
praye to God for the prosperous estate of his mooste excellent
maieste and of all youre good lordships long to indure.

F. *James Bassett to Paget. No place. 2 May, 1556.*
   (Anglesey MSS, vol. ii, fo. 35ʳ.)

My very good lorde, my duety most humblie remembred. I moved
the quenes highnes at the departing of this bearer Master Twyno
your lordeshippes servaunt to vnderstande whither her highnes wold
send or wryte any thing to your lordship by hym, who answered that
forasmoche as her highnes felt not her selfe so wel as she myght wryte
to the kyng, her highnes thought it not convenient to sende any
lettres to any her subiect ther and none to his maiestie, and therfore
to supplie her highnes lettres vnto you, she signified her mynde to
Master Peter by whom you shal perceive how thankfully her maiestie
taketh the service your lordship doth her there. And I thought not to
pretermytte these few lynes to thentent your lordship shold perceiue
by me the cause whye her highnes wrote not vnto you and also that I
forgatte not your lordship. I do assure you at the wryting herof her
maiestie was nothing in such case as I wold wishe for your lordship
knoeth the only thing that wyl remedie her. Thus having no occur-
ences to advertise you other then this bearer can declare by mouth, I
take my leave in hast the ij of May.

Your lordships to commaunde
James Basset.

G. *James Bassett to Paget. No place. 14 November [1556].[1]*
   (Anglesey MSS, vol. ii, fo. 37ʳ–37ᵛ.)

After my most humble recommendacions to your good lordship,
   [1] See letter no. 76.

yesternight betwene vj and vij I receued your lordships lettre and imediatly vpon the receipt therof being called for by the quenes highnes vpon thoccasion of certeyn byls which her maiestie then signed geving me order for the deliuering of them. I having then good oportunytie and fearyng lest if I omytted the same I shold not haue so convenient a tyme ageyn that night, I declared to her maiestie how I had even then receued a pacquette from your lordship and not hauing the laisor to peruse them being so sodenly after the receipt of them called in vnto her highnes, nevertheles being well assured that there was somewhat conteyned in the same either to declare or to deliuer vnto her highnes, I dyd therfore offre the same vnto her highnes to peruse if yt so stode with her pleasure before I saw them myself which her highnes dyd and when she came to that point in your lettre to Sir Ruy Gomes where you make mencion that she ys contented that Darcye shall remayne in saynctuary styll, her highnes said thereunto that she was not absolutely resolued so but that he shold remayne only soo vntyll the kynges comyng, wishing that your lordship shold so wryte it in your lettre. Touching the rest of your so vehement persuasions to Sir Ruy Gomes to be playne with your lordship the quenes highnes dyd nothing lyke ye same at all and said that for her own parte she was most parfightely assured that the kyngs maiestie dothe asmoche as in hym dothe possiblie lye for his lyfe to procure his most spedy retorne, and therfor her highnes cannot by any meanes endure that any person shold speake or thinke otherwise of his maiestie (*fo. 37ᵛ*) and so moche lesse endure that it shold be wrytten specially her maiestie being priuie therunto. And where her highnes and the counsell leekwise dothe conformablye wryte that they confesse the kyng hath most iust & necessarye cause of this his abode & that he wyl not as they are most assured differe the same any one moneth lenger then of force & necessetie he nedes must yt shuld contrary wise by your lettres appere that not only your self but that the moste part here thought otherwise of his maiestie which to put in his highnes hedde in her maiesties opinion may do hurte & no good wherfor seing her highnes hath seen the contents of your lettre she saithe that she cannot in any wise suffre or be pleased that they shuld passe in that sorte & even so commaunded me to signifie vnto your lordship thus. Being glad of your lordships recouery & sory for the sycknes of your servaunt of the small poxe wherby I cannot my selfe come to waight vpon your lordship as els I wold. I do for this tyme most humbly take my leave in hast the xiiij of Novembyr.

Postscript. I do retorne herwith vnto your lordship ij lettres the one from the kyng the other from Quarrey vnto you and also your own ij lettres the one to the duke of Savoy the other to Sir Ruy Gomes.

Your lordships at commaundement
James Bassett

H. *James Bassett to Paget. No place. 15 December, 1556.*[1]
(Anglesey MSS, vol. ii, fo. 39ʳ)

After my most humble commendacions to your lordship. I receved your lordships lettre yesterday in the afternowne with the ij lettres enclosed in the same which I shewed to the quenes maiestie for answer whereof her maiestie commaunded me to signifie vnto you that seing you desyer her advyse she thinkethe in no wyse convenyent you shold make any mencyon in them at all of those iiij poynts which you declare the kynges maiesties presens here wold so greatly further. Her maiestie ys of this opinion for ij respectes, the one ys forasmoche as order was taken before the kyngs departure hense for the doyng of iij of them whereof to mak mencion or to put the kyng in remembrance thereof, before he myght be advertysed that they were in dede donne according as order was taken they shold, yt is in her heghenes judgement a shame and by no meanes convenyent, the other resort that moveth her highnes ys that consideryng there ys not leekwise any resolucion taken in the matter of money what shalbe donne therein her maiestie dothe not thinke yt mete to be tooched in your lettre before you could advertise the full resolucion therof, and for these causes her maiestie wold you sholde in any wise omytte the mencionyng of those iiij poynts in your lordships lettre, as not convenyent to be spoken of before they were either executed or resolued. As for the matter of the marchaunts the same beyng a thing concluded her highnes dothe very well lyke your advertisement thereof. Touching the sending of your stuffe which remayneth here to Grenewich her highnes, consideryng the same hathe contynued here styll, ys very well pleased therewith so that you sende not any that comethe from your house or where the infection hathe been and considering this disease lyngerethe after this sort in your lordships house her highnes feareth it therfore the more. Thus being sorry for this new chaunce of your servants sycknes which wyll prolong your lordships comyng to the courte somewhat the longer. I wyll for this tyme most humblye take my leave in hast the 15 of Decembre.

Your lordships at commaundement
James Bassett

[1] See letter no. 75.

II

THE PARLIAMENTARY DIARY OF
JOHN CLEMENTSON, 1770–1802

edited by

P. D. G. THOMAS, M.A., Ph.D., F.R.Hist.S.

CONTENTS

INTRODUCTION

JOHN CLEMENTSON was Deputy Serjeant at Arms to the House of Commons from 1770 to 1804. Little is known of his personal background, except that his wife was named Mary and that they had at least three children, a son and two daughters. Clementson was apparently seventy when he retired in 1804, and he died on 24 April, 1805 'at his house in the country': this was probably at Copthall in Bedfordshire, for he was living there in 1803.[1]

Clementson served under two Serjeants, Nicholas Bonfoy, Serjeant from 18 October, 1762 until his death on 12 October, 1775, and Edward Coleman, Serjeant from 16 November, 1775 until 1805. Like so many subordinate officials of the time he evidently performed many of the Serjeant's duties himself; and in doing so he made a fleeting and anonymous appearance in one important political crisis. Clementson was the Commons official most closely involved in the House's attempt in 1771 to stop the reporting of Parliamentary debates in the press. It was the Deputy Serjeant who was sent to arrest the first two defiant printers in February, and who was despatched by Speaker Sir Fletcher Norton on 15 March to demand the release of a messenger of the House who had been arrested for attempting to

---

[1] The above is based on information in the possession of the present Deputy Serjeant. Some of it can be verified in the *Gentleman's Magazine*, xlv, p. 503; lx, p. 859; lxi, p. 878; lxxiii, p. 691; lxxv, p. 489.

apprehend a printer within the boundary of the City of London, the incident that was the highlight of the whole controversy.[1]

Clementson was paid no salary and depended on fees and other emoluments: but from 1800 the House of Commons passed an annual Address asking the King to ensure that Clementson's income, including emoluments, would amount to £500.[2] For at least his last ten years in office, moreover, Clementson put his expertise to profitable use by acting as a Parliamentary agent for private bills.[3] In 1804 he was able to bequeath his office to his son, who was appointed Deputy Serjeant on 5 May; and on 7 June the House of Commons unanimously voted an Address asking the King to make some provision for 'John Clementson Esquire, who has for near thirty-five years faithfully and diligently executed the office of Deputy Serjeant at Arms attending this House, and who, on account of his long and laborious services and advanced time of life, has lately resigned the same'.[4] A subsequent Civil List account presented to the House included the sum of £219. 14s. for Clementson, with this explanation: 'rent of a house to midsummer 1806, in lieu of apartments he resigned at the House of Commons'.[5]

This public recognition of Clementson's services confirms the impression given by his diary that he performed his duties with zeal and efficiency. Indeed, he also compiled a formal manuscript account of points of duty and procedure which he left in the Serjeant's office on his resignation and has served as a guide for later generations. Clementson's private diary contains details not in the quasi-official manuscript, but both are primarily concerned with recording the duties of the Serjeant at Arms.[6] Clementson's papers show that in the later eighteenth century the Serjeant was responsible for all the functions listed by Erskine May in the first edition of his *Treatise* in 1844.[7]

His duties are, to attend the speaker with the mace on entering and leaving the house, or going to the House of Lords, or attending her Majesty with addresses; to keep clear the gangway at the

[1] For Clementson's part in the episode see P. D. G. Thomas, 'John Wilkes and the Freedom of the Press (1771)', *Bulletin of the Institute of Historical Research*, xxxiii (1960), pp. 87, 91.

[2] For the 1800 resolution see *Journals of the House of Commons*, lx, p. 790.

[3] O. C. Williams, *The Clerical Organisation of the House of Commons 1661–1850* (Oxford, 1954), p. 185 and n.

[4] *Commons Journals*, lix, p. 326.   [5] *Commons Journals*, lxii, p. 534.

[6] T. G. B. Cocks, 'The Clementson Papers', *Parliamentary Affairs*, vi (1952–3), pp. 216–19.

[7] Thomas Erskine May, *A Treatise Upon the Law, Privilege Proceedings and Usage of Parliament* (1971 reprint of 1844 edition), pp. 162–3.

bar and below it; to take strangers into custody who are irregularly admitted into the House; to give orders to the doorkeepers and other officers under him, for the locking of all doors upon a division; to introduce peers or judges attending within the bar, and messengers from the lords; to attend the sheriffs of London at the bar, on presenting petitions; to bring to the bar, with the mace, prisoners to be reprimanded by the house, or persons in custody to be examined as witnesses. For the better execution of these duties he has a chair close to the bar of the house, and is assisted by a deputy serjeant. Out of the house he is entrusted with the execution of all warrants for the commitment of persons ordered into custody by the house; and for removing them to the Tower or Newgate, or retaining them in his own custody. He maintains order in the lobby and passages of the house, and gives notice to all committees when the house is going to prayers. He has the appointment and supervision of various officers in his department; and, as housekeeper of the house, has charge of all its committee rooms and other buildings, during the sitting of Parliament.

Clementson's diary is a record of Parliamentary practice and procedure, not an account of debates. His usual custom was to note what happened on the first Parliamentary occasion or incident of each kind when he was present. The greater part of the diary, over two-thirds, is therefore concerned with the period from Clementson's appointment in 1770 to the beginning of a new Parliament in 1774.

Clementson, as Deputy Serjeant, was primarily concerned with duties appertaining to the conduct of Parliamentary business, and his diary does not reflect the full range of the Serjeant's responsibilities. The Serjeant at Arms was the executive officer of the House in more than the narrow sense of enforcing its authority against members and non-members alike. The diversification of his functions by the eighteenth century was reflected in the size of the Serjeant's Department, which comprised a Vote Office, a Deputy Serjeant, a Deputy Housekeeper, two Doorkeepers and four Messengers, as well as sundry watchmen, porters and firelighters. The Vote Office was responsible for sending M.P.s copies of the printed *Votes*; and the Deliverer of the Vote had a staff in the early nineteenth century of a Deputy, three clerks and ten Walkmen. The Deputy Housekeeper undertook the supervision of the premises of the House within the Palace of Westminster, and the supply of stationery, fires, candles and refreshments, employing between half-a-dozen and a dozen maids and other servants.[1]

[1] P. Marsden, *The Officers of the Commons, 1363–1965* (London, 1966), pp. 75–92, 139–45.

The diary was presented to the House of Commons Library on 5 March 1952 by Arthur J. Boodle, a descendant of John Clementson; and in 1969 it was handed over to the House of Lords Record Office for preservation in the Victoria Tower. The Clerk of the Records of the House of Lords and the Librarian of the House of Commons have jointly given permission for its publication. I am indebted to the Clerk of the Records, Mr Maurice Bond, and the present Deputy Serjeant at Arms, Colonel Peter Thorne, for their courteous and ready co-operation in supplying me with information in their possession: and to Mrs Margaret White for competent typing of a difficult manuscript.

The diary consists of seventy-five small manuscript pages, this pagination being recorded in square brackets in the text. In order to render the diary more intelligible I have extended abbreviations, added and altered some punctuation, and removed erratic capitalization. Where Clementson himself made some later alterations and erasures I have taken what appeared to be the final version, for the passages crossed out were either erroneous or the same matters of substance less clearly stated.

THE PARLIAMENTARY DIARY OF JOHN CLEMENTSON, 1770-1802

Monday April 2 1770. Having been presented on Saturday the 31st March to Sir Fletcher Norton Speaker of the House of Commons by Nicholas Bonfoy Esquire Serjeant at Arms to the House as his Deputy, Mr. Hill, my predecessor, being incapable on account of his bad state of health to attend any longer, I this day appeared at the House and officiated as Deputy. A division in a Committee upon the State of the Nation on some resolutions moved by Mr. Dowdeswell about the King's Civil List.

In a Committee, the division is in the House, the Ayes to the right side of the House, the Noes to the left side. When the Chairman of the Committee begins to put the Question, you put your hand [2] upon the lock of the Door, and no Member can after that come in or go out. When or just before the Chairman orders the Noes to the right, the Ayes to the left, you open the Door to take the key in, keeping your foot against the Door to prevent any one's entering or going out. You then lock the Door and keep the key till the division is over and the numbers declared.

This evening much confusion and disorder, the minority not choosing to divide but were obliged to do so after much altercation on both sides. The Members after the Chairman had ordered the division not permitting the Tellers to count for some time and disputing and discoursing among themselves sitting with their hats on.[1]

[3] The Serjeant is always on the right hand of the Speaker, and sits opposite in the Coach. Walking he goes next before the Speaker and upon going into the House, he goes a little before the Speaker on the right side, waits at the Bar till the Speaker gets there, bows at the Bar with him to the Chair, secondly under the branch and thirdly at the Table. Then he lays the Mace on the Table and retires below the Bar or to his Seat below the Bar. There are two; the left hand one on coming into the House is the Serjeant's, the seat opposite is the Deputy's. When the Speaker says he is ready to go to Prayers, or, that the Chaplain may be called, the Serjeant goes to the Door and tells the Doorkeeper to call the Chaplain. That done, the Serjeant goes to all the Committees and addressing yourself to the Chairman

---

[1] This disturbance arose because an administration supporter took the unusual and perhaps unprecedented step of insisting on a division against the wishes of the minority. For the incident see my *The House of Commons in the Eighteenth Century* (Oxford, 1971), p. 256.

of each, announce 'The Speaker, Sir, is going to Prayers'. You may then go back to your place and attend the Prayers or not as you think fit, but it is most proper to attend the Prayers lest there should be any noise to disturb the House during that Service. [4] After Prayers the Speaker generally retires to his own Chamber, or sits in the House, at the Table.

When he says he wishes to take the Chair, and there are not 40 Members in the House, the Serjeant goes to the Committees and tells them, 'The Speaker wants to take the Chair', and begs them to walk in just to make a House. If they dont come, the Speaker *can* send the Mace, and on the appearance of the Mace at a Committee it is dissolved of course; but it is usual first to inform the Committees the Speaker intends or threatens to send the Mace, if they dont come.

[5]   When the Speaker takes the Chair, you tell the Doorkeeper, 'The Speaker is in the Chair', who thereupon proclaims the same without Doors.

'Tis the business of the Serjeant to keep the Gangway clear, and desire the Members to take their places.

When the Masters in Chancery come from the Lords, you take the first opportunity of going up to the Table, making your three bows, and there acquainting the Speaker, 'Sir, a Message from the Lords'. [6] You then retire, making 3 bows as before, and after the Speaker has put the Question, which he does by acquainting them, 'There is a Message from the Lords. Is it your pleasure the Messengers be called in? As many are of that opinion say Aye, the contrary opinion say No. The Ayes have it'; then the Speaker directs the Messengers to be called in. You, having given notice to the Doorkeeper to get the Masters ready, go up to the Table bowing for the Mace and return bowing as usual with it across your left arm, go just out of the Door of the House, in the Lobby and taking the right hand side of the Masters proceed with them, the Mace being on your right shoulder, to the Bar, where you make your first bow, next under the branch and the third time at the Table. There you stand with the Mace [7] all the time on your right shoulder, whilst the Masters read their Message. That done you retire backwards with them bowing, as before. You then return the Mace, changing it across your left arm, to its place at the Table, bowing up and back as before.

The only difference when any other person comes on business to the House is that after acquainting the Speaker that 'There is a person from the Treasury or Exchequer or any other place', according to the note he must give you of his name and the office or place he comes from, and the Question having been put as before, you on bringing down the Mace to carry them in put down the Bar if the Doorkeeper or Messenger is not there to do it for you, you bow with the person first on entering within the Door of the House, and next in the midway between that and the Bar, and the third time at the Bar, and bow at the same places on retiring backwards, which you must not do till the Speaker says 'You may withdraw'.

A Prisoner brought to the Bar to be reprimanded is brought in [*8*] in the same manner as any other person only you must be careful not to let him have any sword or stick with him. Formerly as soon as he *was* at the Bar he knelt down and did not rise till he had been reprimanded by the Speaker. But this is not so now.[1]

A Prisoner is never brought in but to receive the Reprimand of the House, which is always on his knees. The House sometimes discharges a Prisoner without appearing at all before them.

[*9*]   On passing private bills, it is not very material to put your hand on the lock on the first and second readings, but on the third reading it is always done, and on the title being read.

But where any private Business is contested or likely so to be, you must be as careful to keep the Door shut on a Question being put as if it was public business.

On all Questions being put of a public nature, either in the [*10*] House or a Committee of the whole House, you must keep the Door fast till the Question is determined.

I have before shewn the nature of a Division in a Committee of the whole House.

A Division of the House differs in this only, that the *Ayes* or *Noes* are directed by the Speaker to go forth into the Lobby. You give notice through the Wick when this is likely to happen for the Doorkeepers and Messengers to have the Lobby or Galleries cleared of all strangers. When the House and Lobby are cleared and the Lobby Doors locked up you open the [*11*] Doors of the House to let out the Ayes or Noes and when all are gone out, you shut up the Doors, having the direction of the Tellers so to do, take in the Key and double lock the Door. Then the Tellers, 4 in Number, 2 on each side, tell the Members in the House. That done, they give in the Number at the Table, then placing themselves just at the Door, a Teller for the Noes on one side and for the Ayes opposite, and a Teller for the Ayes on one side and the Noes opposite, the Serjeant unlocks and opens the Doors and the Members in the Lobby are then told in. Then a proclamation is made by the Doorkeeper, if there are any more [*12*] Members to go in. None appearing, the Door is shut again,

---

[1] Clementson added a footnote. 'This is altered. Vide resolution of 16 March 1772.' See *infra*, pp. 155–6. In the text he inserted this doubt. 'Query if he kneels unless the Order is to be reprimanded *on his knees*.'

and the Tellers bowing up to the Table declare the numbers on both sides, which being requested by the Speaker, he declares that the Majority Ayes or Noes have it.

The Speaker does not put the Question till the Galleries are cleared and all Strangers gone out. Sometimes the Serjeant is obliged to go and clear the Galleries of Strangers but cannot leave the Door unless the Speaker directs him so to do.

[13] A Witness examined in a Committee. The Chairman directs Mr. A—— to be called in, the Serjeant (having a Bar made for the Witness to stand at) goes to the Door and directs the Doorkeeper to call Mr. A—— (the Witness) who advances to the Bar. *N.B.* Care must be taken that he directs himself to the Chairman, and a Messenger or Doorkeeper must stand by the side of the Witness.

When a Witness is examined before the House it is done in the same manner. Upon hearing a contested Election, whether Mr. A—— the [14] Sitting Member is duly returned or not, Mr. A—— the sitting Member must go out of the House before the Question is put.

You must remember to go up to the Table, or to the Speaker, during a debate on the contrary side of the House from that which any Member is speaking from, and on the contrary side which any Counsel is pleading from.

When the candles are to be lighted in the branch, you having ordered the branch to be lowered, go up to and stand just under it, to prevent any Member from being hurt by its coming upon them in moving from their places. You make two Bows, and the like on the return.

[15] Candles are placed on each side the Bar, when Counsel attend the House.

When any person has papers from two different offices or departments, though the same person comes with both, they can't be delivered together; but after having delivered one, you return the Mace and again acquaint the Speaker, 'There is a person with papers from —', who having put the Question, you introduce the person again as before.

If more than one Petition is to be presented by the Sheriffs of the City of London who are the common Messengers to the House or if the sheriffs are Members, then the Petitions are sent by some Aldermen and Common Council;[1] they must present only one at a time at the Bar, which having done, they retire as all other persons, and the House is again informed by the Serjeant, that the Sheriffs or some Aldermen and several of the Common Council of the City of London,

---

[1] Clementson has 'Counsel' or 'Counsellors' throughout.

as the case is, are at the Doors and they are a second time introduced
to the Bar in the usual form.

[16]   *The mode* of carrying private Bills through the House.

Petitions for Inclosures, changing of a Name and Naturalization
are presented by a Member from his place, opening of the contents
of the Petition, and after the Speaker has put the Question, the
Member goes to the Bar and making three bows delivers the Petition
to the Clerk to be read; then the Member moves for a Bill to be
brought in.

Petitions for a Turnpike, changing of Estates, etc, are to be presented in the same form, but they are referred to a private Committee,
which Committee may sit the same day and must consist of eight
Members. The Report may be made the next day (that the allegations
of the Petition are true) at the Bar, the Report to be delivered in at
the Table and read [17] and a Bill moved for by the Member who
makes the Report.

The Bills as well for Turnpikes as Inclosures etc. may be presented
at the Bar as soon as prepared and delivered in at the Table and read
the first time.

Before a bill can be read a second time, three whole days must
intervene. It may be read a second time the fourth day, viz. if presented and read the first time on Monday it may be read the second
time on Friday and committed.

Which Committee cannot sit in less than eight days after the
second reading and Notice of their sitting must be stuck up in the
Lobby.

The Report of the Committee may be made as soon after their
sitting as the Chairman pleases and after the Report is agreed to by
the House [18] the Bill is ordered to be ingrossed and may be read a
third time and passed the next day, if the ingrossment is ready.

All Bills to be presented at the Bar. No question put for bringing
them to the Table.

All Reports to be made at the Bar and the Speaker to put the
Question before they are brought up to the Table.

N.B. No time is necessary to intervene between the first and
second Reading or between the second Reading and Committment
of Public Bills. They may be read the first time one day and the
second time the next day etc.

[19]   *13 November 1770.* The first day of Sessions. *The Speaker*
comes to the House in his gold gown, does not take the Chair till the
Black Rod comes. No Prayers this day, not being a House. When the
Black Rod comes into the Lobby the Serjeant takes the Key in, and

holding the Key up in his hands shakes it to let the Speaker know the Black Rod is coming. The Speaker thereupon gets into the Chair. The Black Rod having delivered his Message the Serjeant bows up to the Table, takes the Mace and goes before the Speaker as usual to the House of Lords. When he gets within the Door of the Lords' House, the Serjeant makes his reverence to the Throne or Commissioners and the Messenger takes the Mace and puts up by the side of the Clock. After the King has made his Speech, the Speaker returns, and the Mace is carried before him as usual back to the House of Commons.

[20]   The Speaker after bowing up to the Table retires to his Chamber and puts off his gold gown and returns in his silken one. He then for the first time upon account of the new Act of Parliament of last sessions for the Speaker's issuing his Warrant for a new Writ on the deaths of any Member acquainted the House with the Warrants he had issued on the deaths of members during the recess and the dates of them. After that several new Members were sworn, a bill was then read, prepared by the Clerk of the House, for preventing clandestine outlawries the first time and ordered to be read a second time. After this the Speaker acquainted the House he had been up to the House of Peers where His Majesty had made a most gracious Speech from the Throne of which for greater certainty he had procured a copy which he read a first [time][1] [21] and put the Question 'If it was the pleasure of the House that he should read it a second time'; upon which an Address is moved for and seconded and then the debate goes on as all others.

Strangers are admitted the first day, there being no Order to the contrary; so full this day, not room for the Members.

When the King himself goes to the House of Peers, the Speaker goes upon being sent for by the Black Rod in his golden gown to the Lords' House and makes three reverences to the King on the Throne. But when Bills pass by Commission he goes in his common black silk gown and makes three reverences as before at going to the Bar but only one on retiring and that on condition that the three Lords Commissioners get up and take off their Hats to the Commons. This Mr. Hill told me was the rule.

[22]   *28 November 1770* In a debate on the Act for regulating the trials of controverted elections or returns, a doubt arose whether after a Petition presented to the House complaining of an undue return, and a day appointed for hearing the complaint, and the notice served on Mr. Bell one of the Members who had not taken his

---

[1] Omitted by Clementson.

seat, and he having written to Mr. Lascelles that he gave up the contest and should not trouble himself about it, the House could let the sitting Member for Scarborough Sir James Pennyman withdraw his Petition and order the Clerk of the Crown to alter the return, or whether it must (though no contest) go to the Committee to be chosen according to the directions of the Act to be by them decided. The House ordered the Petition to be withdrawn and the Clerk of the Crown to alter the return.

[23]   In this debate great warmth arose between Mr. Wedderburn and Mr. C. Fox. The first charged the latter with having attempted to make the memory of his late deceased friend Mr. Grenville ridiculous by the objections started to his Bill for the Trials of Elections etc. and repeated words spoken. The latter denied the words. He insisted he never had spoken such words and that the first well knew that he had not used such words. With great heat this was said. The Speaker called to order. The House fired. Mr. C. Fox got up from his seat. The Speaker ordered me to lock the Door, then to lock the Gallery Door, that neither might go out till they each had promised no further notice should be taken of what had happened. They both did so and Mr. C. Fox [24] asked pardon of the House for being disorderly and thereupon all was quiet.[1]

10 December 1770[2] The Lords on the motion of Lord [Gower][3] had their standing order for not admitting Strangers read and put in force and their House was thereupon cleared and among the rest Members of the House of Commons were not permitted to continue in the House but told that they as well as everybody else must withdraw. Soon after several Lords came to the House of Commons, the House then in a Committee. Mr. George Onslow broke in upon the business of the Committee and acquainted them of the Members of the House of [25] Commons being turned out from the House of Lords and he thereupon moved to have the standing order of the House of Commons read for the exclusion of all Strangers, which being done Sir Charles Whitworth the Chairman of the Committee ordered the Serjeant to clear the House of all Strangers particularly *Peers*, and all the House was cleared accordingly and among others Lord Rockingham, Duke of Portland, Dukes of Bolton and Richmond; and no Strangers were admitted from this day till the adjourn-

[1] For this episode, see Henry Cavendish's diary. British Museum, Egerton MS. 222, pp. 355–63 (third pagination).
[2] Clementson has 9 December. For the incident see the sources listed in P. D. G. Thomas, *Sources for Debates of the House of Commons 1768–1774, Bulletin of the Institute of Historical Research, Special Supplement no. 4* (1959), p. 28.
[3] Omitted by Clementson.

C M—L

ment before the Holidays except on the Mutiny Bill a few Officers by leave of the Speaker. Strangers were admitted but not Lords after the Holidays but the Lords still continued to shut their [26] Doors against all Strangers (Members of the House of Commons as well as others) till the end of this session of Parliament.

During this dispute several Motions were made in the House by Lord George Germain and Lord George Cavendish and Mr. Dunning relating to the matters in dispute but nothing was done.

[31]¹ *Call of the House.* 5 February 1771.

House was called over alphabetically by the Clerk, immediately after which the absentees were twice called over; many had excuses made for them, others were abroad, others had not taken their Seats, others were defaulters: this took up two hours.

N.B. A Committee sat (if not two) during part of this business, but undoubtedly the Speaker would have done right to have dissolved all Committees, and perhaps it would have been proper to have directed the Serjeant to summon Members with the Mace from Westminster Hall etc.

Members present	474
Excused	49
Not taken their Seats	5
Abroad	19
To attend this day sevennight	11
	558

[32] For Serjeants fees on bringing a person to the Bar to be reprimanded immediately vide *Journals* 16 June 1746.²

Fee of	6. 8.	for bringing to the Bar
Caption fee	3. 6. 8.	
One day in custody	1. 6. 8.	
	£5. 0. 0.	

For every day after the first when a person is in Custody £1 only. Vide Table of fees.

¹ Pages 27–30 of the MS. are omitted. They merely comprise extracts from the *Commons Journals* of 4 and 14 April 1707 and 22 December 1711 concerning resolutions by the House relating to the enforcement of fees by the Serjeant at Arms from persons ordered into custody. See *Commons Journals*, xv, pp. 376, 386; xvii, p. 23.
² A Committee appointed to inquire into the fees of the Serjeant and messengers

[34]¹   *Mourning 26 February 1772*

Court in *Cuff* Mourning for the Princess Dowager of Wales, the King's Mother who died on 8 February.

The King came to pass land tax and other Bills 26 February. The Speaker went in his black crape gown, not in his gold as at other times. When a Court Mourning without Cuffs he goes in the gold gown.

On the Dowager's death the 8th which happened on a Saturday morning the House being then adjourned to Monday. The House met on the Monday the 10th, did all the private business and some public till Lord North the Minister came. He then acquainted the House with the death of the Dowager, moved an Address to the King on the melancholy occasion which was agreed to Nem: Con: and ordered to be presented by the Members who were Privy Councillors. And then Lord North moved to adjourn immediately.

[35]   *Tuesday the 11th February*. A Bill to prohibit the exportation of corn and others were passed by Commission, the Corn Bill of last session being expired.

The Speaker doubted whether he should not have gone to Court, the Sunday sevennight after the Dowager's death, the 16th [she was buried the 15th]. Held clearly he should not.

The Speaker went the day after the Dowager died to Court and had his name put down, a Lord of the King's Bedchamber and a Lady of the Queen's sitting for the King and Queen. And afterwards to the Princess of Brunswick but *not in form as Speaker* but in a private manner. *All Members* should have gone and pay their compliments the next day the 9th or 10th and have their names taken down.

25 February.   Thanks of the House of 31 January for Dr. Nowell's Sermon of 30th ordered to be expunged after a division for the order of the day to be read.²

For the Order   41
Against   152

[36]   Prisoners and persons in Custody not to kneel unless ordered. *16 March 1772*.   Resolved *nem. con.* That, when any person shall

---

made its report to the House that day: but the House overruled its recommendations and established the fees stated by Clementson. *Commons Journals*, xxv, pp. 170–1.

¹ Page 33 of the MS. is omitted, as being an extract from the *Commons Journals* for 21 December 1640 concerning the treatment and behaviour of the Lord Keeper when he then addressed the House. *Commons Journals*, ii, p. 55.

² *Commons Journals*, xxxiii, p. 509. The sermon was widely held to have been unconstitutional in its advocacy of non-resistance to the sovereign. For the debate see the sources listed in Thomas, *Sources for Debates . . . 1768–1774*, p. 45.

from henceforth be brought to the Bar of this House, to receive any Judgment of this House or to be discharged from the Custody of the Serjeant at Arms attending this House or from any Imprisonment inflicted by Order of the House such person shall receive such Judgment, or the Order of the House for his Discharge *standing* at the Bar, unless it shall be otherwise directed in the Order of the House made for that purpose.[1]

[*37*]   An improper Message from the Lords.

1 April 1772.   A Message being brought from the Lords by Mr. Anguish (a Master in Chancery) and Mr. Strutt the Clerk Assistant of the House of Lords. The Messengers were called in and delivered their Message, and then they withdrew. And Notice being taken that the said Message was not brought by the Messengers usually sent with Messages from the House of Lords to this House. And Objection being made against Mr. Speaker's now reporting the said Message to the House. The said Message was not reported. Ordered *Nem. Con.* That a Committee be appointed to examine into the precedents with respect to the Messengers by whom Messages have been brought from the Lords to this House and to report the same to the House with what proceedings have been had thereupon. And a Committee was appointed accordingly with powers to send for persons, etc.

[*38*]   Ordered That it be an Instruction to the Committee that they do take into their consideration the treatment offered to Mr. Speaker and the Members of this House upon the first day of this Session of Parliament and to other Members of this House attending their duty in the House of Lords during this Session of Parliament when Bills have been passed by his Majesty or by Commission and to report the same to the House.[2]

2nd April 1772.   Two Members of the above Committee came down from the Speaker's Chamber where the Committee was sitting to desire Mr. Speaker would attend to be examined touching the treatment offered to him. The Speaker told them he would attend as soon as Prayers were over. He did so and went up unattended and without the Mace and was examined, the Speaker's Chamber being part of the House; but if he stirs out of the Door of the House the Mace attends him.

[*39*]   *9 April 1772.* Resolved *nem: con:* That no Bill relating to Trade or the Alteration of the Laws concerning Trade, be brought into the

---

[1] This is an extract from *Commons Journals*, xxxiii, p. 594, with emphasis by Clementson on the word 'standing'.

[2] This entry is almost identical with *Commons Journals*, xxxiii, pp. 645–6.

House until the Proposition shall have been first considered in a Committee of the Whole House and agreed unto by the House. A Standing Order.

Report made from the Committee and after reading the Report, a Motion was made and the Question being put that the Bills brought from the House of Lords on Wednesday the 1st day of this instant April be sent back to the Lords and that their Lordships be acquainted, that this House hath ordered the said Bills to be returned to their Lordships on account of their having been sent to this House by Messengers not usually employed in bringing Messages from the House of Lords to this House. It passed in the Negative.[1]

Ordered That a Message be sent to the Lords to acquaint them that this House having received a Message from their Lordships on Wednesday the 1st day [40] of this instant April, which was brought by a Master in Chancery and the Clerk Assistant of the House of Lords and being desirous of preserving a good correspondence with their Lordships, have sent this Message to acquaint their Lordships that this House doth take notice of this unusual method of sending Messages to this House and desire that the same may not hereafter be drawn into precedent.

Ordered that Mr. Ongley do carry the said [message].[2]

Then a Motion was made and the Question being put that a Conference be desired with the Lords, on matters tending to preserve a good correspondence between the two Houses. It passed in the Negative.[3]

13 April 1772.   A Message from the Lords by Mr. Holford and Mr. Cuddon, that the Lords having considered the Message sent by this House [*41*] their Lordships for Answer thereunto say, That the Lords ordered their Message of the 1st of this month to be carried to the House of Commons in the usual manner: and their Lordships have found upon enquiry that one Master in Chancery being ill, their Message was carried by only one Master in Chancery and the Clerk Assistant of the House of Lords; and the Lords desire the Commons may be informed that the Lords have nothing more at heart than to maintain a good correspondence between the two Houses and do not mean to introduce any precedent contrary to the usage of Parliament. Ordered That Mr. Speaker do now report the Message brought from the Lords upon Wednesday the 1st of this instant April. Mr. Speaker accordingly reported.[4]

[1] By 107 votes to 57.   [2] Omitted by Clementson.
[3] By 117 votes to 51. For the report and proceedings thereon see *Commons Journals*, xxxiii, pp. 679–82.
[4] This is an extract from *Commons Journals*, xxxiii, p. 690.

All this happened at the time both the Houses had kept their Doors shut and would not permit the Members of either House to be admitted, which dispute began 9 December 1770 and still continuing.

[*42*]   *21 May 1772.*   A puisne Judge not a peer attending the House to give evidence. In a Committee on Mr. Fenwick's bill. He is introduced by the Serjeant on his right hand without the Mace being a Committee. The Bar on his making the third reverence is lifted up and the Judge is told by the Chairman, there is a chair for him to repose himself *upon* not *in*. The chair is previously set by the Serjeant about a yard within the Bar on the right hand side coming into the House. *N.B.* The Judge did not sit down nor was he covered as is the case when a peer attends to give evidence.

   N.B. When a peer attends the chair is placed in the same manner on the *left* hand side coming in to the House, on the right of the Speaker's Chair.

[*43*]   Witness ill permitted to sit at the Bar.

12 February 1773.   In the course of the examination of witnesses relating to the military force sent to drive away the Caribbs from the Island of St. Vincent and the conduct of the Caribbs. Charles Payne Sharpe was examined at the Bar and he declaring that he was unable to stand at the Bar owing to the bad state of his health, was indulged with a chair at the Bar, in which he was at times permitted to sit. His examination lasted above three hours.

[*45*][1]   *17 February 1773.* House was called over as usual, previous to which the Serjeant was sent with the Mace to the Speaker's Chambers placed adjacent and Westminster Hall.

> Members present
> Excused
> Not taken their Seats
> Leave of Absence
> Abroad
> To attend this day ⎫
> fortnight   ⎭

[*46*]   *17th and 18 February 1774.* The Reverend Mr. John Horne being in custody of the Serjeant for not attending brought to the Bar with the Mace as usual to hear the charge against him. The Serjeant standing by him all the time with the Mace rested it for the most part on the floor.

   Mr. Woodfall who also was in the Serjeant's custody brought in,

---

[1] Page 44 of the MS. is blank.

as an evidence with Mr. Horne by the Serjeant with the Mace. Other witnesses called in and examined. Several questions proposed by the Members to be asked Mr. Woodfall as no one but the Speaker can ask any questions, the Mace being off the Table, except that 'The person at the Bar do withdraw'. [47] At length the examination of the witnesses was upon a Question left wholly to the Speaker.

The Serjeant with the Mace brought Mr. Horne in every time to the Bar in the usual manner and stood at the Bar with the Mace rested on the floor during all the time of Mr. Horne's being at the Bar.

[48] *New Parliament,* summoned to meet Tuesday 29 November 1774.

The first day at 10 o'clock precisely Earl Talbot the Lord Steward came to the Court of Wards where there was only a Common Committee around Chair for him and Mr. Hatsell, Mr. Ley in their gowns and the Deputy Clerk of the Crown in his gown and all the other Clerks of the House attended.

The Deputy Clerk of the Crown (having delivered the Return Book) administered the oaths to several of the Members before the Lord Steward, and having sworn a competent number, he executed a Commission appointing the Members so sworn his Deputies to swear others; that being done the Lord Steward and Deputy Clerk of the Crown went away.

The Members were then sworn before the Commissioners, the Clerks out of Doors etc administering the oaths and about half past one the Members sworn assembled in the House.

[49] *N.B.* The Members get blank Qualifications in the Room where they are sworn, the form of which is as follows.

'The Lands Tenements and Hereditaments whereby I make out my Qualification to serve as a Knight Citizen or Burgess in the present Parliament do lie in [here insert the parishes and county] and I do declare my Estate in the same to be of the annual Value of [three or six hundred pounds] above reprizes.'

This must be filled up and signed by the Member, but is not wanted till they are sworn *in the House,* and then they deliver it to the Clerk so signed and swear to it.

N.B. The Scotch dont swear to their Qualification, nor the eldest son of a man qualified.

About two the Black Rod came, knocked at the Door, was let in and made his *three* Bows as usual and delivered his Message [50] 'commanding the House to attend his Majesty immediately in the House of Peers'.

Several Members went up with Mr. Hatsell the Clerk. The Lord Chancellor then told them his Majesty did not think fit to declare the causes of his calling them together until they had *chosen a Speaker*.

On the return of the Members to the House Lord Guernsey moved that Sir Fletcher Norton might again take the Chair and was seconded by Lord Robert Spencer. Sir Fletcher made a handsome Speech for the honor they were about to do him, begging their assistance and support etc. The Clerk then put the Question which was carried *Nem. Con.* Lord Guernsey and Lord Robert took the Speaker Elect from his seat and placing him between them and making three bows lead him to the Chair. *N.B.* He should have been brought down to the Bar between the two Lords and should have made three reverences to the Chair as usual.

[*51*] The Speaker Elect being seated in the Chair the Mace which was all the time (before any body came to the House) put under Table as in a Committee was by the Serjeant taken from under and put upon the Table. After the Speaker Elect had mentioned to the House some matters respecting the usual Prayer he was to make to the King on behalf of the Commons the House was adjourned by the Speaker Elect till the next morning. The Speaker Elect went from the House as any other Member without the Mace, which is taken away and kept by the Serjeant. The Deputy Housekeeper kept the Mace.

Wednesday 30 November at one Mr. Speaker Elect appointed to be and was at the House, not in his gown and large wig but in black suit and a tye wig. The Mace was placed *upon* the Table before the meeting of the House.

After the Black Rod came with the King's commands Mr. Speaker Elect (who had [*52*] before taken the Chair) went up to the House of Lords without any gown or large wig to be presented to the King for his approbation. He should have been presented by the gentlemen who moved and seconded the motion for his being Speaker but Mr. Rigby and I forgot the other Member supported Mr. Speaker Elect on each side to the Bar of the House of Lords, Lord Guernsey and Lord Robert Spencer not being in the House.

I took the Mace from the Table and went before Mr. Speaker Elect with the Mace laid upon my *right arm* unadvanced but on the Speaker's return from the House of Lords, I carried the Mace upon my shoulder and bowed up to the Table with *Mr. Speaker as usual*.

The business which was done at the House of Lords was the King's approbation of Sir Fletcher Norton to be Speaker, and that being over and the Speaker having [*53*] made the usual Prayer for the Commons, and his Majesty by his Chancellor having consented to it, his Majesty made his Speech.

When the Speaker returned to the House, he took the Chair and did not as at other times report the King's Speech but took the Oaths and made and subscribed etc. alone; and after he had so done, the clerk from the Return Book called over the names of the Members beginning with Bedfordshire and went on alphabetically and such Members as were present came to the Table (with a written paper containing an account of the qualification signed by such of the Members as are required to give in their qualification) and were sworn 40 and 50 at a time. [54] Each batch of 40 or 50 takes an hour at least. Two batches were sworn the first day and then the House adjourned till the next; you cannot begin to swear a batch *after* four o'clock.

Thursday 1 December. The Speaker came *for the first time in his gown and large wig* and the Chaplain, Secretary and Trainbearer. Had Prayers for the first time. The Speaker came at twelve. Swore four batches. The Clerk after going through the names according to the Return Book began again and again, leaving out the names of such as were sworn.

Friday 2 December. Members sworn as before.

Monday 5th December. Members sworn. 'A Bill for the more effectual preventing Clandestine Outlawries' was read first time and ordered to be read second.
[55]   Then the Common Orders, among the rest that all persons who will question returns shall do so within 14 days next. And that all who are returned for 2 or more places should make their election by this day three weeks. And that all returned upon Double Returns withdraw till their returns are determined.

After the usual Orders were made the Speaker this day reported the King's Speech. An Address moved for as usual.

Tuesday 6 December. Petitions received touching elections, without a Question put according to the true construction of the Act 10. Geo. 3 for regulating the Trials of controverted Elections or Returns of Members to serve in Parliament.
[56]   Agreed that Petitions against
                    Double Returns should be first heard.
                    Against Returns only, next.
And (though not this day) I think it was understood some days after that Petitions against persons who were returned for two places should take the preference of others.

And *it was Ordered* that whenever more than one Petition shall at the same time be offered to be presented, Mr. Speaker shall direct such Petitions to be all delivered in at the Table and the names of the

Counties Cities Boroughs or places to which such Petitions shall relate shall be written on several pieces of paper of an equal size and the same pieces of paper shall be then rolled up and put by the Clerk into a glass or box and then publicly drawn by the Clerk and the said several Petitions shall be read in the Order in which [57] the said names shall be drawn respectively.

Several Petitions were accordingly delivered in at the Table and the names of the places being rolled up and put into a glass were drawn by the Clerk.

Wednesday 7 December. Mr. Speaker went up with the Address on the King's Speech and being in *deep Cuff Mourning* for the death of his mother, he went to St. James's in his black gown only.

If he is in a slighter Mourning he then goes in his gold tufted gown but in Cuffs he never puts on any but a black one.

Petitions against Elections etc. were received till Monday 19th December (that day inclusive) when the 14 days expired.

[58] *Tuesday 20th December 1774.*

Several writs were moved, one or two on deaths and others where Members were returned for two places and had made their Election which place they would serve for.

This day a Petition was presented stating particular circumstances and praying leave to present a Petition against the Election for the Boroughs of Elgin etc. in North Britain which had not arrived time enough to be presented to the House *yesterday* whilst the House was sitting but was on that day lodged with the Clerk of the House and therefore and for other reasons hoped that the House would in the present instance dispense with their Order of the 5th instant.

This matter was debated this day very much but in a thin House [59] the Attorney and Solicitor General[1] and Mr. Dunning warmly supporting the side of the Petition but on dividing whether the debate should be renewed *tomorrow* or 26 January, an amendment moved by Solicitor-General.

> Ayes for tomorrow   29
> Noes   13[2]

Then a Division on the original Motion and there not being a House the House adjourned.[3]

Friday, 23 December. The same debate renewed by the same persons, the Solicitor-General claiming it as a Right, the Petition having been

---

[1] Edward Thurlow and Alexander Wedderburn.

[2] *Commons Journals*, xxxv, p. 59. Clementson omitted the figures.

[3] The voting-figures were 9–23. *Commons Journals*, xxxv, p. 59. The quorum of the House was 40.

on the 14th day left with the Clerk but the Petition was rejected after full debate.

Ayes   24
Noes   55[1]

Mr. R. Fuller and Mr. Welbore Ellis two old Members in the Majority.

This day orders discharged for referring the Petitions of Mr. Bigge and of [60] several of the freemen and electors of Morpeth which were ordered to be taken into consideration on the 24 January next at the same time that the Petition of the Honourable William Byron complaining of an *undue return only*, and which Petition of Mr. Byron had got a priority on account of its being against the return only. After a debate.

[61]   *18 January 1775*.[2] The Speaker being in Cuff Mourning for his mother's death did not go to Court today being the Queen's birthday.

23 January 1775. On this day the Petition against the Morpeth return ordered to be taken into consideration. The Court being sitting in the new Election Room for trying the double return of Milbourne Port, the Mace was not sent there till after notice had been given to that Committee; and they adjourned for an hour and came into the House to make up the 100.

I have been with the Mace into the Election Committee Rooms when the 100 have not been in the House but I have always given them previous notice by a Messenger.

62]   *Thursday 11 February 1779. Call of the House.*

Called over alphabetically; absentees called over; many had excuses made for them which were allowed, some abroad, one not taken his seat, others Defaulters.

Present	470
Excused	74
Ordered to attend	12
Not taken his seat	1
	1
	558

Near two hours in all.

[63]   *Friday 12th February 1779*.

Ordered. That the *Thanks* of this House be given to the *Honourable Admiral Augustus Keppel*, for his distinguished Courage, Conduct

[1] *Commons Journals*, xxxv, p. 62. Clementson omitted the figures.

[2] Clementson has 19 January. The Queen's real birthday was on 18 May, but it was officially celebrated on 18 January. J. Brooke, *King George III* (London, 1972), p. 290.

and Ability, in defending this Kingdom in the Course of the last Summer, effectually protecting its Trade and more particularly for his having gloriously upheld the Honour of the British Flag on the 27th and 28th of July last.[1]

N.B. This was occasioned by a charge made against Admiral Keppel by Vice Admiral Sir Hugh Palliser for misconduct and neglect of duty in the action of the 27th and 28th July and brought by the Vice Admiral, after Admiral Keppel in the House of Commons had said his signals were not regarded by the Vice Admiral, though flying his signals from three till eight o'clock.

The Court Martial sat at Portsmouth in the Governor's house there, (an Act of Parliament having passed for the purpose of proceeding with this trial on shore if the Commissioners of the Admiralty thought fit so to direct) from the 7th of January 1779 to the 11th of February following. When the Court were unanimously of opinion that the charge against Admiral Keppel was ill grounded and malicious.

[64] *Thursday 18th February 1779.*

Admiral Keppel (having previously by letter communicated his intention to the Speaker) came to the House attended by his brother the General and Admiral Pigot and taking his place where he sat when he received an account of the Court Martial having been ordered for his Trial on the charges exhibited against him by Sir Hugh Palliser.

Mr. Speaker (though no particular Order was made for the Thanks to be given the Admiral by him) *standing up and being uncovered,* the Admiral being on his Legs and uncovered, gave him the Thanks in a Speech which was answered by the Admiral. After which Colonel Barré moved that what the Speaker had said on the occasion and the Admiral's answer should be printed in the *Votes* of this day.[2]

N.B. No business likely to be debated was done till the Admiral came. Not being well, he did not get to the House till 4 o'clock and went away directly after he had made his Speech. Mr. Wilkes this day made his annual motion touching the Rights of Electors, which was by him postponed till Mr. Keppel went as there was a division on the Question and consequently Strangers must have been all turned out, who were numerous. [65] N.B. This was a civility of Mr. Wilkes to the Strangers in the Gallery who must (had he made the motion before the Admiral came) have been all turned out.

[1] This is an extract from *Commons Journals,* xxxvii, p. 139.
[2] For the two speeches see *Commons Journals,* xxxvii, pp. 150–1.

[66]   *6 May 1779.* The Earl of Cornwallis was examined in a Committee on the American Papers laid before the House, being the correspondence between Sir William Howe and Lord George Germain, on the subject matter of those papers.

On the question being agreed to for the Earl's being called in, an armed chair was put within the Bar by the Doorkeeper, inclining to the left side coming into the House before you get to the Gangway.

And the Earl was introduced by the Serjeant without the Mace in the following manner. The Doors thrown open. The Bar being then down was immediately on Lord Cornwallis appearing at the Door lifted up. Then Lord Cornwallis with the Serjeant without the Mace advanced to the place where the Bar usually is, making the common three Bows and then [67] Mr. Frederick Montagu the Chairman acquainted Lord Cornwallis that there was a chair for his Lordship to repose himself *in.*

His Lordship thereupon seated himself in the chair and put on his Hat but on the questions asked by Members being repeated to his Lordship by the Chairman, his Lordship arose and uncovered gave his answers, and when he had so done, seated and covered himself as before.

On his first examination the *Bar* by mistake was not *put down* during his Lordship's being examined but on the Earl's retiring at the motion of a Member previous to his being again introduced it was taken notice of by Mr. Rigby to the Chairman and after Lord Cornwallis had taken the chair, the Bar was put down as usual all the time the examination lasted. [68] On Lord Cornwallis's retiring, he makes three bows with the Serjeant at his right from the Bar to the Door as usual.

Agreed that a peer of Scotland, though not one of the *Sixteen* being a British peer, has the same indulgence and favor shewn to him and the same ceremonies as a English peer.

27 May 1779. Lord Balcarras a Scotch peer not one of the Sixteen was examined in a Committee on the American papers. An *armed* chair was put for him within the Bar. He was introduced by the Serjeant without the Mace and sat down and covered himself and had all the indulgence and ceremony as an English peer.

[69]   In 1775 on Mr. Wood the Messenger's death Serjeant sold the place to William Shells for five hundred pounds.

[70]   *2 June 1792.* On a joint Address of both Houses. The hour fixed by the King to receive it is communicated to the House of Commons by a Message from the Lords. On the day, previous to the time appointed, the Chancellor goes in state from the House of Lords with

such of the Members of that House as think proper to attend him. On hearing from a Messenger who is sent to watch their motions that the Lords are nearly gone, the Serjeant acquaints the Speaker that the Lords are gone and it may not be [71] amiss that he do acquaint the Speaker when the Lords first begin to move to prepare him. The Speaker then follows in his State Coach with such of the Members accompanying him as choose to attend. When at St. James's they wait till the King is ready to receive them, and then the *two Speakers* go together. The Chancellor reads the Address, the Speaker close at his left hand, the Black Rod at the Speaker's left hand. On a joint Address the mover of the Address has no place.

[72]   *Tuesday 9 February 1802.* On Sir John Mitford's being appointed Lord Chancellor of Ireland he sent a letter this day to Mr. Ley the Deputy Clerk of the House to inform him thereof, which letter at 4 o'clock when the House was assembled with the assent of the House Mr. Ley read. And immediately afterwards the Serjeant brought in the Mace and put it under the Table as in a Committee and then the Chancellor of the Exchequer (Mr. Addington) rose and informed the House that his Majesty under the circumstances of the case gave the House leave to proceed to the choice of a new Speaker and to present him to his Majesty for his approbation on the Thursday following at 2 o'clock and moved to adjourn till tomorrow. Mace left in Bellamy's custody.

Wednesday 10 February 1802. House began to assemble at half past three, Mr. Ley and Clerks, Mr. Colman and self, there at that time dressed and the Mace being brought by Bellamy the Deputy House-keeper and put in Mr. Colman's seat was at four o'clock taken by the Serjeant from thence and put under the Table as before. [73] And then the Master of the Rolls Sir William Grant moved that the Right Honourable Charles Abbot do take the Chair of this House as Speaker. Mr. Baker Member for Hertfordshire seconded. Mr. Sheridan moved for Mr. Charles Dundas and Lord George A. H. Cavendish seconded, but Mr. Dundas begged that his friends would not press it and made his excuses and thereupon the Question for Mr. Abbot taking the Chair passed without a Division and Mr. Abbot was led up to the Chair by the Master of the Rolls and Mr. Baker and before he sat in the Chair he made a Speech thanking the House for the honor they had done him and that he would exert his utmost abilities to fulfil the duties of the Chair and immediately the Serjeant went up to the Table and took the Mace from under the Table and put it upon the Table.[1]

[1] For Abbot's election see *Commons Journals*, lvii, p. 93.

And the House was by the Speaker Elect adjourned till tomorrow, and [he] went away as a common Member [74] without any ceremony, the Mace continuing on the Table till after the adjournment. Mr. Bellamy the Deputy Housekeeper took it away and it remained in his custody.

The late Speaker Sir John Mitford was at Court this day and kissed the King's hand on being appointed Lord Chancellor of Ireland and a peer of the United Kingdom by the title of Lord Redesdale.

The late Speaker sent me a note to say he had ordered his servants to have the door of his official House open for the Speaker Elect to go into it and to have two rooms ready to receive him, the Library and that which leads to it where the Officers usually meet, as he thought it would be more pleasant than for him to go by Mrs. Bennett's room. I sent to the servants to inform them that the House was adjourned [75] and to be ready to show Mr. Abbot the Speaker Elect into the rooms.

Thursday 11 February. The Speaker Elect came to the Speaker's official House in St. Stephen's Court and the Officers met him there at half past two, he in a Tye wig, black dressed suit and sword. We attended him without Mace, out of compliment only.

On his coming to the House (*Prayers*) Mr. Barton the Chaplain ill and not able to attend, a Friend Mr. [blank] attended and read Prayers for him.

At [blank] the Black Rod summoned the House to attend in the House of Peers to hear the Commission read, for approving the choice of Mr. Abbot to be Speaker.

III

REPORT ON BOLIVIA, 1827

by

JOSEPH BARCLAY PENTLAND

edited by

J. VALERIE FIFER, B.A., Ph.D., F.R.G.S.

CONTENTS

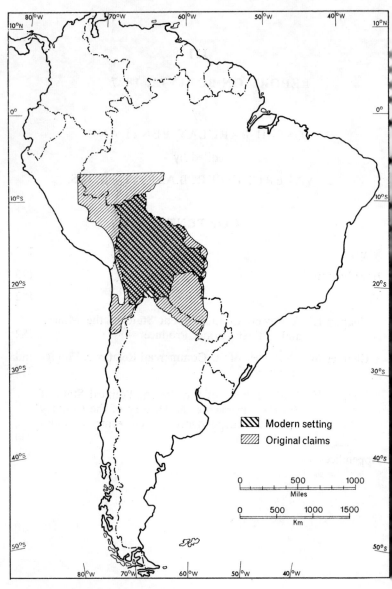

1 Bolivia: modern setting and original claims (Figures 1–3 are taken from
J. V. Fifer, *Bolivia: Land, Location, and Politics since 1825*, Cambridge, 1972)

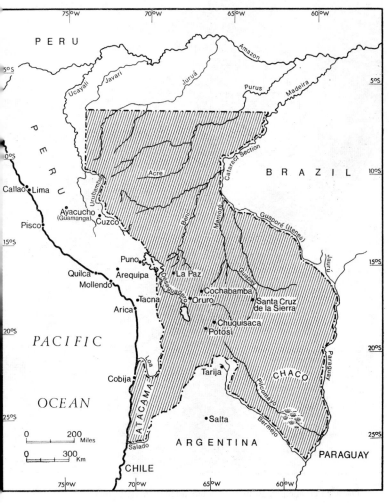

2 The area claimed by Bolivia at independence in 1825

Territorial claims were based on the limits of the colonial *audiencia*, or Presidency, of Charcas in 1810. Tarija was incorporated in 1826

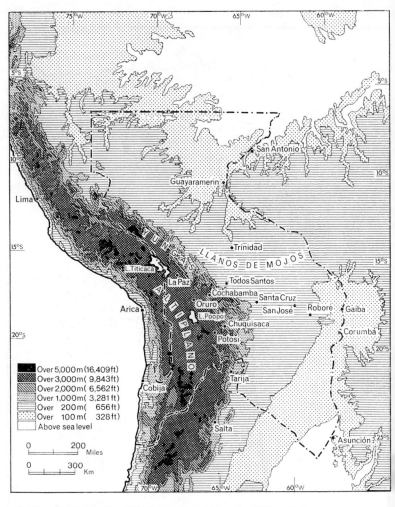

3 The area claimed by Bolivia at independence in 1825: relief

INTRODUCTION

PENTLAND's Report fills almost the whole of volume F.O. 61/12 in the Public Record Office's Foreign Office archive collection, and is significant as the first major description of Bolivia at a very early period in its history. Joseph Barclay Pentland (1797–1873) left England for Peru in 1825, travelling as private secretary to Charles Milner Ricketts, the British Consul General then taking up his post at Lima. Ricketts had especially requested Pentland's services at the time of his own appointment and received a favourable response:

In reference to your request for permission to take Mr Pentland, a gentleman of considerable scientific attainments, with you to Lima in the capacity of your private secretary, with a small annual salary, and also that he might be furnished with a moderate sum of money to provide himself with books and instruments to assist him in the scientific researches which he proposes to make in Peru, I am directed by Mr Secretary Canning to acquaint you that he is willing to grant a sum not exceeding £200 to Mr Pentland for the purchase of books and instruments, and that, for the present, you are authorised to make to him an allowance at the rate of £300 a year . . . Mr Canning however directs me to state distinctly to you that he cannot consider Mr Pentland as a public servant, nor as having any claim upon H.M.'s Government for future employment in consequence of this permission.[1]

Ricketts and his party arrived in Lima in January 1826 and shortly afterwards the Consul General instructed Pentland to begin preparations for a fact-finding tour of Bolivia, known before its independence in August 1825 as Upper or Alto Peru.

Between the years 1810 and 1825, the changing political map of Latin America had recorded the progressive break-up of the old Iberian empires in the New World, and plotted the emergence of a new, more complex pattern of nation states shaped for the most part by the ground-plan of the former principal colonial administrative divisions. By the early 1820s, therefore, with independence either effected by the armies of liberation, or confidently anticipated by

[1] Foreign Office memorandum to C. M. Ricketts, London, 5 July, 1825, P.R.O., F.O. 61/5. Ricketts was appointed as Consul General for Peru in succession to Thomas Rowcroft (apptd. 10 October, 1823), killed accidentally after dark by patriot sentries outside Lima in December 1824.

foreign observers, there was a swift and mounting demand for accurate information of every kind about this huge, still virtually unknown
sub-continent. Above all, the British Government needed competent,
objective assessments of the internal affairs of the new states: the
prospects for their political stability, their resources, communications
and trade. Spain's own long-established restrictive attitudes, its
limited domestic manufacturing base and official imperial trading
monopoly, had together left Middle and South America's true commercial potential largely unmeasured, and only partly exploited by
contraband trade. This was now to be legalized and expanded, and
clearly offered attractive possibilities to British merchants and
industrialists actively seeking new export markets overseas. Mexico
and South America particularly were regarded as potential growth
areas. Thus the total lack of any systematic and co-ordinated British
intelligence concerning conditions in Latin America as a whole
called for new light to be shed on the western world's 'dark continent'—light to illumine the paths of commerce, however, not
primarily those of political power.

Between 1823 and 1825, Canning established a number of con-
sulates and other commissions of inquiry at selected key centres in
Latin America, with instructions to submit detailed reports on the
trade and commercial prospects of the new states.[1] Once the statements and returns had been received in London, copies of the more
important and carefully researched sections were forwarded by the
Foreign Office to the Board of Trade. A long and comprehensive
report was despatched to Canning by Ricketts in December 1826 on
the commerce and condition of Peru, *i.e.* Lower Peru.[2] The Consul
General had already forwarded to London a short preliminary survey of Upper Peru (Bolivia) in May of that year, but the pressures of
work and great distances involved had meant that the summary was
drawn together quickly from a number of secondary sources, and
lacked evidence of personal acquaintance with the country.[3] Acknow-
ledging the brevity of the report, Ricketts sought formal approval of
his decision to send Pentland into Upper Peru

> for the purpose of obtaining a knowledge of its natural productions,
> which may in fact be said to be unknown, as no scientific person

[1] See *British Consular Reports on the Trade and Politics of Latin America,*
1824–1826, ed. R. A. Humphreys (Camden, 3rd ser., lxiii, 1940), which provides a
detailed and invaluable study of the documents from the Spanish American
states despatched to London in that three-year period. The edited 1827 Report on
Bolivia which follows thus forms a short supplement to Humphreys's volume.

[2] *Ibid.,* Document vi, 27 December, 1826, pp. 107–206 (P.R.O., F.O. 61/8).

[3] *Ibid.,* Document vii, 30 May, 1826, pp. 207–25 (P.R.O., F.O. 61/7).

has heretofore given any detailed description of them. The objects to which I propose to direct his special attention are: the determination by astronomical means of the geographical position of the different places, and the construction of a map of the provinces; the examination of the country geologically, and a description of the extent and capability of the mines, with reference to the advantages of machinery and to the probability of the employment of British capital in working them; the examination of vegetable and animal productions for the purpose of ascertaining what descriptions of bark, dyewoods, etc., and wool, etc. may answer for exports; and the collection of objects of interest for the British Museum. In addition to this I shall direct Mr Pentland to collect particular information regarding the commerce of the respective provinces, and those subjects which may be beneficial to the British interests. As His Excellency General Bolívar is particularly desirous that a scientific person should make a circuit of the country and give a report on the capability of the mines with a view to their valuation and ultimate sale, I propose to embrace the opportunity of His Excellency's next visit to Chuquisaca to send Mr Pentland thither, proceeding by sea to Arica, and returning by way of Cuzco, Guamanga, and Pasco to Lima.[1]

Pentland departed for Bolivia in September 1826 and remained there until April 1827.[2] During the greater part of these seven months in both the dry and the rainy season, he travelled extensively through Bolivia's Andean territory, concentrating his investigations in the most densely populated parts of the country as Ricketts had subsequently instructed him to do, although these represented considerably less than one-quarter of the total national area claimed at independence (Figs 2–3). Even then, Bolivia contained virtually no wheeled vehicles, or cart and carriage roads of any kind, yet Pentland records little of the adventure and physical hardship involved in touring some two thousand miles by mule across wretchedly exposed plateaus and along steep, narrow mountain trails, often at elevations of more than 12,000 feet above sea level. A more vivid picture of the wear and

[1] C. M. Ricketts to George Canning, Lima, 30 May, 1826, P.R.O., F.O. 61/7. In the event, Pentland took a different route into Bolivia, *via* Arequipa, Puno and Lake Titicaca to La Paz, Oruro, Potosí, Chuquisaca, Cochabamba, back to La Paz, and thence down again into Peru by way of the Tacna oasis to the port of Arica. He returned by sea to Callao, arriving at Lima in May 1827. Pentland was later to return to Bolivia following his appointment (1836–9) as Britain's first Consul General there.

[2] Pentland travelled alone on behalf of the British Government, not in the company of Woodbine Parish, Consul General at Buenos Aires, as stated in the *D.N.B.*

tear experienced *en route* may be drawn from the simple itemized expense account submitted separately. Pentland is less reticent, however, in his appreciation of the landscape, and the wonder inspired by the grandeur, beauty and extraordinary scenic variety of the central Andes. The journey led Ricketts's secretary into some of the most rugged, lofty and secluded regions of the western hemisphere and, as the work develops, his substantial reporting on man and land in Bolivia, 'a great new state in the interior of the South American continent', builds into a volume of considerable interest. Given the prevailing conditions and time limit imposed, Pentland's labours produced a document from which much valuable information and comment about contemporary conditions may be obtained.

The Report is divided into five chapters:

  I *A brief Historical Review of the Political Events which preceded the Independence of Bolivia.*

  II *A Geographical and Statistical Description of the Republic.*

  III *A Review of the present state of the Mines, and of their former produce.*

  IV *A Review of the Commercial Relations, foreign and domestic.*

  V *A short view of the present political state of Bolivia, embracing the History of the country since its independence, its Government, Laws, and Institutions.*

The first two chapters have been omitted from this edited report since they comprise more general material now readily available elsewhere, although this in no way detracts from their usefulness to Pentland's contemporaries. The opening summary recalls Bolivia's earlier colonial history as the rich, silver-producing *audiencia*, or Presidency, of Charcas, which remained part of the Viceroyalty of Peru for over two hundred years, but which was transferred to the newly-created Viceroyalty of the Río de la Plata in 1776 and administered from Buenos Aires until the beginning of the revolutionary phase. Local insurrection, occasional sharp exchange, and sporadic mountain guerrilla activity between 1809 and 1825 characterized Upper Peru's revolutionary period, which proved to be the most protracted if not the most violent of the struggles by South American patriots for emancipation from Spanish rule.

Pentland's second chapter, after briefly recording the boundaries of the new republic with Brazil, Argentina, Peru, Chile, and Paraguay, provided his superiors with a sound, basic, first-hand geographical account of highland Bolivia about which so little was reliably known, despite the early fame and prodigious wealth of its 'silver city' of Potosí. As for lowland Bolivia, that huge ultramontane plains tract lying silent and remote in the continental interior, few had ever penetrated it from any direction. Except for occasional mission reports, travellers' accounts, and frequently inaccurate map fragments, the low, flat savannas, swamps and tropical forests spreading beyond the east Andean slope towards the Amazon and Paraguay rivers remained *terra incognita*. Indeed, the most serious flaw in Pentland's summary of the drainage network of the *oriente* was his complete failure to record the cataract section on the Mamoré and Madeira rivers: 230 miles broken by eighteen sets of falls and rapids which effectively interrupted Bolivia's most important and direct navigable routeway into the Amazon (Fig. 2). Pentland inevitably concentrated his investigation in the western *cordilleras*, presenting such data on the geology and topography as could be assembled from personal survey, colonial records and other sources. Scientific interests which had first been pursued at Armagh in his native Ireland, and later in London and Paris, encouraged Pentland to make several surveys of the more imposing peaks in the Cordillera Real, the first individual to undertake such work.[1] He did not construct a map of the Bolivian provinces as Ricketts had initially proposed, for the task was impossible in the time available, but three ink and sepia-wash annotated relief profiles were included among the thirteen enclosures submitted in the final report.[2]

[1] J. B. Pentland, 'On the general outline and physical configuration of the Bolivian Andes; with observations on the line of perpetual snow upon the Andes, between 15° and 20° South latitude', *Journal of the Royal Geographical Society of London*, v (1835), pp. 70–89.

[2] The enclosures comprise:
1. Section or profile of the Peruvian Andes and of the adjoining provinces of Peru and Bolivia, between the 14th and 16th parallels of South latitude.
2. Section or profile of the Peruvian Andes and of the adjoining provinces of Peru and Bolivia, between the 16th and 18th parallels of South latitude.
3. Section or profile of the provinces of Bolivia bordering in the Andes (road from Peru to Buenos Ayres) from the shores of the Lake of Titicaca to the town of Salta and the plains of Buenos Ayres, between the 16th and 25th parallels of South latitude.
4. Plans and elevations of Peruvian ruins, Lake Titicaca.
5. Table of the geographical position of the most remarkable places in Bolivia, and in the neighbouring provinces of Lower Peru determined by astronomical observations.
6. Table showing the height above the sea of the most remarkable places of Bolivia, and of the adjoining provinces of Lower Peru, as determined by J. B. Pentland.
7. Table exhibiting the present division of the Bolivian Republic into Departments, Provinces and Cantons.
8. Statement showing the quantity of silver produced by the mines of Upper Peru from the earliest period, exhibiting the amount of duties paid to the Crown of Spain on this metal, and the amount of silver registered at the

A National Census was in progress, and from returns already to hand the projected total population was estimated at between 1,100,000 and 1,200,000 persons: 200,000 white Spaniards and creoles; 100,000 *mestizos*; 800,000 Indians, and about 7000 negroes. The recording of relatively small numbers of *mestizos*, in fact that considerable proportion of mixed white and Indian stock, revealed the difficulty of categorizing accurately such an element in the country's racial composition. The population of the city of La Paz was given as 40,000; Cochabamba, 30,000; Chuquisaca (also known as Sucre), 12,000; Potosí, 9000; Santa Cruz de la Sierra, 9000; Oruro 4600. The dominance of La Paz and Cochabamba reflected their greater accessibility from Peru and the major Pacific ports. Chuquisaca's growth had been slow; despite its prestigious role as the seat of the Spanish colonial *audiencia*, close to Potosí, for nearly three hundred years, its archbishopric, its famous two hundred-year-old University of San Francisco Xavier, and its recent confirmation as the new capital of Bolivia in 1825, this attractive old town remained isolated and distant from the chief commercial centres. In a well observed section on the Department of La Paz, Pentland expands upon the Lake Titicaca region, and describes in some detail the ruined Inca and pre-Inca settlement sites and extensive terrace systems on the islands and margins of the lake, all of which had plainly awed and fascinated him.

The agricultural survey records the extraordinary range of climates and products which Pentland noted on his reconnaissance: the distribution and limits of cultivation of cereals, fruits, vegetables, fibre, and tree crops, and the locations of the more favourable areas for grazing and cultivation in the warm, sheltered, irrigated intermontane basins. The apparent future commercial possibilities for plantation agriculture in the deep, humid tropical valleys dissecting the east Andean slope are emphasized, for Pentland had been greatly im-

---

Treasury of Potosí from 1545 to 1824 compiled from official documents [Appendix I].
9. Statement exhibiting the total quantity of silver produced by the mines of Upper Peru from the earliest period, including the amount estimated to have been exported by contraband and the quantity furnished by the other mines of those provinces not included in Enclosure 8 [Appendix II].
10. Statement exhibiting the amount of the precious metals coined at the Mint of Potosí from 1800 to 1826 [Appendix III].
11. Law respecting the duties to be levied on importations through Cobija (Chuquisaca, 24 February, 1827).
12. *República Boliviana: Colección oficial de Leyes, Decretos, y Órdenes del Gobierno* (Chuquisaca, 21 January, 1827).
13. *Constitución de la República Boliviana* (Chuquisaca, 25 November, 1826).

pressed by the variety of tropical products he found growing wild. Regular observations upon rural settlement and land use were made as he travelled between the principal towns and mining centres.[1] Life at high altitudes was a subject of special interest since Pentland was surprised to find as much as one-third of the total population living permanently between altitudes of 12,500 and 14,000 feet, 'not only in isolated dwellings but in hamlets and villages'. Seasonally occupied sites were common up to 15,000 feet in the high summer pastures grazed by llama and alpaca herds. This early geographical and associated statistical description thus provided a first basic inventory in English of the physical features, wild life, field and forest products, and settlement distribution of highland Bolivia, and offered a useful introduction to the more specific studies which followed.

Chapters III and IV of the Pentland Report were copied and despatched by the Foreign Office to the Board of Trade in April 1828; together with the final Chapter V they comprise more than two-thirds of the original document, and undoubtedly have the most to tell scholars about economic, commercial and political conditions in Bolivia in the mid-1820s. In many respects, despite the aftermath of Revolution, the years 1826 and 1827 were a uniquely favourable period in which to assess Bolivia's future prospects. The organization of the country's internal affairs had begun well under Antonio José de Sucre, the Colombian[2] hero of the decisive victory over Spanish forces at Ayacucho in December 1824. After that triumph Bolívar had instructed Sucre to proceed south-eastward into Upper Peru to eradicate the remaining centres of Royalist resistance lodged in the high central *sierras* close to Potosí. During his long march into Upper Peru, Sucre had given strong support to the region's desire for self-determination and subsequently, in opposition to Bolívar's own wishes, to Upper Peru's persistent demand for complete independence. An authoritative and popular figure, Sucre accepted the Presidency of Bolivia on 1 January, 1826, agreeing to hold office until Bolivia's independence was confirmed and the country's institutions successfully established. He resigned the Presidency on 18 April, 1828 and four months later left Bolivia to return to his home in Quito. Tragically, in less than two years, June 1830, as

[1] Pentland does not appear to have visited the towns of Santa Cruz de la Sierra or Tarija, and only brief descriptions of them are included. Tarija's determination to be incorporated into Bolivia had originally been challenged by Argentina (and by Bolívar), but it was effective by September 1826.

[2] I.e. from Gran Colombia, the name of the extensive new state which Bolívar had established on the boundary of the colonial Viceroyalty of New Granada. It soon broke up, however, into three separate components: Colombia, Venezuela and Ecuador. Sucre was born at Cumaná, Venezuela.

violence swept again through Gran Colombia, the Grand Marshal of Ayacucho was assassinated on a mountain trail between Quito and Bogotá.

During his brief but highly significant association with Bolivia, however, Sucre proved himself to be an able and dedicated administrator. He impressed those who met him, including Pentland, two years his junior, by his realism, judgment and practical grasp of affairs. Certainly, the energy with which Sucre set about establishing order, introducing reform, planning transport improvements, opening schools and colleges, and encouraging overseas interests in Bolivia, resulted in any assessment made in 1826-7 of the country's long-term future prospects being cautiously optimistic. Neither Sucre, nor Pentland, however, could ignore the problems. The long period of revolutionary unrest in Bolivia had had a disastrous effect on the mines: maintenance had deteriorated, production declined and much work been abandoned. Many mines were flooded, primitively equipped, short of labour and of fuel, while Bolivia's slender internal investment capacity now showed every sign of being attracted more to commercial than to mining enterprise. Transport to and from the coast was a formidable undertaking, costly, exhausting, and time-consuming. Yet already the competition of European manufactured goods was stifling much small domestic production. In such a situation Pentland discerned encouraging prospects for British trade with Bolivia, a poor country it was true, but still one possessing considerable resources and an apparently stable, favourably disposed administration.

Warnings of hazards to come, however, were already visible to those who could recognize them as such. Sucre, the sympathetic foreigner, had made no secret of his resolve to relinquish office and leave Bolivia in August 1828, by which time it was hoped that the ground-work for viable internal and external policies would have been securely laid. But in the conduct of Bolivian affairs with the other new South American states, rivals now it appeared rather than allies, President Sucre's burdens were heavy. His attempts to purchase or bargain for possession of Arica, the traditional and most convenient port for Upper Peru, were firmly rejected by Lima. Bolivia was left to make the best of the tiny, remote landing-place at Cobija, its legal colonial inheritance (Fig. 2). Sucre, like so many who followed him, was to continue to negotiate unsuccessfully for Arica, and soon the extreme seriousness of Bolivia's essentially landlocked position, with its transit costs and tariff load, became apparent. At the time of Sucre's departure, Bolivia was already plunged into conflict with Peru in what marked the beginning of a disastrously long period of internal intrigue and violence, goaded by frustrating, intermittent struggle with neighbouring states.

Thus, the timing of the Pentland Report is significant. In 1826-7, despite a post-Revolution catalogue of difficulty, backwardness and neglect, some qualified optimism appeared justified. There was still sufficient indication of a determination and an ability to succeed in the goals that had sustained belief in independence for Upper Peru. Mining investment and increased mining revenues would gradually have to finance the solutions to the host of problems demanding attention, not least those of transport. But if goodwill and good management continued, then long-term prospects for development were bright. In view of the country's subsequent misfortunes, it is fitting that this brief, far from despairing interlude in Bolivia's early history remains recorded in the pages of the Pentland Report.

Note on Editing

Save in the very few cases of unintended error the original spelling has been retained. Capitalization and punctuation have been modernized. Editor's corrections and other insertions in the text are indicated by square brackets.

REPORT ON BOLIVIA, 1827,
BY JOSEPH BARCLAY PENTLAND

CHAPTER III

A REVIEW OF THE PRESENT
STATE OF THE MINES, AND
OF THEIR FORMER PRODUCE

IN the review of the mines of Bolivia which I am directed by your instructions to furnish, I shall follow the administrative division of the Republic into Departments and Provinces as detailed in an earlier part of this report, in order to prevent a confusion which might arise in adopting the division of the Mining Tribunal into Mining Intendancies, *asientos*, etc.

The following table presents a list of the most remarkable mining districts:

Departments	Mining Districts	
La Paz	(i)	Tipuani
	(ii)	Illimani
	(iii)	Berenguela
	(iv)	Corocoro
	(v)	Sicasica
Oruro	(vi)	Oruro
	(vii)	Poopó
Potosí	(viii)	Potosí
	(ix)	Porco
	(x)	Ciporro
	(xi)	Portugalete
	(xii)	Lipez
	(xiii)	Atacama
	(xiv)	Aullagas
	(xv)	Moromoro
	(xvi)	Ocuri
Cochabamba	(xvii)	Choquecamata

(i) TIPUANI. The gold mines of Tipuani, as they are improperly called, consist of stream works situated on each side of the river of the same name in the Province of Larecaja. The gold is disseminated in the form of scales of dust, and of masses of various sizes in a bed of clay which reposes on slate, the rock in which the valley was originally excavated. The thickness of this auriferous mass varies from 4 to 12 feet, and upon it reposes a considerable deposit of sand and gravel containing also a minute quantity of the same precious metal. The actual mode of working is by removing the upper beds of sand and gravel until the auriferous bed is laid bare. The argiles of which it is formed is carried on the backs of Indians to the river's edge, where the gold is subsequently separated by washing. The labour is principally performed by Indians who are brought from the opposite side of the cordillera [*i.e.* from the *altiplano*] and by a few negroes, the property of individuals resident at Tipuani.[1] The extraction of the auriferous clays occupies the months of May, June, July, August, and September, and the washing or separation of the gold the months of October and November; during the remainder of the year all works are suspended arising from the perpetual rains which prevail during the summer and autumnal months.

It will be seen that the different operations in use are of the most simple, and I may add rudest, description. Everything is performed by manual labour, and consequently at a heavy expense; the pits from their vicinity to the river become often inundated, and abandoned from ignorance of the means to extract the water. To remedy the many inconveniences attendant on the present mode of working I have recommended (a) the use of barrows, spades and shovels which will economise the expense of manual labour, (b) the introduction of pumps of the chain kind for the removal of the water from the pits, and (c) I have suggested a more economical mode of washing the argiles which, by diminishing the use of manual labour, will prevent theft on the part of the washers, at present a source of very serious loss to the proprietors of stream works. The introduction of machinery similar to that employed in the tin stream works of

[1] Earlier, Pentland had written, 'The negro population is chiefly confined to the eastern provinces of the Dept. of La Paz, where they were formerly introduced as slaves; they are employed in the cultivation of the coca plant . . . The total number of negroes throughout Bolivia scarcely reaches 7000, of whom 4700 are slaves. By the 11th Article of the Constitution, slavery is abolished throughout Bolivia, and by a subsequent law Congress has extended this enactment of the Constitution, and regulated the mode in which those who remain in the state of slavery . . . are to gradually emancipate themselves by indemnifying their owners from the proceeds of their labour for the loss sustained by their freedom' (*Report*, chap. ii). The slaves in Bolivia had been introduced, or escaped, from Lower Peru where they had worked mostly on the sugar estates. Apart from those living close to the Brazilian border, Bolivia's very small negro population is still concentrated in the headwater valleys of the Beni river between Tipuani, Coroico and Suapi.

Cornwall would answer many of those objects, and their establishment at Tipuani will be attended with every facility.

The quantity of gold produced before the Revolution by the Tipuani stream works has often exceeded one million dollars annually.[1] During the past year (1826), when only two individuals continued to work, 62 arrobas[2] or about 420,000 dollars-worth of gold were obtained in six months. The expense of labour in the present difficulty of procuring workmen amounts to from two-thirds to three-fourths of the value of the gold produced. In order to ascertain the profits which might be expected by embarking capital in the stream works of Tipuani, I directed the overseer of Mr. Begg's[3] property there to send me a statement of one day's workings, by which it appears that the expenses incurred amounted to 113 dollars 6 reales,[4] whilst the value of the gold produced was 180 dollars affording a net profit consequently of 58 per cent. This fact will allow of forming some idea of the profits which may be at present derived from the stream works of Tipuani even under the many disadvantages which they labour, and of the immense returns which may be calculated on from the introduction of the improvements already adverted to.

From reports which I have received, not only do the banks of the rivers Tipuani and Mapiri, but those of the Cuca [Cooca], Coroico, and in general of all the streams descending from the Eastern Cordillera in the Provinces of Larecaja and Yungas, abound in the same auriferous deposits. But few are now worked except those of Tipuani, and I am persuaded that no point of the American continent offers greater prospects of success to the introduction of European capital than the gold stream works of this district.

It is expected that the produce of the stream works of Tipuani will approach near to 800,000 dollars during the present year. The produce of the other stream works of Larecaja and Yungas has not exceeded 50,000 dollars so that in 1826, the total amount produced from the stream works of the Department of La Paz may be estimated at 500,000 dollars, or £100,000 sterling.

(ii) ILLIMANI. The gigantic mountain of Illimani which, in the centre of the Province of Yungas and of the Department of La Paz,

---

[1] The rate of exchange of the U.S. dollar was then $5 to £1. The Bolivian silver peso at this period also had an exchange value of about 5 to the Pound Sterling, so that the terms dollar and peso could be, and were, used interchangeably.

[2] arroba: a unit of weight, about 25 lbs.

[3] John Begg, a British merchant, with headquarters in Lima and agencies at Arica, Tacna and Arequipa.

[4] real: a small Spanish silver coin, 8 to the dollar or peso. About 6d.

rises to an elevation of 24,200 [22,700] feet as mentioned in a preceding part of this report, is traversed by numerous veins of quartz in which masses of native gold and of auriferous pyrites are disseminated. Prior to the Conquest these veins appear to have been worked to a considerable extent, approaching an elevation of 17,000 feet. In the 17th century an immense mass of rock was detached on the northern side of the mountain by lightning, when large quantities of gold were collected from the sides of one of those veins which was rent assunder. The working of these and other veins has been since undertaken at various times, and successively abandoned; a small quantity of gold was obtained in this way in 1825 and 1826, but so inconsiderable as not to defray the expenses incurred in its extraction.

There prevails a tradition in the country that considerable treasures were deposited in a small lake situated on the side of this mountain (at an elevation of 15,950 feet) by the aborigines, after the death of Atahualpa and the conquest of Cuzco, in order to preserve the objects of their religious worship from the Spaniards. On the strength of this tradition some persons undertook to drain off the water of the lake, and for this purpose towards the end of the last century an individual cut an adit, and actually laid bare a considerable portion of its area. No well-authenticated proof exists that any part of the expected treasures was met with, but the sand which formed the bottom of the lake, where it was laid bare, was found to contain a sufficient quantity of gold to pay the expenses of the adit. On the death of that individual the lake became the property of the State, which has granted a lease of it to Colonel O'Brien and Mr. Begg. When I visited Illimani in December 1826 I pointed out how the remaining water of the lake may be drawn off but I possess considerable doubt that the lessees are likely to meet with the expected treasure, since the tradition on which their hopes are solely founded merits little credit, unsupported by other testimony.

It is my opinion that much brighter chances of success will be found in the formation of stream works at the base of Illimani, on the alluvial deposits which fill many of the valleys surrounding the mountain, and which have been produced by the destruction of the strata and of the many auriferous veins traversing them during a long succession of ages. From works of this kind I am persuaded large quantities of gold may be obtained, and the country around offers every facility for the establishment of the necessary machinery, and an abundance of workmen. The working of the auriferous veins must always be attended with great difficulty arising from their excessive elevation where the barometer descends to $16\frac{1}{2}$

C M—N

inches, and where human beings can only exist during a limited period.[1]

(iii) BERENGUELA. The silver mines of San Juan de Berenguela in the Province of Pacajes, are situated on the eastern declivity of the Western Cordillera of the Andes, near to the village of Santiago de Machaca. The mines of Berenguela were formerly very productive. The ores consisting of argentiferous sulphurets [sulphides] of lead and of copper, and of antimonial and red silver, averaged from 6 to 7 ounces of silver per quintal [100 pounds] of ore. The veins were of inconsiderable thickness, and the works suffered much from infiltrations of water which rendered their working difficult. At the present day these mines are almost entirely abandoned from want of capital to drain off the water which has accumulated in them. Until the necessary adits could be completed to drain them effectively, the introduction of pumps would be attended with great advantage and would permit of many rich mines being worked in Berenguela which are now abandoned.

I have not been able to ascertain the amount of silver produced in this district for any considerable time but about the year 1780 it exceeded 25,000 marks[2] annually, or 212,000 dollars. At present the produce of the mines of Berenguela is very trifling, scarcely reaching 100 marks per month, or 10,000 dollars yearly. This quantity however would be increased even in their present abandoned state, if a more constant supply of quicksilver could be reckoned on, and at a less exorbitant price than that which it now bears.[3]

(iv) COROCORO. The copper mines of Corocoro situated in the Province of Pacajes have furnished for many years the large quantities of this metal consumed in the two Perus. They are placed on beds of native oxide and green carbonate of copper in the midst of the red sandstone formation; the native metal is alone worked, the people of the country being ignorant of the means for the extraction of the copper from its other ores. Many of the Corocoro mines have lately become the property of two British merchants. The poorer descriptions of ore are extremely abundant and are soon likely to be turned to advantage since the recent discovery of coal in the neigh-

---

[1] $16\frac{1}{2}$ inches of mercury in barometric reading approximates to an altitude of 18,000 feet. Above this height, the human body is no longer able to compensate indefinitely for lack of oxygen, and no permanent human settlement is recorded anywhere in the world at such altitudes.

[2] Mark (*marco*): a unit of weight for gold and silver, 8 Spanish ounces (equalling 8.112 English ounces avoirdupois).

[3] *Infra*, pp. 201–2, 231–2.

bourhood.[1] The great distance of those mines from the sea will in a measure preclude the export of their copper to a foreign market so that their importance will chiefly depend on the home consumption of this metal.

(v) SICASICA. The two principal mining districts of this province are Pacuani, 5 leagues north-east, and Laurani, 2 leagues south-west, of the town of Sicasica. The mines of Pacuani are situated on veins which traverse a very compact variety of the metalliferous porphyry; many of them were worked formerly and some still remain in a state of activity, but here as elsewhere the greater number have become abandoned from the effects of the Revolution. The veins seldom exceed a few inches in thickness, but this is compensated for by the richness of their ores consisting of argentiferous galenas and sulphurets of copper, and of antimonial and white silver, the whole averaging from 15 to 150 ounces of silver per 100 lbs of ores. They possess the great advantages also of being free from water, and of being situated in a district where an abundance of miners is to be met with.

The mines of Laurani belong to an insulated group of porphyritic hills at the north-west base of which the town of Sicasica is situated. Those hills are traversed by innumerable veins of the same metallic ores as those mentioned in the preceding paragraph, the richness and abundance of the ores increasing with the depth of the mines. The ordinary classes of ore give from 40 to 50 ounces of silver per 100 lbs, whilst others give as much as 15 per cent of the same metal. In the eighteenth century, upwards of two hundred mines were worked in the hills of Laurani. Many of them are now abandoned, partly arising from the late unsettled state of the country, but chiefly from the circumstances of the best mines being watered. Only five or six are worked at present and when I visited this district in November 1826 these few gave very handsome returns, even at the exorbitant price of quicksilver at that period. I am persuaded that there is not one point in Bolivia which offers greater advantages to a foreign mining company than the mineral district of Laurani, since by completing one or two adits at a comparatively trifling expense, numerous mines now inundated might be rendered productive, and new ones opened at inferior levels, where the metallic ores are more abundant.

The ores of Pacuani and Laurani are carried to the metallurgical establishments of Belén on the river of Aysayo, 6 leagues distant,

---

[1] The carbonized plant remains of the Corocoro group, seen by Pentland, were not found subsequently to indicate the presence of coal measures.

where the silver is separated by the method of amalgamation, a process ill-adapted to ores of their description.

In former times the mines around Sicasica produced 50,000 marks or 425,000 dollars-worth of silver annually, and under better management might at the present day be made to produce a larger quantity. It does not appear, however, that more than 5,000 marks, or 42,500 dollars, was obtained in each of the years 1825 and 1826. I have reason to believe that in the years 1827 and 1828 the produce of the mines of Pacuani and Laurani will fall little short of three times that sum.

To the south-east of Sicasica are situated the mines of La Silla (the Saddle), a conical mountain of porphyry which rises on the banks of the Desaguadero; they are now entirely abandoned, but are said to have been formerly very productive.

(vi) ORURO. The mineral district of Oruro is situated close to the town of that name, and formerly occupied an important place among the mining establishments of Upper Peru. The mines of Oruro are now abandoned. They had already begun to fall off before the Revolution, when many of them having penetrated below the level of the surrounding plain, they became inundated, and it was found impossible to drain them by means of adits. When I visited Oruro last December, the only work carried on consisted in collecting fragments of ore from the rubbish formerly rejected as too poor, and from this a small quantity of silver is annually procured. But in the early part of 1827 a large vein was discovered, which it is expected will produce 400 marks weekly, or nearly [2]00,000 dollars during the present year. The great depth to which the best mines of Oruro have penetrated below the plain of the Desaguadero renders it impossible to drain them by means of adits. Pumps might be introduced which would effect this object, and by such means I am persuaded many of the richest veins might be still worked, and the mines of Oruro once more rendered productive, but at no place is capital less abundant than at Oruro, and it is probable that as far as its present inhabitants are concerned its mines will long remain in their present state of abandon.

(vii) POOPÓ. The mines of Poopó, a mineral district situated 5 leagues south of Oruro, are in the same state as the latter. They formerly produced very large quantities of silver, and their decadence as well as that of the Oruro mines in a measure arose from the memorable rebellion of the aborigines in 1780 and 1781 under Juan [José] Condorcanqui or Tupac Amarú.[1] This movement which pene-

[1] José Gabriel Condorcanqui, adopting the title Tupac Amarú II after his

trated throughout the entire extent of the mountainous provinces of the two Perus, reached Oruro, where an opulent family of miners by name of Rodríguez, became implicated in the rebellion. The heads of the family were arrested and executed and at their death their mines, the most considerable of those two districts, became abandoned, and have remained in the same state to the present day.

The average annual produce of the mines of Oruro and Poopó between the years 1820 and 1825 amounted to 62,600 dollars; it has little increased since that time, but it is difficult to ascertain the exact amount as the whole of the silver produced is carried by contraband to Arica, in return for iron, quicksilver and mining implements.

A very large quantity of tin has been obtained of late years at Oruro and in its vicinity, from the residues rejected in former times after the separation of the silver from its ores by the process of amalgamation. These residues (*relaves*) contain a considerable proportion of oxide of tin which is separated by washing and afterwards reduced to a metallic state by the same process as that employed in England and in Saxony. In this way 400 tons of tin have been procured annually for many years past. A small quantity has been also obtained from the tin mines of Huanuni, 9 leagues south-east of Oruro, which from its greater purity is preferred to that of Oruro, the latter being rendered brittle and unfit for many purposes by a trifling admixture of copper, which it is difficult to separate. The amount of tin, the produce of Oruro, exported from Arica in 1825 and 1826 has averaged 7,000 quintals, worth 4,000 dollars annually; but as the residues from which the greater part of it has been obtained are now nearly worked out and the mines of Huanuni abandoned, the export of tin from Oruro must decrease considerably and its extraction cease in a few years.[1]

(viii) POTOSÍ. The mining district of Potosí, which has acquired so great celebrity from the immense amount of silver which it has produced, was discovered soon after the Conquest about [in] the year

---

sixteenth-century Inca ancestor, led a major revolt against the Spaniards which began near Cuzco in November 1780. Indian rebellion against harsh treatment, abuse, taxation and forced labour broke out in many Andean centres, but was concentrated in Upper and Lower Peru. After initial victories, resistance was crushed in May 1781.

[1] Exports of tin from Oruro and Huanuni (normally *via* Arica) were maintained at almost exactly the same levels, however, for several years and began to rise in the second half of the nineteenth century. When the railway from Antofagasta on the Chilean (formerly Bolivian) coast at length reached Oruro in 1892, tin exports increased dramatically and soon assumed their dominant role in the Bolivian economy. See J. V. Fifer, *Bolivia: Land, Location, and Politics since 1825* (Cambridge, 1972), pp. 49, 68–71, 245–9.

1545. It consists of the Cerro [Rico] or Mountain of Potosí, at the northern base of which the city to which it has given its name is situated. This mountain, which rises in the form of a sugar-loaf in the midst of the Andes to an elevation of 16,080 [15,800] British feet, is traversed by three principal veins, and several others less regular and important. In many places the entire mass of the porphyritic rock is penetrated with metallic substances.

Immediately after the discovery of the principal veins, excavations were opened upon them in a most rude and unscientific manner, not in the form of shafts and galleries, but of open excavations not unlike our modern quarry works. By this mode of working many lives were lost from the falling in of the sides of the veins. The richest description of ores alone was selected, and the veins were necessarily abandoned at an inconsiderable depth from the surface. It does not appear how long this injudicious system was pursued, but it must necessarily have led to the exhaustion of the more superficial portions of the different veins. It was then that more regular operations were entered on; researches were made to discover new veins and to reach the old ones by subterraneous shafts and galleries. The number of mines increased rapidly and during the 17th and commencement of the 18th century, the mines of Potosí were the most productive in the known world. Their prosperity remained nearly stationary up to the commencement of the 19th century. The improvements introduced into the metallurgical operations caused many ores formerly rejected as too poor to be now eagerly sought after, and at the close of the 18th century, at a time when peace and tranquillity reigned throughout the colonial possessions of Spain, the mines of the Potosí district alone furnished about two million dollars annually.[1] Up to the year 1809 the average produce of those mines had not materially decreased but on the breaking out of the Revolution about this latter

[1] The discovery of silver at Potosí proved to be one of the greatest mineral strikes of all time. Studies of the city, its mines and production include L. Hanke, *The Imperial City of Potosí* (The Hague, 1956); L. Hanke and G. Mendoza (eds.), *Bartolomé Arzáns de Orsúa y Vela's History of Potosí*, 3 vols. (Providence, R.1., 1965); B. W. Diffie, 'Estimates of Potosí Mineral Production 1545–1555', *Hispanic American Historical Review*, xx, 1940, pp. 275–82; G. B. Cobb, 'Supply and Transportation for the Potosí Mines, 1545–1640', *Hispanic American Historical Review*, xxix, 1949, pp. 25–45; also, 'Potosí, a South American Mining Frontier', in *Greater America. Essays in honor of Herbert Eugene Bolton* (Univ. of California Press, Berkeley and Los Angeles, 1945), pp. 39–58; J. Lynch, *Spanish Colonial Administration, 1782–1810. The Intendant System in the Viceroyalty of the Rió de la Plata* (London, 1958), *passim*. Alexander von Humboldt's estimate of average annual silver production at Potosí, 1779–89, was 3,676,330 *pesos*. See *Essai Politique sur le Royaume de la Nouvelle-Espagne* (2nd ed.; iii, Paris, 1827), p. 377.

period, Potosí, from its vicinity to the Buenos Ayrian provinces, was constantly the scene of excesses of either party. Its respectable and peaceable inhabitants, the principal miners, were obliged to abandon it and from that time the produce of its mines decreased rapidly.

In 1790, the Spanish Government sent out a commission of Germans to examine and report on the state of the mines in the two Perus.[1] By their advice a gallery or adit was undertaken for the purpose of draining the richest mines of Potosí, and of attacking the inferior part of the three veins above mentioned, where they had been abandoned. The project was an excellent one, and if carried into effect, would have restored to the mines of Potosí their former celebrity and have made it a second Guanajuato. After having expended a very large sum in cutting 926 yards of this adit it was abandoned, partly from jealousies raised against its German projectors, partly from its not having produced the wished-for effect, as soon as was expected, but chiefly from the poverty of the Treasury, at the expense of which the work was commenced upon. This adit, now the property of the State, is the most perfect specimen of mining architecture in South America and does great credit to those who constructed it. Its continuation under certain modifications of the original plan is likely to be attended with success in the hands of intelligent European miners, and I doubt not of its being turned one day or other to great advantage.

It is to be regretted that the *Potosí, La Paz and Peruvian Mining Association* formed in London at the commencement of 1825 did not direct its attention to an undertaking of this kind, which it only required capital to effect. Instead it expended immense sums on an extravagant establishment, and in the purchase of machinery totally unsuited to the localities, a great part of which could never have been transported from the coast into the interior of the continent, or if it had reached its destination was little suited for the objects

[1] This was the Nordenflycht mission (led by Baron von Nordenflycht, a Swedish mineralogist), which visited some of the principal mining centres in Upper and Lower Peru between 1789 and 1793. The experienced German mining engineer and metallurgist, Anton Zacharias Helms, a senior member of the party, criticized the workings at Potosí: 'All the operations at the mines of Potosí, the stamping, sifting, washing, quickening and roasting the ore are conducted in so slovenly, wasteful, and unscientific a manner.' Flooding was a major problem, and advice was given on drainage techniques as well as on improved methods of amalgamation. The mission was most unpopular among the local mine-owners. See A. Z. Helms, *Travels from Buenos Ayres, by Potosí, to Lima* (English translation, London, 1806, first published Dresden, 1798), pp. 39–50. Also, R. M. Buechler, 'Technical Aid to Upper Peru: the Nordenflicht Expedition', *Journal of Latin American Studies*, v (1973), pp. 37–77.

proposed.[1] Undertakings of this magnitude are the only ones where the resources of a wealthy company are likely to be advantageously employed at Potosí; in every other respect the local experience of the native miner will probably triumph over the advantages of European science, at least for a time.

The mountain of Potosí is excavated in every direction. At one period as many as eight thousand mines are recorded to have been opened in its extent [*i.e.* right to its summit], if such works can be called mines, since they in no way resemble those of the Old World, consisting in narrow, tortuous shafts and galleries carried on without any system, following the ore where it was to be met with. This immense number has considerably diminished, many have fallen in, others have been abandoned whilst several remain inundated, without their proprietors possessing the means to clear off the water. In January 1827, only six mines, properly speaking, were in a state of activity furnishing ores containing from 3 to 4 ounces per 100 lbs, whilst the great mass of silver which Potosí now produces is obtained from a class of ores called *pacos* and *rodados* collected on the surface of the mountain, and which were rejected as too poor at the time of the great prosperity of the mines.[2] These *pacos* and *rodados* contain little more than $1/1250$ or $1/1500$ of their weight in silver, but as they are obtained without difficulty and at a trifling expense, and as they exist in great abundance over the surface of the Cerro, they seldom

[1] Edmond Temple, secretary of the *Potosí, La Paz and Peruvian Mining Association*, called it 'one of the nine hundred and ninety-nine speculations of the all-speculating year 1825'. The Company was launched in London on 27 April, 1825, its capital said to be £1,000,000 and its purpose 'to work mines of gold, silver, platina, quicksilver, copper, and other minerals in the provinces of Potosí and La Paz, and generally in Upper and Lower Peru'. The company's President was Juan García del Río, the Vice-President General James Paroissien, both of whom had been officially commissioned by Peru in 1821 to encourage European interest and investment in Peruvian mining enterprises. Paroissien had seen Potosí in 1810 when he joined the first unsuccessful Argentine expedition to liberate Upper Peru from Spain. The new company failed in 1826, quickly bankrupted by ignorance of local conditions, prodigal spending and transport difficulties; its general incompetence and misfortune resulted in considerable loss of confidence in the region among potential investors overseas. For details, see E. Temple, *Travels in various parts of Peru, including a year's residence in Potosí*, 2 vols. (London, 1830), and *A Brief Account of the Proceedings of the Potosí, La Paz, and Peruvian Mining Association, drawn up at the request of the Shareholders, by their late Secretary Edmond Temple* (London, 1829); also R. A. Humphreys, *Liberation in South America, 1806–1827. The career of James Paroissien* (London, 1952). Temple records meeting Pentland in Potosí (i, p. 300), although Pentland makes no mention of this in his report. Also *infra*, pp. 208–11.

[2] *paco*: a brown iron oxide containing particles of silver. The name is probably derived from 'alpaca' (Span., from Quechua, *paco*) because of the similarity in colour. *rodado*: scattered fragments of ore.

fail to give a return of 20 and 25 per cent. The ores extracted from the few mines which are worked, although containing in general a larger proportion of silver, seldom afford so handsome or so certain a profit to the miner. The *rodados* consist in general of portions of the sides of the veins, and of the porphyritic rock in which some metallic particles are disseminated. These scattered fragments of ore are formed of sulphuret and native silver, and of that variety of ore called *paco*, an hydrate of iron resulting from the decomposition of argentiferous pyrites. At the present day, four-fifths of the silver produced in the Potosí mineral district is obtained from this class of ores.

There are now in Potosí and in its suburbs 15 metallurgical establishments (*ingenios*) for the separation of the silver from its ores in operation, besides a great number in a state of ruin. Each of the *ingenios* at work produces from 80 to 100 marks weekly. The number of persons actually employed does not reach 2,000, of whom 1,450 are employed in the mines and in separating the ore in the mountain, and 450 in the 15 metallurgical establishments above mentioned.

The quantity of silver produced by the 15 *ingenios* amounted in 1826 to 53,130 marks, besides which about 1,000 marks are weekly obtained by individuals in their own houses from ores collected by a species of theft so that the total amount of silver may be assessed at 100,000 marks, or nearly 900,000 dollars, as the produce of the mines of Potosí during the past years.

It is impossible to ascertain the exact quantity of silver which the mines of Potosí have produced since their discovery, the registers which might have afforded this information having been destroyed during the Revolution. Statements I am aware have been published by Baron de Humboldt and others, but they are founded on error, insofar as instead of representing the produce of the mines of the Potosí district *alone*, they embrace the total of the silver coined at the Mint of that city, which comprises also that produced by many of the other mines of Upper Peru.

Of many causes which have contributed to the decadence of these mines, none has had a greater influence than the injudicious manner in which the three principal veins were worked after their discovery, and the difficulty which has attended on clearing out the old works at a subsequent period, from ignorance on the part of those who undertook it. The decreasing capital arising from the ruin of many of the mines during the Revolutionary struggle, and the want of confidence in the different governments which have succeeded each other during the eventful period, have also contributed of latter years to the reduced state in which those celebrated mines were situated when the provinces of Upper Peru declared their independence.

It is a prevailing idea, but a most erroneous one, that the mines of Potosí have been worked out, and that their future prosperity must fall off under any circumstances. This notion, imbibed by persons who have not visited the locality, appears to be unfounded, and I cannot adduce a more convincing proof that it is, than that at the present day at the close of the Revolution which has desolated Potosí more than any other province of Upper Peru, the produce of its mines has gone on increasing since tranquillity has been restored, and that this increase in the past years has amounted to 260,000 dollars. This increase has continued during the first three months of 1827 whilst I remained in Bolivia, and there is every reason for believing that instead of 900,000 dollars which these mines produced in 1826, their produce will reach, if it does not exceed, 1,300,000 dollars in 1827.

From enquiries which I instituted when at Potosí, the working of the *rodados* scattered over the surface of the Cerro, without entering on mining operations properly speaking, would furnish alone 20,000 marks of silver monthly, or nearly two million dollars annually, supposing the necessary supply of quicksilver to be obtainable at a moderate price, the introduction of certain improvements in the process of amalgamation, and the necessary number of workmen. I do not hazard this as my own opinion; it is the result of information received from respectable persons long engaged in mining operations, who have no object in drawing too flattering a picture of the branch of industry in which they are engaged.

Many of the drawbacks under which this district has laboured being removed, and as those which still continue will gradually cease to exist, I am persuaded that with returning peace and tranquillity the mines of Potosí may be made to produce, under an improved system of mining, and under certain improvements of the metallurgical process, a much greater quantity of silver than they now do; and by continuing the great adit and attacking the three principal veins at inferior levels, the day will yet arrive, when the mines of Potosí will regain their former celebrity, and attain a degree of importance in no wise inferior to that of the most productive mining districts of the New World.

(ix) PORCO. The mines of Porco appear to have been worked long prior to the Conquest and to have furnished a considerable part of the silver in use at the Court of the Incas. They had passed into the hands of some Biscayan adventurers prior to 1545 who abandoned them for those of Potosí. They continued to be worked for many years afterwards, but on the principal mine falling in, when many

lives were lost, the mines of Porco were abandoned and have remained so until the present day.

(x) CIPORRO. The mines of Marca or of Ciporro [or Siporo], the
property of a Spanish nobleman, the Marqués de Cazares, are situated at a short distance from Potosí. They formerly produced very
large quantities of silver, the principal ore being an argentiferous
bournonite[1] containing a large proportion of this precious metal;
these mines abound also in argentiferous sulphurets of lead and
copper. The mines of Ciporro have remained abandoned during the
Revolution, and the possession being now disputed, it is probable
that they will remain for some years longer in the same state.

(xi) PORTUGALETE. On the prolongation of the porphyritic chain
of Potosí and of Porco into the Province of Chichas, several important
mining establishments are situated, including those of Portugalete
which in point of importance occupy after Potosí, the first place
among the mines of Bolivia. These mines owe their present prosperity to an enterprising Biscayan miner who during his residence
at Portugalete has realized a handsome fortune, and introduced
various improvements into the process of amalgamation, a circumstance to which the productive state of these mines is mainly to be
attributed.

The ores of Portugalete consist chiefly of argentiferous galenas
and grey copper, containing 3 to 5 ounces of silver per 100 pounds.
The produce of these mines now averages 4,400 marks of silver
monthly or, in the course of the year, upwards of 400,000 dollars;
and as it is proposed to introduce the Saxon mode of amalgamation[2] this amount will thereby be increased considerably, and
it is calculated that their produce in 1827 will exceed 700,000
dollars.

(xii) LIPEZ. This province, situated in the centre of the Andes, contains several mining districts, which the inclemency of its climate,
the absence of population, and the want of the necessaries of life
have caused to remain for the most part abandoned. The *Mineral de*

---

[1] An antimonial sulphide of lead and copper, named after Count Bournon, the
French mineralogist who first described the rock in Cornwall in 1804.

[2] In 1784–7, improved methods of amalgamation were developed in Saxony by
Ignaz Born. These involved the treatment of the silver ore with mercury, salt,
roasted iron or copper pyrites, and water in closed containers, instead of in the
open air. The Saxon method, therefore, was largely one of mechanical improvement whose chief advantages were marked reductions in the consumption of
mercury and salt, as well as considerable saving in physical effort and processing
time. Also *supra*, p. 191n. and *infra*, p. 204.

Ubina situated 45 leagues from Potosí is said to equal the richest mining district of Bolivia in the abundance of its ores. The mines near to San Cristobal, the capital of the province, those of Concha and of Tomave have been worked and subsequently abandoned, and at the present day no regular work is carried on in any mining district of this province, although the inhabitants still extract a small quantity of silver to the amount of 4,000 marks, or 35,000 dollars, annually.

(xiii) ATACAMA. The principal mining riches of Atacama consist in its copper ores which are extremely abundant but have not been hitherto worked, there being no demand for that metal. The opening of the port of Cobija[1] will be attended with beneficial advantages to this branch of industry in procuring a market for the only important article of export which this miserable province possesses. Silver mines are also said to exist in the Province of Atacama but I am not aware of their having been worked. Iron mines were also reported to exist and to have been worked by the inhabitants of Atacama, who were said to extract an excellent quality of that metal which has been carried into the Province of Salta. The existence of these mines is not true; the iron which the people of Atacama have carried into the neighbouring provinces being procured from an immense mass of native iron of meteoric origin resembling entirely that discovered in Siberia by Pallas,[2] and similar to the large fragment of native iron which lies near to the town of Santiago del Estero in the Buenos Ayrian Province of that name, which was described many years ago by Señor Ruben de Celis.

(xiv) AULLAGAS. The mines which surround the miserable village of Aullagas in the Province of Chayanta, at one period were only inferior to those of Potosí in importance. They are situated on metalliferous veins traversing from east to west an insulated porphyritic mountain which in some measure resembles that of Potosí and like the latter is also placed at a very great elevation. The climate is consequently cold and the country unproductive, but as it is placed in the centre of a populous district, it possesses the great advantage of furnishing an abundant supply of miners at modest wages. Before the Revolution, some of the mines of Aullagas were highly productive, furnishing a large proportion of the silver coined annually at Potosí. They were then chiefly in the hands of Spaniards or of per-

---

[1] *Infra*, pp. 221-4.
[2] Peter Simon Pallas (1741–1811), the German naturalist and traveller, who made the discovery while on the celebrated scientific expedition from St. Petersburg into Siberia, 1768–74.

sons attached to the Royal cause who were compelled to abandon them on the entrance into Upper Peru of the expedition of Belgrano, which for months desolated the Province of Chayanta. The ravages committed by this and the subsequent Buenos Ayrian expedition in 1815, and the occupation of the province afterwards by a large armed force under the Viceroy [earlier General] Pezuela, prevented the working of the mines from being entered on.[1] In this state they have remained until the present day when the mines of Aullagas do not produce one mark of silver.

In 1826, a company of merchants was formed with a capital of 60,000 dollars, to complete an adit leading to the shaft of La Gallofa, one of the most celebrated mines of this district, the former produce of which is almost fabulous, but which had remained unworked for several years. This adit is likely to be completed during the present year when it is expected that the mines of Aullagas will not yield even to those of Potosí in productiveness. Besides the mine of Gallofa, those of Colquechaca and of Taxardo gave large returns until within the last twenty years, the former the property of a German miner whom the political events of the times obliged to abandon it.

The ores of the Aullagas mines consist of native silver of antimonial and red silver ore, of sulphuret of silver, and of argentiferous sulphurets of lead and of copper. These ores have been hitherto exclusively worked by the process of amalgamation, and here the introduction of the smelting furnace would prove particularly advantageous, especially as the ores can be easily transported into the adjoining valleys where combustible may be obtained in sufficient quantity at 5 or 6 leagues from the mines. I do not know a more favourable situation for a mining company possessed of from 150,000 to 200,000 dollars than the district of Aullagas; the mines of Taxardo, of Colquechaca, and of Gallofa might be had on very advantageous terms from their present proprietors who do not themselves possess the necessary capital to place them in a state of activity. The mines of Colquechaca, by the introduction of pumps of the simplest and less expensive kind, would in a short time produce a sufficient quantity

---

[1] In all, three expeditions were despatched from Buenos Aires between 1810 and 1815 in an effort to liberate Upper Peru from Royalist control, and retain the region's economic and strategic advantages within the Argentine sphere. Balcarce and Castelli led the 1810 expedition, Belgrano that of 1812–13, and Rondeau the final expedition in 1815. Hostility aroused in Upper Peru by the savage conduct, particularly of the first Argentine expedition, the great distances and altitudes involved, the unexpected strength of the Royalist forces in Upper Peru, and existing heavy commitments in Chile and the Banda Oriental (Uruguay) all combined to deter Buenos Aires from mounting any further liberating campaigns in the region.

of silver to enable a company to work the other mines without any considerable additional outlay, and to obtain larger quantities of silver than the mines of Aullagas ever before produced. Aullagas possesses advantages not frequently to be met with, in its position in the midst of a province abounding in agricultural productions, in a numerous and peaceable population, in an advantageous situation for the construction of the necessary machinery to be employed in the extraction of the silver from its ores, and in the abundance of combustible for these operations.

(xv) MOROMORO. To the east of Aullagas are situated the mines of Moromoro and Maragua which in addition to their silver ores produce others of cobalt, antimony and arsenic. The ores of antimony, containing a minute proportion of gold, were formerly worked for this precious metal but at the present day the silver ores of Maragua are the only ones which are extracted. The mines of Maragua produced in the past year 5,000 marks of silver, or about 45,000 dollars.

(xvi) OCURI. Near to the Indian village of Ocuri in the same Province of Chayanta several silver mines were formerly worked, all of which are now abandoned. According to some German miners who examined this district, considerable veins of oxide of tin exist in porphyritic mountains near to this village, but the scarcity of fuel at this great elevation and the great distance of Ocuri from the sea coast, the only market for the purchase of this metal, render it probable that the tin mines, however productive they may be, will long continue abandoned.

In addition to the mines above mentioned, there exist several others less important in the Province of Chayanta; two leagues north of Chayanta are situated the antimony mines of Capasilca which formerly produced a large amount of gold; near to the villages of Chipasa and Pocoata are numerous gold stream works still productive.

The rainy season having prevented my visiting the Province of Chayanta, the information which I have given respecting its mines has been derived principally from persons resident at Chuquisaca and Potosí engaged in mining operations in that province. A large quantity of gold is actually produced from the different stream works of Chayanta, which His Excellency General Sucre has informed me amounted in 1826 to nearly 400,000 dollars.

As a mining province, that of Chayanta holds the next rank to Potosí amongst those of Bolivia; with returning order and tranquillity, and with the aid of European capital and science, the mines of Aullagas, Maragua and Ocuri will not yield in importance to any other of the Republic. The increasing commercial intercourse with foreigners will procure for this province a market for some of her mineral productions now neglected, such as cobalt and antimony, and in taking a prospective glance over the many mining resources of this province, I think I am justified in saying that under the present Government, before five years shall have passed over, the produce of the gold and silver mines of Chayanta will reach 1,500,000 dollars.

(xvii) CHOQUECAMATA. In the many valleys of the Department of Cochabamba which descend from the Eastern Cordillera of the Andes, and from the mountains of the Yuracares Indians, small quantities of gold have been and are still collected; but the only regular undertaking which this Department possessed was that of Choquecamata in the Province of Ayopaya. The mines of Choque-camata, as they were improperly called, consisted in stream works similar to those of Tipuani; they are said to have produced as much as two and three millions of dollars in gold in one year during the last century. About twenty years ago, two German mineralogists sent out to explore the mines of Peru by the Spanish Government, undertook the working of the Choquecamata stream works. After having expended large sums in constructing an aqueduct to convey the necessary water to the excavations, they were obliged to abandon them, the Government refusing them any further assistance. In this state they still remain, although I have been assured they offer very great advantages and might even now be commenced on without any considerable outlay.

In the detailed review which I have taken in the preceding pages I trust that I have furnished you with the principal information respecting the mines of Bolivia which I am directed by your instructions to obtain, in addition to which I have to inform you that I have collected the ores of the different mines which I have visited and which I have now the honor to transmit to you. In conclusion it remains for me to examine under a more general point of view the present state of the mines of Bolivia: the disadvantages under which they now labour, how far these disadvantages may be removed by the introduction of European science and industry, to determine the quantity of the precious metals which the mines of Bolivia formerly produced, that which they produce at present, and that which they may produce hereafter, and finally the advantages which may result from the introduction of foreign capital, and the benefits to be derived by foreigners by embarking in this branch of Bolivian industry.

The disadvantages or drawbacks under which the mining industry of Bolivia labours at the present day may be classed under want of capital, scarcity of workmen, irregularity in the supply of quicksilver, want of knowledge among those engaged in mining operations, and the high duties levied by the Government on the produce of the mines.

No cause has operated more forcibly towards this decadence of the mines than the want of capital, a necessary consequence of the lengthened contest in which the provinces of Upper Peru have been engaged. On no class of its inhabitants has it fallen with more severity than on the proprietors of mines, and to it is to be attributed the abandoned state of many of the most productive mines of the Republic. Since the restoration of tranquillity, many who do possess capital have preferred embarking it in commercial transactions which may now be said to absorb the great mass of the capital possessed by the citizens of Bolivia. But as the profits arising from trade [esp. in domestic manufactures] are gradually decreasing, and as severe losses have been experienced through ignorance, it is natural to expect that a large proportion of the capital embarked in foreign commerce will be directed into some channel of national industry, and no other offers greater temptations or more brilliant prospects of success than the working of the mines.

Considerable apprehensions are entertained by the proprietors of some of the mining districts, that a limited and inadequate supply of workmen will be the necessary consequence of the abolition of the forced labour to which the indigenous population was subjected under the ancient system. You will be probably aware that the *mita*, or compulsory labour of the Indians, existed up to the time of the Declaration of Independence, and still remains in force in some provinces of Lower Peru, whilst it has been abolished throughout Bolivia. A cause, however, which has more contributed to the decrease in the number of miners than the abolition of the *mita*, is the harsh treatment which this as well as every other class of the aborigines have experienced from either party during the Revolution, and which has forced a large proportion of those inhabitating the towns and mining districts to fly into the remote and more tranquil regions of the Andes. From this cause some mining districts have suffered, such as Potosí, whilst in many others no such decrease is complained of. To remedy, however, the inconveniences which might arise in some points from the abolition of the *mita*, the Bolivian Congress and Executive have promulgated regulations in the respective duties of the proprietors of the mines and of their Indian workmen which have already been attended with beneficial results. It will require some time, however, to induce the Indian, rendered timid and suspicious from former ill-treatment, to return to his former dwellings. Already, however, does he see peace and tranquillity diffusing itself, he begins to understand that there now are laws to prevent oppression from the white population, and that under the new order of things he is a free member of society and no longer to be subjected to slavery, and to that brutal treatment which was but too often his recompense under his former masters. He will gradually desert, therefore, his mountain haunts to enjoy a more civilized life. I am of opinion, therefore, that the want of workmen now experienced in some mining districts will be of short duration and that the apprehensions entertained as touching the decrease of mining industry on this head will prove unfounded.

Among the causes which have materially contributed to the decreasing produce of the mines of late years, that arising from the irregularity in the supply of quicksilver deserves particular notice. During the dominion of Spain, the sale of quicksilver in every part of her American colonies belonged to the Treasury, a want of this necessary metal was therefore seldom experienced and as the Government derived a large revenue from the duties levied on the precious metals, it was its interest to secure a constant supply of quicksilver to the miners at a moderate price.[1] The newly constituted Government not possessing the necessary funds to continue this very useful system, the trade in quicksilver has passed into the hands of individuals and ceased to be a monopoly. The consequences have been that supplies have become most irregular and the prices exorbitant, so much so, that it may be said that in one-half of the mines of Bolivia the works were suspended at the end of 1826 and commencement of 1827 from a total want of this metal. While the monopoly of quicksilver remained in the hands of the Government under the former system its price never exceeded 73 dollars per 100 lbs even in the most remote districts, whilst in the years 1825 and 1826 it has varied from 120 to 150 dollars, a circumstance which in itself is sufficient to explain the decrease in the produce of the silver mines when compared to what it has been in the past century.[2] Various

[1] Mercury for the mining industry in Upper Peru came from the famous quicksilver deposits at Huancavelica in Lower Peru, where in 1570 Spain had established a State monopoly in production and distribution of this metal on which the amalgamation process for obtaining silver and gold from medium- and low-grade ores depended.

[2] The situation had deteriorated during the Revolutionary period. The trebling of the price of Peruvian quicksilver by 1819 had been accompanied by severe new credit restrictions on mining and mercury-amalgamation enterprises in Upper Peru. As the wars of independence continued, Potosí's Bank of San Carlos, founded by royal decree in 1782, recalled many loans in the early 1820s, thus accelerating the economic collapse of the region. See Tibor Wittman, 'Andean Nations in the Making', *Etudes Historiques* (Hungarian Academy of Sciences, 1970), pp. 157–82.

plans have been proposed to remedy the evil complained of, and the Bolivian Executive is about to enter on a contract for a regular supply of this metal from the mines of Europe.

To remedy the inconveniences arising from the want of knowledge in the art of mining, the Bolivian Government has established two Schools of Mines, one at Potosí and another at La Paz. It is the wish of His Excellency General Sucre to introduce European professors into those establishments, and for that purpose he has requested that I should engage a fit person in England to place at their head, and to procure the necessary instruments. In these schools a number of pupils will receive a gratuitous education and will be afterwards distributed throughout the mining districts of the Republic. This diffusion of knowledge will be attended with very beneficial effects to this important branch of national industry, and will change a blind art into one established on more certain and fixed principles, and in destroying the prejudices which exist in the minds of many against mining speculations from the uncertainty which has hitherto attended them, will direct a larger mass of the capital of the country into this channel of Bolivian industry. The great division of mining property in the two Perus amongst a number of persons who only hold a kind of life tenure of the property, may be reckoned as one of the most serious drawbacks which have attended the mining prosperity of those countries. The object of each person engaged in mining has been consequently to obtain in his own life-time as large a quantity of the precious metals as he could, without having any regard to the modes of working, the safety of his workmen, or the interests of those who surround him. This, added to the want of knowledge of the art of mining, has caused most of the works to be carried on in a rude and barbarous manner, consisting of tortuous shafts and galleries badly ventilated and where every thing is done by manual labour. The most simple machinery is as unknown as the more complicated combinations of the steam engine. The art of mines in fact remains at the present day nearly in the same state as it existed three centuries ago, when the first Biscayan miners introduced the improvements of their country on the rude operations of Indians.

The high duties levied on the precious metals form a general and very just cause of complaint amongst the proprietors of mines. These duties are the same as during the Spanish Government: silver pays a duty of $11\frac{1}{2}$ per cent under the name of *Derechos de Cobos y Diezmos*, besides 4 *reales* on each mark as Mint dues to defray the expenses of coinage; amounting in all to nearly $18\frac{1}{2}$ per cent whilst the duties on gold amount to $8\frac{1}{2}$ per cent, or nearly one-half of that levied on silver.

In addition, the export duty on coinage leaving the country amounts to 2 per cent since as the law now stands, the precious metals are not permitted to be exported under any other form. The duties on precious metals have always formed an important branch of the public revenue of the Spanish colonies, and which it will be difficult to do away with entirely in the present state of the Bolivian finances. It is in contemplation to propose to the ensuing Congress the reduction of the present duties, and both His Excellency General Sucre and the Minister of Finance are well disposed to diminish or even repeal such an impolitic taxation as an encouragement to this most important branch of national industry.

The use of machinery in the mines of Bolivia appears to me, generally speaking, inapplicable as regards those works already begun. The application of machinery in every mine is two-fold: for the removal of the water, and for the extraction of the ores, rubbish, etc. To attain the first of these objects, the general practice has been to cut adits or draining galleries, whilst manual labour has been exclusively employed in effecting the second. Adits are certainly better for draining off the water from mines than the more complicated description of machinery, since they are constant in their action and in general easily executed. They are, besides, the only mode applicable to the present tortuous and irregular form of the shafts and galleries. To aid them in their operation, the introduction of pumps would be attended with great advantage in every mining district of the Republic for the purpose of conveying the water from inferior levels into the canal of the adits. This is the only improvement which appears to me applicable towards the draining of many excellent mines as far as machinery is concerned, and which remain abandoned from a total ignorance of their use and construction.

The application of machinery in the extraction of the ores is still more limited; in all mines already commenced upon, their removal must still be effected by manual labour. In some few instances, short railways might be formed in the galleries or along those adits of sufficient width, for the transport of the ores; but such exceptions do not bear against the general fact that in the present state of the mines of Bolivia, the more complicated description of machinery cannot be applied with advantage, either in the extraction of the water, or in the removal of the ores, rubbish, etc. But if the applications of European science are not likely to be attended with advantage in facilitating the miners' operations, such is not the case as regards those of the metallurgist, where the introduction of many processes for the separation of the silver from its ores are likely to be attended with beneficial effects to the mining industry of Bolivia.

The process of amalgamation, or that effected by means of quick-silver, is exclusively followed in the extraction of the silver. This method which is well adapted to the poorer description of ores, or to those in which the silver and some of its combinations are disseminated in small quantity through a large mass of rock, becomes inapplicable to the richer ores where this precious metal is combined in large quantity with copper, lead, iron and mineralized by sulphur, as is the case in the majority of ores of the Bolivian mineral districts. Those ores consume a large quantity of quicksilver, the expense incurred consequently is great, and the metals with which the silver is combined are lost to the miner. To obviate these several disadvantages, smelting furnaces may be introduced to immense advantage in those places where fuel is to be met with, as in the districts of Sicasica, Aullagas and Portugalete, and I am persuaded that their introduction will add fully one-third to the produce of these districts in silver, a large quantity of lead and copper now lost will be obtained, and Bolivia will be released from the heavy tax which she now pays to Europe for quicksilver. There are, however, many ores of silver which it will be still more profitable to treat by the process of amalgamation. Here the Saxon method will be attended with great advantage over that actually in use; it will reduce the loss of quicksilver sustained from 10 per cent to $\frac{1}{2}$ per cent, it will diminish by three-fourths the expense of manual labour actually incurred, and it will enable the miner to work five times the quantity of ore which he now does. In the more remote districts, the complicated operations of the Saxon amalgamation may not be easily established. There, the present system of amalgamation may nevertheless be modified to advantage by calcining the ores with salt, by diminishing manual labour in the mixing of the amalgamating mass by means of mules and horses, or by changing the amalgamation in open air for the more expeditious process effected by heating the amalgamating matter in metallic boilers.[1]

Such are the principal ameliorations and improvements which appear to me to be required towards the future prosperity of the mines of Bolivia. In what precedes I have not referred to the many mines which remain to be discovered, or to those which have been little worked since their discovery. To both, every improvement in European mining is necessarily applicable. In them foreign capital will be profitably employed and perhaps to more advantage than in mines already commenced upon, but even these latter present a

---

[1] *Supra*, p. 195, n 2. Born's Saxon method of amalgamation had called for a multiple-barrel machine in which rotating shafts turned wooden barrels containing the mixture.

wide field for the investment of European capital, and for the application of European science and enterprise.

FORMER PRODUCE OF THE MINES

During my residence at Potosí I obtained a document exhibiting for each year the amount of duties levied on the silver registered at the Treasury of that city, from the earliest period up to the year 1800. From this and other official returns I have formed the annexed statement which represents the amount of silver registered at Potosí and the duties levied on it by the Spanish Government during the 280 years which the provinces of Upper Peru continued annexed to the Crown of Spain [*Appendix I*]. As the official statements which exist, however, only embrace the produce of the mines of the Potosí district, and of those in the more immediate vicinity, it is estimated that the produce of the other mines of Upper Peru amounted to one-fourth of the quantity registered at Potosí. It is also estimated that during the same period the amount of silver conveyed clandestinely from the country often reached one-half of the quantity which paid duties, and which is the only part noticed in the foregoing statement. Taking these circumstances into consideration, I have formed the second statement [*Appendix II*] which exhibits the total produce of the mines of Upper Peru in silver alone, from the earliest period until the separation of these provinces from Spain, from which it will be seen that the mines of Upper Peru have furnished to Europe since the Conquest the enormous sum of 1,614,045,538 dollars, or £322,809,108 sterling, forming a mass of pure silver weighing upwards of 46,000 tons.

There exists no document showing the quantity of gold produced during the same period. Indeed, a very small proportion of that collected remained in the country, arising from the exorbitant duties levied on it at an early period, and which led to nearly the whole of this metal being smuggled by European traders who frequented the coasts, or by the Portuguese colonists of the Brazilian provinces. From the amount coined of late years [*Appendix III*], there is reason to believe that since the discovery of the stream works on the eastern side of the Andes about the commencement of the 17th century, the amount of gold produced in the provinces of Upper Peru has seldom fallen short of 500,000 dollars, or £100,000 sterling, annually.

PRESENT PRODUCE OF THE MINES

The preceding documents [*Appendices I and II*] exhibit the quantity of the precious metals produced until the end of 1824 as far as can be obtained from the official returns which exist. Since then, the prosperity of the mines has gone on increasing, the following amount in silver having been registered at Potosí in the past two years:

1825 Marks 146,870 ($1,303,471)
1826 Marks 177,127 ($1,572,002)

But as this only included the silver of the mines of Potosí and of those in its immediate vicinity, it will be necessary to add to it the amount produced by the other mines of the Republic, and that which has been carried out of the country by contraband. From enquiries which I have made it appears that at least two-thirds of the amount registered has been produced by the other mines of Bolivia and smuggled to Arica and Buenos Ayres, so that for the past two years in question the total produce of the silver mines may be assumed at:

1825 Marks 244,780 ($2,172,424)
1826 Marks 295,202 ($2,619,918)

The amount of gold produced of late years is still more difficult to ascertain, since the entire quantity collected has been carried out of the country clandestinely. I have already shown however that the stream works of Tipuani and of other parts of the Department of La Paz have furnished to the amount of 500,000 dollars in 1826, and that from reports which I have received from General Sucre, those of Chayanta have produced nearly 400,000 dollars of the same metal during the past year. The total produce of the gold works of Bolivia may be estimated during the year 1826 at 800,000 dollars; and consequently the amount of the precious metals furnished by the provinces of Bolivia in 1826 will stand thus:

Silver $2,619,918 (£523,984)
Gold $ 800,000 (£160,000)
Total $3,419,918 (£683,984)

As to the future produce of the Bolivian mines, I have already shown that there is every reason to suppose there will be during the present year a considerable increase on that of the past, and I think this augmentation, on the most moderate calculation, may be reckoned at one-fourth the amount of last year's produce, so that we may conclude that the mines of Bolivia will furnish upward of 4,000,000 dollars, or £800,000, in the current year.

When we consider the many drawbacks under which these mines have hitherto laboured, the blind ignorance which has prevailed amongst those engaged in mining operations, and the rude processes used in the separation of the silver from its ores, it is impossible not to look forward to a very large augmentation in the produce of the precious metals on their removal, when the resources of the arts and sciences of Europe from which this branch of industry has remained debarred shall have been called in to its assistance.

I have endeavoured to point out the capabilities which the mines of Bolivia possess in the preceding pages of this report, and it only remains for me to express my opinion that in the midst of the peace, tranquillity and contentment now rapidly diffusing themselves throughout the Republic, the produce of its mines will continue to increase, and that before ten years shall have passed over, it will exceed what it did at any former period; I think I am not over-sanguine in my expectations in fixing the future amount of the Bolivian precious metals at 10,000,000 dollars, or £2,000,000 sterling. The mines of Bolivia offer a wide field for the employment of European capital and one from which large returns are likely to be obtained. Mines to any extent may be procured by the foreigner at a trifling expense among those possessed by the State, whilst individuals holding mines will be always ready to enter into advantageous terms with those who may undertake to work them. In the whole list of mining undertakings to which British capital has been applied within the last four years, I do not know a country which offers to the foreign miner the same advantages as those possessed by Bolivia. No country contains more productive mines under proper management, peace and harmony reign throughout the Republic, prosperity is rapidly diffusing itself, the foreigner will meet with every protection from the Government, and will be treated with kindness and hospitality by the inhabitants. Those petty jealousies which exist against foreigners in the maritime provinces of the late Spanish colonies are scarcely to be met with in Bolivia, and the introduction of foreign arts and sciences aided by foreign capital will be looked upon more as a blessing than as a detriment by those engaged in the same branch of industry.

The Bolivian Executive possesses extensive powers from the Legislature respecting encouragement to be granted to those foreigners who may embark in mining undertakings. I have received repeated assurances from the President of the Republic and from the members of the Government that it will be ever-ready to grant, as it has already done to foreigners, the same proprietory right in the possession of mines, as that secured by the existing laws to its own citizens.

MINING COMPANIES

Although in the preceding description of the several mining districts I have adverted generally to such mines in the working of which British capital had been employed, it is necessary to add a few observations for the purpose of showing the [degree of] success which has attended the British mining speculations.

Of the many companies formed in England during the years 1823, 1824 and 1825 for the purpose of working the mines of the New World, only two appear to have directed their attention to the mineral riches of Upper Peru, *viz.* the *Chilian and Peruvian Mining Association* and the *Potosí, La Paz, and Peruvian Mining Association.*

(i) The *Chilian and Peruvian Mining Association* had scarcely been formed, when it despatched an agent invested with extensive powers to contract for, and purchase, mines in Chile and in the two Perus. This person arrived at Buenos Ayres in 1825 from whence he proceeded by way of Salta to Potosí, at the former of which places he entered into contracts for some mines and for others situated in the Upper Peruvian provinces. But having deviated from his instructions, he was recalled by his employers and the contracts into which he had entered being in general conditional, were not ratified by the Directors of the Company at home.[1]

(ii) The *Potosí, La Paz, and Peruvian Mining Association.*[2] Of the unfortunate fate of this Company you are already informed, and as it may be the subject of much enquiry, it may not be unnecessary for me to notice here the leading circumstances attendant on its failure. It was formed in London in the early part of 1825. The proprietors were the two political agents of the Republic of Peru, who had been

---

[1] The Company's agent was Capt. Joseph Andrews, who recorded his experiences in *Journey from Buenos Ayres, through the Provinces of Córdova, Tucumán, and Salta, to Potosí, thence by the deserts of Caranja to Arica, and subsequently, to Santiago de Chili and Coquimbo, undertaken on behalf of the Chilian and Peruvian Mining Association in the years 1825–26,* 2 vols. (London, 1827).

Andrews modified and extended his itinerary, visiting Potosí and its mines between 15 October and 17 November, 1825. There he met Bolívar, Sucre and 'all the heroes of the Andes', ii, pp. 88–130. Later (pp. 197 and 203), Andrews records making the acquaintance of Pentland between 27 January and 2 February, 1826, when they travelled together in Chile on a return journey between Valparaiso and Santiago. Pentland had been instructed by Consul General Ricketts, who had arrived in Lima on 15 January, 1826, to make a short survey in Chile. Andrews noted, 'I now left Santiago in company with Mr. Pentland, before spoken of, who took an occasional shot when the carriage halted, in pursuit of his professional objects. For my own part I was too gloomy to enjoy any thing, brooding over the loss of my own humble efforts in the company's service, and seeing nothing propitious in prospect.'

[2] *Supra,* pp. 191–2.

sent by the Government of that country under the protectorate of General San Martín, to establish friendly relations with Great Britain, and who subsequently raised the first Peruvian loan in this country. The gentlemen were Don J. García del Río and General Paroissien, the latter an Englishman and a General of Brigade in the Peruvian service. On their assurances and representations, an Association was formed and mines were purchased from two Spanish noblemen who had possessed property at Potosí for the sum of £10,000 sterling. A nominal capital of one million pounds sterling was subscribed of which a first instalment of £50,000 was immediately paid; García was appointed President of the Association, and Paroissien Vice-President, Managing Director, and Chief Commissioner in Peru with a salary of £2,500. A second Commissioner, surveyors, engineers, mining officers, surgeons, secretaries, bookkeepers, clerks, assayers, chandlers, carpenters, gardeners, mechanics of every kind, with a proportionate number of Durham and Cornish miners were engaged, and no expense was spared in providing every thing that could contribute to the comforts and even to the luxuries of the officers of the Association.

A supply of iron, quicksilver, and of mining utensils was purchased, the latter in general little adapted to the mode of working pursued in these countries, a part of which could never have been carried into the mining districts arising from the difficulty of transporting packages beyond a determined weight across the Andes. A ship was taken up to convey the operatives, machinery, etc. to Arica at onerous charter. Delays took place in the time of her sailing and the voyage was long and protracted, and the expense incurred consequently great. At Arica, the Commissioners learned that the contracts which had been entered into for mines at Potosí were of little or no value as one of the proprietors had forfeited his title to the property which he disposed of to the Company, and that the other Spaniard had made over to them mines which then belonged to another branch of his family. An embargo was placed on the cargo immediately after the arrival of the ship at Arica for the payment of freight; and a second embargo was soon after placed on it by a merchant of Buenos Ayres who had advanced about £12,000 sterling to the agents of the Association on the faith of bills which the Directors in England had refused to accept. To meet this latter demand, and to minister to the wants of the many persons employed by the Company, the cargo was sold, and at a considerable loss, since most of the articles were unsuited to the market whilst the major part of the machinery was found perfectly useless, and still remains on the sands of Arica.

Although the value of this investment originally amounted to £24,000 sterling, it has not produced two-thirds of that sum after paying storage and commission charges, custom-house duties, etc. Of the persons employed by this Company, many have already returned to England, some have died,[1] whilst most of those who have sojourned at Arica have suffered severely from the effects of its pestilential climate. The whole of the first instalment of £50,000 sterling was expended on the cargo freight of the vessel, outfits to the persons engaged, calculating the heavy arrears of salary due to the officers of the Company, the expense of furnishing their passages back to Europe, and on several outstanding debts at Potosí and Arica. The Directors in England will still have to make good an amount falling little short of £30,000 sterling which, added to the preceding outlay of £50,000, will form a total of £80,000 sterling for ever lost to this Association.

Had the Potosí Mining Association gone judiciously to work by sending out in the first instance a few individuals under the direction of a person possessed of some practical knowledge in the art of mining, with a moderate establishment and a limited number of mechanics and miners to point out the more simple improvements of European mining to the Indian labourers, and have furnished to its agent a sufficient sum of money to meet the purchase of mines, to pay workmen, and with an assortment of the mining utensils immediately required, the Potosí Company by confining its operations to that district alone would I am persuaded have covered, ere this, the original outlay and have prospered. The native miner of Potosí derives at the present time a profit of from 20 to 25 per cent on the capital employed, and a company of foreigners possessed of capital, of superior knowledge, and enjoying every privilege and protection, may be reasonably expected to derive still greater advantages for its labours.

The Bolivian Government and His Excellency General Sucre manifested a lively interest in the proceedings and prosperity of this Association. Every favor sought by its agents from the authorities of the Republic was instantly acceded to, and for the first time I believe in Spanish America the old restrictive laws of the mining codes as relating to the possession of mineral property by foreigners were dispensed with, and the same privileges and advantages granted to them as those enjoyed by the citizens of Bolivia.[2] The agents of the

---

[1] Including Paroissien, who died at sea *en route* for England from Chile, 23 September, 1827. See Humphreys, *Liberation in South America*, p. 161.

[2] According to Edmond Temple, *Travels*, i, p. 401, President Sucre's comment on the Company's failure had been, 'I know not on which side folly is most

Potosí Company have continued to experience every facility and protection from the Executive and other local authorities, as well as hospitality and goodwill from every class of the Bolivian community.

GOLD STREAM WORKS

Several British merchants have entered into contracts for the gold *lavaderos*, or stream works, situated in the valley of Tipuani. Messrs Cochrane, Robertson & Co. of Lima purchased one half-share in some extensive *lavaderos* held by a person named Villarroel, stipulating to pay 280,000 dollars, or £56,000, and to furnish the funds required for carrying into effect certain projected works. Of the above amount 80,000 dollars (£16,000) were advanced, but owing to some embarrassment in the British firm, it was found impossible to make good any further advances, which has led to the contract being annulled. Therefore, excepting an inconsiderable amount realized from the workings of last year, the sum of 80,000 dollars advanced may be considered as lost to Messrs Cochrane & Co.

The House of Messrs J. Begg & Co., of Lima and Arica, purchased about the same time the property of a Spaniard at Tipuani where he is said to have realized very considerable wealth, and from which he was driven by the political events of 1825. This property, the most extensive in the district, consisting of extensive *lavaderos* and of rich plantations of cocoa trees, cost only 12,000 dollars or £2,400 sterling, and appears from every information which I have been able to collect, a very valuable acquisition. Messrs Begg & Co. intend to expend a certain amount during the present year for the purpose of ascertaining the capabilities of the different stream works as preparatory to the introduction of an improved mode of extracting and

glaring, or which party is most to blame—whether those who raised and dispatched this expedition without money, or those who embarked in it and left their homes without considering how they were to be supported, much less how they were to carry their gigantic plans into effect! *Los señores Ingleses* must have been reading the history of El Dorado with a little more credulity than it deserves, if they imagined that the precious metals were to be obtained without labour and expense; for, although it is true that they abound in this country, they cannot be had for *nothing*, any more than the materials of which we build our houses.'
Bolívar had ruled (2 August, 1825) that mines not worked for a year and a day were forfeited to the State which could then derive revenue from their sale or lease. On this subject, see also J. Miller, *Memoirs of General Miller in the service of the Republic of Peru*, 2 vols. (London, 1828, enlarged edit. 1829), ii, pp. 256–9 and 271–2; and G. Ovando-Sanz, 'British Interests in Potosí, 1825–1828; unpublished documents from the Archivo de Potosí', *Hispanic American Historical Review*, xlv (1965), pp. 64–87.

washing the auriferous soils, as noticed in the foregoing part of this report.

An Englishman named Page has associated himself with a native of Peru in the purchase of some gold *lavaderos* at Tipuani, in which they have expended a few thousand dollars. I am uninformed of the success which has attended their undertaking, as likewise of the precise amount invested in this purchase.

The firm of Messrs J. Begg & Co. above spoken of has, in company with a Buenos Ayrian merchant residing at La Paz, purchased a tract of auriferous soil at the base of the mountain of Illimani, and at the same time rented a small lake in the same district (in which the Indians are reported to have deposited large treasures at the period of the Conquest by the Spaniards) for an annual sum of 2,500 dollars. As the chances of succeeding in procuring this treasure are doubtful, it is probable that the British firm will ultimately withdraw itself from the copartnery.

COPPER MINES

A number of the copper mines of Corocoro in the province of Pacajes have been purchased by Messrs Begg & Co. for the trifling amount of 1,000 dollars, or £200, with the coal strata of Paxaqui in the same neighbourhood for the still more trifling sum of 150 dollars, or £30. In the event of the coal mines proving productive, as there is every reason to expect,[1] it is proposed to establish smelting works in the vale of Corocoro where copper ores may be procured in great abundance, and from which a large supply of copper may be obtained at the low rate of 4 or 5 dollars (16 to 20 shillings) per quintal. Production would not only be for the extensive consumption of the Bolivian and Peruvian provinces, but may also furnish an important article of foreign export to the European and East India markets, since it can be transported at a moderate expense to Arica or Iquique, the nearest ports on the shores of the Pacific.

The preceding observations will show that little benefit has heretofore attended the investment of British capital in the mining undertakings of this Republic, but it is evident that where failure has been the consequence, it cannot in any case be attributed to the poverty or unproductive state of the mines. Of the few mining undertakings still in the hands of British subjects, and I will notice particularly those at Tipuani, I entertain the most sanguine anticipation. In the description which I have given of the capabilities of the several mining districts in the foregoing pages of this report, I have

[1] *Supra*, p. 187n.

shown enough to prove that, under judicious management, British capital may be invested to very great advantage in the mines of Bolivia. No part of the South American continent offers at the present day a wider field for mining speculation than the Upper Peruvian provinces, under the protection of a liberal and enlightened Government which will extend its aid and protection to the foreign capitalist, and place him on an equal footing with its own citizens.

CHAPTER IV

A REVIEW OF THE COMMERCIAL RELATIONS, FOREIGN AND DOMESTIC

THE commercial relations of Bolivia may be classed under the three following heads: first, the trade which exists between the respective provinces of the Republic; second, that which is carried on with the states which surround her; and third, her foreign or ultramarine commerce.

INTERNAL TRADE

The objects of the home or interior trade consist of agricultural productions and manufactures. Of the former, the two principal are coca and grain, the produce of the eastern Departments which is carried in very large quantities into the more elevated regions of the Andes where mining operations fix a considerable mass of the population in the midst of unproductive districts. The trade in grain alone, from the Departments of Cochabamba and Chuquisaca, to those of Oruro and La Paz, amounts to 300,000 dollars annually.

The most important branch of the interior trade of the Republic is that of coca, which is cultivated in the eastern provinces of La Paz. The coca is the dried leaf of a shrub little known, the use of which is as essential to the Indian as his food; he chews it in the same way as the betel nut is used by the people of the East. The trade in coca is chiefly confined to the town of La Paz. It appears from the official returns of the Custom House of the latter place, that in the year 1826, the commerce in coca amounted to 719,800 dollars, or £143,960 sterling.[1]

The Department of Santa Cruz carried on a considerable traffic in sugar and cocoa with the more western provinces. This trade now

[1] Pentland had earlier noted that it was from the coca trade that the wealthy merchants in La Paz derived their principal income.

labours under great drawbacks from the distant situation of Santa Cruz, and the consequent difficulties of communication in a country where roads can scarcely be said to exist. The amount of sugar, cocoa and wax [*i.e.* beeswax], the produce of the Department of Santa Cruz, imported into the western Departments is estimated at 80,000 dollars, or £16,000 annually.

The remaining trade in agricultural productions consists of wines which are produced in the Province of Cinti [Department of Chuquisaca], and the small quantity of cocoa which is brought to La Paz from the Provinces of Apolobamba [or Caupolicán] and Moxos by way of Sorata and Pelechuco.

The only manufactures which deserve notice in a commercial point of view are those of Cochabamba and Moxos. The manufactures of Cochabamba consist chiefly of coarse cotton cloths (called *tocuyos* and barracans) made from cotton-wool, the produce of the maritime provinces of Lower Peru. The *tocuyos* are a kind of coarse, un-bleached cotton resembling the inferior description of North American calicoes; the barracan is a narrow blue calico much worn by the Indians, and not unlike the blue gurrahs of India. The consumption of these two articles was formerly very great, not only through Bolivia, but in the Peruvian, Chilian and Buenos Ayrian provinces, and it is said to have exceeded one million dollars annually. They were manufactured at Cochabamba and at Tarata in the same Department, and occupied upwards of 20,000 persons. At present their consumption is comparatively trifling and does not reach 80,000 dollars. This rapid decrease is owing to the introduction of British and Indian cotton goods, especially of that kind of glazed calico called Madopolams [Madapollams][1] of British manufacture, which may be said to have taken the place of the undyed *tocuyos* among all classes. The consumption of the dyed cottons of Cochabamba has not decreased in the same proportion, no similar article having been imported from Europe. But there is little doubt that the blue Indian calicoes will reduce the consumption of the barracans of Cochabamba, especially since the price of indigo has increased, and since the supply of this dye is procured with greater difficulty in Bolivia.

The Department of Cochabamba manufactures also glass and soap in which an active trade is kept up with the other provinces. The manufacturing of glass at Paredon produces an article of very inferior quality, from the want of care observed in its fabrication. Its con-

---

[1] Madapollam was a cotton cloth, intermediate between a calico and a muslin, which took its name from Madhavapalam on the delta of the Godavari river, south India.

sumption is in general amongst the middle and lower orders, and although it may have fallen off since the opening of the trade with Europe, the great distance from the sea coast and the difficulties of communication entail too heavy charges on the importation of European glassware to permit of its being generally used, particularly in the more remote provinces. The demand for the glassware of Paredon remains still considerable, and is likely to become even greater, since the Government has placed the manufacturing in the hands of a European artist, who will find in the country around all the necessary materials for making a glass of good quality, and at a cheap rate.

Soap is prepared in considerable quantities from the oil and soda which are produced in the same Department. This soap has been heretofore of extensive consumption throughout the provinces of Upper Peru. Within the last two years however, a considerable quantity of British soap, and some North American, has been imported into Arica, and carried from thence to La Paz, Oruro and Potosí, where it has met a ready sale to the exclusion of that of Cochabamba. The trade in this article merits the attention of the British merchant, as it is one of very extensive consumption in the interior provinces of both Upper and Lower Peru.

The manufactures of Moxos were introduced by the Jesuits amongst the Indians of that extensive province, and have reached an astonishing degree of perfection. They consist of cottons, in the form of ponchos, table-cloths, napkins, sheets, hammocks, etc., all of which are highly prized for their beauty and durability. The cotton is produced in the same province. This branch of industry now labours under great disadvantages from being placed in the hands of the civil Governors, which enhanced the price, and confined the consumption of these manufactures to the higher classes.[1]

The manufactures of Cochabamba and of Moxos hold the first rank among those of the Republic as forming objects of its interior commerce. There are others, however, but of much less importance than the two former; thus Oruro possesses a manufactory of tin vessels; Corocoro in the Province of Pacajes, of copper utensils; Sorata of ponchos, and Potosí of ironmongery, but none of those is

---

[1] Pentland noted that thirteen missions had originally been founded in the old Jesuit Mission-Reserve Province of Moxos (Mojos), and ten in the Province of Chiquitos, lying to the south and south-east. By decree of 18 November, 1842, the Province of Moxos formed the basis of Bolivia's new Beni Department. The Province of Chiquitos remained in the Department of Santa Cruz, which was officially created (with those of Chuquisaca, La Paz, Cochabamba, and Potosí) on 23 January, 1826.

sufficient to merit a place in a general review of the manufactures of the Republic as connected with its interior trade.

At the present day, the total amount of the manufacturing industry of Bolivia does not reach 300,000 dollars, or £60,000 sterling, formed out of the following items:

Cotton manufactures of Cochabamba	$ 80,000
Soap, glass, pottery, etc.	$ 30,000
Manufactures of Moxos	$ 40,000
Ponchos of Sorata, Copacabana and Cochabamba	$ 50,000
Tin manufactures of Oruro	$ 10,000
Copper manufactures of Corocoro	$ 25,000
Ironware of Potosí	$ 10,000
	$245,000

TRADE WITH THE NEIGHBOURING STATES

Brazil. The inhabitants of the Provinces of Chiquitos and Moxós, bordering on the Brazilian Empire, were interdicted under severe penalties from holding any commercial intercourse with the Portuguese possessions under their former Government. This system of non-intercourse has been abolished, but as the population of the countries forming the frontiers of each state is very thinly scattered over an immense extent of country, it is probable that under present circumstances the communications will not become much more frequent than formerly. The only article of traffic possessed by either country is salt, which is collected from the salt marshes of Santiago and of San José in the Province of Chiquitos, where it is procured by solar evaporation to the amount of 3,000 *arrobas* annually. This salt is consumed by the inhabitants of the Mato Grosso, and constitutes the only object of commerce which exists at the present day between the Bolivian and Brazilian provinces.

Buenos Ayres. During the many years when Upper Peru formed a part of the Buenos Ayrian Viceroyalty, an extensive commercial intercourse was kept up between the limiting provinces of these two countries. It consisted of the export from Upper Peru of the manufactures of Cochabamba and of Moxos, in return for which it imported great numbers of black cattle and horses from the Provinces of Rioja and Tucumán, and large quantities of *yerba* [*maté*], the growth of Paraguay. The European manufacturer having secured to the people of the Buenos Ayrian Provinces cotton goods of better quality and at a cheaper rate than those of Cochabamba, the trade in manufactures has ceased entirely. The difficulty of procuring the Paraguay tea has obliged the inhabitants of Upper Peru to search for a substitute here as elsewhere. This they have found in common tea, now growing into general use, whilst the *yerba*, formerly an article of the first necessity, is seldom used, and the quantity imported at the present day extremely trifling. The only branch of commerce which now exists between the Bolivian and Argentine provinces is that in mules and horses, and even this is very inconsiderable since in 1826 not more than 2,000 mules and horses were imported into Bolivia, forming an amount of 36,000 dollars.[1]

Lower Peru. The trade between Bolivia and the neighbouring Departments of Lower Peru still continues to be carried on to a considerable extent, the Governments of these two republics having agreed to impose a duty of 6 per cent on the produce and manufactures of the respective states.

The imports from Lower Peru consist of cotton-wool, the produce of the valleys of Sama and Locumba on the shores of the Pacific, of wines and brandies from Moquegua, and of the woolen manufactures of the Provinces of Puno and Cuzco. All the cotton-wool consumed in the manufactures of Cochabamba is grown in the maritime provinces of Lower Peru, whence it is carried in the rough unpicked state [*i.e.* not ginned] to Paria, a small town in the Province of Oruro,[2] whither the inhabitants of Cochabamba resort to purchase it. By a return made to me by the *corregidor* of Paria, the quantity imported in 1826 amounted to 8,000 loads or 800,000 lbs. From this it will be necessary to deduct one-half for the weight of the seed contained in it in the rough state, which will reduce the quantity of clean cotton-wool employed in the Cochabamba manufactures to 400,000 lbs, or 200 tons. The price of this cotton in the unpicked state averages 32 *reales* per 100 lbs delivered at Paria, or 18 *reales* on the coast of Peru, making the value of the total import to Paria 18,000 dollars. About one-quarter of the same amount is introduced into the Departments of La Paz and Potosí, so that the total value of the cotton-wool imported from Lower Peru may be estimated at 24,000 dollars.

The fertile valleys of Moquegua and of Tambo north of Arica produce large quantities of wines and brandies, which they export to Upper Peru. In a country like Bolivia where inebriety is the prevailing vice of the Indian population, the consumption of ardent spirits is necessarily great, and forms one of the most extensive

[1] The northward movement of Argentine livestock into Bolivia (mules, horses, cattle, sheep, and asses), *via* Jujuy and Salta, quickly revived, however.

[2] The Department of Oruro had been created by decree of 5 September, 1826.

C M—P

imports from the state of Lower Peru. The commerce in brandy occupies the great mass of the inhabitants in the two above-mentioned valleys, who transport it on mules over the Western Cordillera to La Paz, Oruro and Potosí.

The Peruvian manufactures imported into Bolivia consist of the coarse woolen cloths fabricated about Cuzco, Guamanga and Andahuaylas, and of carpeting, rugs and woolen ponchos from Puno and Lampa. The woolen cloths of Cuzco (*bayetas del Cusco*) [baizes] are narrow and of a coarse quality, dyed blue, and manufactured from the wool which is produced in the extensive plains of the Andes about Lampa and Puno. These manufactures have been gradually falling into ruin since the opening of the trade with Europe and their chief consumption is now confined to the more secluded districts of Lower Peru. Wherever they have come into competition with cloths of European manufacture, their consumption has rapidly decreased, arising from the cheapness and superior dye and finish of the latter. I have been assured by Don L. de la Cotero, one of the most wealthy and experienced Spanish merchants of Peru, that prior to the expulsion of the Spaniards from Upper Peru when the trade with Pacific ports was forbidden, he himself was in the practice of importing from Cuzco to Potosí woolen manufactures to the amount of 480,000 and 500,000 dollars (£100,000) annually.[1] At the present day, the import of the same articles to the whole of Bolivia does not reach 50,000 dollars, or £10,000 sterling.

From returns furnished by the Bolivian Custom Houses it appears that the amount of importations in 1826 from Lower Peru was nearly as follows:

Cotton-wool	$ 24,000
Brandies and woolen manufactures	$390,000
	$414,000

The chief articles of export to the provinces of Lower Peru which Bolivia possesses are her agricultural productions. Of those, a large quantity of flour and Indian corn is carried from the Department of Cochabamba to the maritime provinces of Lower Peru, and to those

[1] Cotero's headquarters were at Arequipa, Peru, where according to C. M. Ricketts's report to Canning, 27 December, 1826 (F.O. 61/8) this merchant had monopolized trade 'owing to his influence with Viceroy La Serna; and the consequence of the high prices which he charged on his goods was that the merchants of Buenos Aires were enabled to supply the articles required in Upper Peru at a cheaper rate'. Cotero had temporarily been able to boost the port of Quilca, *Reports*, p. 173 and *infra*. The Pacific ports were in fact reopened to Upper Peru after 1810.

of Puno and Chucuito. Bolivian manufactures still find their way to the same provinces, where the deep-rooted prejudices of the Indian population cause them to be sometimes preferred to the better articles of foreign manufacture. The trade in manufactures is, however, rapidly falling off, and is at present chiefly confined to Cochabamba ponchos, which are with reason preferred to those of European fabric, both for their beauty and durability. Large quantities of the coca leaf were formerly carried from Bolivia into Lower Peru, but since the cultivation of this plant has been introduced into the deep valleys of the Department of Cuzco, the exports of this article have decreased considerably, and are now confined to the Provinces of Arica, Chucuito and Puno.

The value of the exports from Bolivia to Lower Peru does not exceed 150,000 dollars, leaving a balance in favor of the latter country of 264,000 dollars (£52,800), which Bolivia is obliged to make good in specie.

COMMERCE WITH FOREIGN COUNTRIES

The geographical position which the Bolivian Republic occupies in the centre of the American continent, possessing a very limited extent of sea coast, and that barren and devoid of population, without an established port, has necessitated its inhabitants to draw their supplies of foreign merchandise from the ports of the maritime provinces of Peru and Buenos Ayres. This was still more necessary at a time when the Provinces of Upper Peru were annexed to either of those countries, and when it became the policy of Spain to reduce the points for the introduction of foreign merchandise to the fewest possible, in order to secure the monopoly of the trade of her South American possessions to her own subjects, and to guard against contraband on the part of the foreigners. It is thus that we find the commercial intercourse of the inhabitants of Upper Peru limited either to the ports of Arica and Quilca during the time when the Presidency of Charcas formed a part of the Viceroyalty of Peru, or to that of Buenos Ayres at a subsequent period.

Upon annexation of the Provinces of Upper Peru to the Viceroyalty of La Plata in 1776, a total change took place in the channels through which the foreign commerce of the latter passed. During the lengthened period when Upper Peru formed a part of the Peruvian Viceroyalty, these provinces received their foreign supplies and exported their treasure from the ports of the Pacific. But once annexed to Buenos Ayres, the principal port of Arica was closed by an order emanating from the Council of the Indies, which forbade any further foreign trade with the Viceroyalty of Peru, and directed that the Provinces of Upper Peru should henceforward receive their supplies of foreign merchandise from Buenos Ayres.[1] This trade continued until the Revolution broke out in 1809 and 1810, when the Provinces of La Plata established their separation from the mother country, and then endeavoured to secure that of the Upper Peruvian provinces also. The unsuccessful issue of the expeditions under Balcarce, Belgrano and Rondeau confirmed the Spaniards in the possession of the Presidency of Charcas, which was again annexed to the Viceroyalty of Peru, whilst the foreign commerce began to flow once more from the shores of the Pacific. During the struggle which continued in Upper Peru subsequent to the defeat of the Buenos Ayrian expedition in 1815, a considerable trade was carried on under the authority of the Spanish Government from Arica and Arequipa to these provinces, and from the ports of Iquique, Cobija and Copiapó by contraband.

With the destruction of the last Spanish force remaining in South America in 1825, that under General Olañeta, the new Republic of Upper Peru found its foreign commerce divided between the ports of Peru, and that of Buenos Ayres. As soon as tranquillity was established, the relations with Buenos Ayres became more frequent so that during the years 1825 and the early part of 1826, the trade to Bolivia was nearly equally divided between Buenos Ayres and the Pacific ports. The blockade of the river Plate caused the imports to fall off from that quarter,[2] and to increase proportionally from the ports of Peru, and especially from Arica where several British merchants had formed establishments about this period. In 1826 the Constituent Congress of Bolivia, in retaliation for the mysterious and disdainful conduct shown to the Bolivian Minister at Buenos Ayres by the Executive of the Argentine Republic, passed a law imposing a duty of 40 per cent on all merchandise coming from South American countries which had not formally acknowledged the independence of Bolivia. This law, which was intended to apply particularly to

[1] Trade between Upper and Lower Peru was not completely severed after the former's transfer to the Viceroyalty of the Río de la Plata. The import of foodstuffs, textiles and fibres from Lower Peru, the through-trade in imported foreign manufactured goods, and the export of small quantities of minted gold and silver from Potosí all remained legitimate. But the prohibition in July 1777 on the export of gold and silver bullion from Upper Peru except through Buenos Aires effectively channelled most of the trade of those provinces, including the return flow of European imports, through that port. See Lynch, *Spanish Colonial Administration, 1782–1810*, pp. 40–5.

[2] Disputed ownership of the Banda Oriental (which became the independent State of Uruguay on 25 August, 1828) led to Brazil's declaration of war against Argentina in December 1825, and its blockade of the Plate river ports.

Buenos Ayres, has come into force at the commencement of 1827, and has put a stop to all commercial intercourse between the Buenos Ayrian and Bolivian provinces.[1]

The foreign trade to Bolivia is carried on exclusively from the port of Arica at the present day, the imports from Quilca by way of Arequipa being extremely trifling. On all articles of foreign produce destined for the Bolivian market imported through Arica, the same exorbitant duties are levied as if intended for the consumption of Lower Peru, no difference being made in this latter country between duties on transit and consumption. This system obliges Bolivia to pay a most onerous tax to Peru for the use of one of her ports, whilst it excludes the inhabitants from the use of many articles of European manufacture which they would possess under a better regulated system. These inconveniences, arising from the want of an established port in her own territory, induced His Excellency General Sucre to enter into negotiations for the possession of the port of Arica. A treaty was agreed on at Chuquisaca between the Bolivian Executive and Peruvian Chargé d'Affaires in November 1826 to that effect, Bolivia ceding two of her provinces [Copacabana and Apolobamba] in exchange for those of Arica and Tarapacá, and taking on herself 5,000,000 dollars, or one-half of the foreign debt of Lower Peru. The ratification of this treaty was refused by the Government of the latter country in opposition to the wishes of the inhabitants of the ceded provinces, and Bolivia is now obliged to have recourse to one of the ports of her own territory in the Province of Atacama.[2]

The port of Cobija is looked upon as the best calculated for this object.[3] It is said to be in every respect adapted for shipping, although it now labours under great disadvantages arising from its scanty population, its situation in an unproductive country, and its not possessing at present a sufficient supply of fresh water for a larger population. It is also situated at a considerable distance from

[1] Argentina had refused to recognize Bolivia on the grounds that it was still occupied by Colombian troops and that its new President, Sucre, was a foreigner. The principal points of discord, however, were that an independent Upper Peru violated the general principle of *uti possidetis de jure 1810*, and, more particularly, that Bolivia's ownership of the Province of Tarija was still disputed.

[2] Bolivia had offered to exchange its portion of Lake Titicaca north of the Tiquina Strait, together with the Copacabana peninsula and Apolobamba (Caupolicán) province, for ownership of Peru's provinces of Arica and Tarapacá. If agreed, this would have given Bolivia a Pacific seaboard totalling some 600 miles (to 18°S), in order to include the plain and port of Arica on which the whole transaction pivoted. Not surprisingly, President Sucre's proposals were rejected by Peru under Andrés Santa Cruz.

[3] For a discussion of Bolivia's struggle at this time to establish a port on the Pacific, see Fifer, *Bolivia*, pp. 36–51.

the large towns and populous districts of the interior. When Bolívar was occupied in settling the affairs of Upper Peru in 1825, he sent Colonel O'Connor, a British Engineer Officer in the service of Colombia, to report on the practicability of forming Cobija into a port. I have perused this report in which Colonel O'Connor gives his opinion that although Cobija is not at present in a state to receive shipping owing to the disadvantages above mentioned, yet he is decidedly of opinion that as a commercial centre it possesses many advantages in its salubrious climate, its good anchorage, and the abundant pasturage for beasts of burthen in the vicinity. A plentiful supply of fresh water may be procured by sinking wells in the neigh-bourhood of the port.[1] He further states that the road leading into the interior is in general good, and might be rendered fit for wheeled vehicles to within 25 leagues of Potosí, and that food, pasturage and water may be procured at short stages by constructing posthouses on the roads. Colonel O'Connor estimates that 202,270 dollars would suffice to execute the necessary works at Cobija to place it in a situation to receive shipping, and to construct the necessary post-houses on the road leading into the interior as far as Potosí. I have been also informed by the Prefect of Oruro, that the road from Cobija is still better to this latter town, than that leading to Potosí, that it is also shorter, and traverses a part of the Cordillera which is open at all seasons of the year. By this road the communications between Cobija and the northern Department of La Paz will be facilitated through the navigation of the river Desaguadero of which I shall speak hereafter.[2]

In order to grant every encouragement to trade through Cobija, the Bolivian Congress passed a law by which all foreign imports through this port are only subjected to a duty of 2 per cent *ad valorem*.[3] This in itself offers a sufficient inducement to the native merchant to draw his supplies from Cobija, when it is considered that all imports from Buenos Ayres *now* pay a duty of 55 per cent, and those from the Peruvian Pacific ports from 45 to 92 per cent.[4]

---

[1] Francis Burdett O'Connor, Sucre's Irish *aide-de-camp*, could have had no evidence for these last statements. Cobija is one of the driest sites on the Atacama coast; quantities of fresh water, food and fodder had always to be imported from the Calama oasis in the interior, or coastwise from Arica and Valparaiso.

[2] *Infra*, p. 227.

[3] Law dated 24 February, 1827.

[4] Merchants were to complain, however, that the heavy losses, delays and damage to goods suffered during the six hundred-mile journey between Cobija and the Andean towns rendered the port unacceptable to them on virtually any terms. Cobija was particularly remote from the major commercial centres of La Paz and Cochabamba whose trade ties were with Arica and Arequipa.

The Bolivian Government is extremely anxious to place Cobija in a state to receive shipping. In order to do so, it is proposed to apply any excedent of the revenue to this object, or to raise a loan among the native merchants of the amount required. No anchorage or port dues are to be levied for the present, and to encourage the foreign merchants to remove to this port, a decree is about to be published imposing from October 1827 an additional duty on all foreign merchandise brought into the Bolivian provinces through the ports of Peru. The strict enforcement of this decree must inevitably lead to the ruin of Arica, and will probably induce the foreign agents at that port to remove to Cobija (Atacama).[1]

It is admitted on all sides that the port of Cobija possesses advantages over that of Arica, for example in its position relative to the Provinces of Salta and Tucumán, whence beasts of burthen employed in the transport of merchandise into the interior may easily be procured at a cheaper rate than on the coast of Peru. The distance from Cobija to Salta is 80 leagues, and the road is represented as good and level.[2] The opening of this port will enable the northern province of the Buenos Ayrian federation to export several products, such as hides, horns, hair, wool, to the European market.[3] This trade is at present prohibited by the difficulty of transport to the port of Buenos Ayres. Cobija will also furnish an outlet for the copper of Atacama, which may be obtained in large quantities. The low duties imposed on importations through Cobija will also give rise to an extensive contraband trade with the provinces of Lower Peru, whilst its vicinity to the Provinces of Salta and Tucumán will cause the latter to draw a large proportion of their foreign supplies from it, all of which circumstances must add to the importance of Cobija as a place of commerce.

Notwithstanding all those advantages adduced by the friends to

[1] Pentland's comment echoes one of President Sucre's oft-repeated pronouncements designed to bring pressure to bear upon Peru to cede Arica to Bolivia: 'Bolivia's acquisition of Arica is of the utmost importance. It will be a magnificent port for Bolivia, especially with a good road to Cochabamba. But if Peru retains it, we may declare Cobija a free port which will cause Arica to decline.' Sucre to Bolívar, Chuquisaca, 11 May, 1826, *Cartas de Sucre al Libertador*, ed. D. F. O'Leary, 2 vols. (Madrid, 1919), ii, 1826–30, pp. 8–9. The unlikelihood of such a prospect was clear both to Lima and to Sucre, whose pleas fell on deaf ears.

[2] Since the trail is trans-Andean, this presumably meant well graded.

[3] East-west trade between northern Argentina and what in time became the Chilean desert remained small until the nitrate boom revolutionized the economy of Atacama, 1880–1918. Then, the trailing west of mules, cattle and hides from the Chaco lands of northern Argentina, Paraguay and eastern Bolivia flourished, together with the movement of *peón* labour to the nitrate and copper works. It was not to become a trade route to Europe for Argentine products, however.

this measure, strong prejudices exist against it amongst the native merchants, unwilling to depart from the commercial routine in which for years they have been engaged. I feel confident, however, that should Bolivia fail in getting possession of Arica, which recent political events have rendered still more probable than before, her Government will strain every nerve and make every sacrifice to render Cobija suitable to receive the foreign products consumed in her territory, and to release her citizens from the very heavy tribute which they have hitherto paid, and are still paying, to their neighbours as transit duties. The hardship of the present system will be evident when it is known that in the years 1825 and 1826 Bolivia has paid to Lower Peru duties amounting to 820,000 dollars, or £164,000, on articles of foreign manufactures, and 300,000 dollars during the same period to Buenos Ayres. As I have said before, the principal supplies of European manufacture have been received of late years from Arica, where the foreign merchants or importers reside. The merchants of the interior frequent the coast at stated intervals, where they purchase their supplies partly for ready money, but a large proportion on credits of six, nine and twelve months, the native merchant remitting to the foreign agent the value in specie and in other Bolivian produce, and receiving fresh supplies of goods in return. A running account is thus kept up, and severe losses are sometimes sustained by the foreigner from his ignorance of the state of the trade in the interior of the country, and from the want of caution observed in granting credits to individuals little known to him. I am not exactly informed of the amount of bad outstanding debts due to British merchants by the traders of Bolivia, but I have understood from the agents at Arica that they are inconsiderable.

There are at present at Arica nine British agencies (branches of those established at Valparaiso and Lima), one French, one German, two Buenos Ayrian, and two North American Houses. Their commercial transactions are confined to Arica and to Tacna, situated 40 miles inland, no foreign agents having yet settled in the interior provinces of Bolivia.

COMMUNICATION WITH THE INTERIOR

The road leading from Arica into the Bolivian provinces traverses the Western Cordillera of the Andes. The ascent for the first two days is precipitous until it reaches an elevation of 14,800 feet above the sea, near to the volcano and village of Tacora, whence it descends gradually to gain the elevated table-land or valley of the Desaguadero. Frequent accidents occur in the first portion of this road, until it attains this great elevation, from the dangerous nature of many of the passes. This might be remedied by widening the path and constructing arches over the torrents which descend from the Andes, but it appears to me to be impossible to form a cart road over this part of the chain, as was once contemplated, where in the course of a few leagues the track ascends nearly 10,000 feet. Communication might be considerably facilitated, and a cart road formed from Tacora to La Paz, Oruro and Potosí without any considerable outlay, as the country is level and presents few difficulties. Should such a work be ever undertaken it will be necessary to build post-houses, and to place supplies of forage at each, as the greater part of the country which such a road would traverse is placed at an enormous elevation, and is wholly unproductive.

The transport of every description of foreign merchandise is effected by means of mules, which carry on an average 250 lbs and travel about 20 miles each day. The expense of transport is considerable, whether on goods brought from Buenos Ayres or Arica, arising from the great distance of the one, and the difficult roads which separate the second from the populous towns of Bolivia. The amount, however, forms a matter of little importance in the centre of the Republic, whether the supplies are received from the Río de la Plata or from the shores of the Pacific, the great distance at which Buenos Ayres is placed being nearly compensated for in the better roads, and greater facilities of communication which it possesses. Supposing Bolivia not to possess a port in her own territory, and the transport duties to be the same at Buenos Ayres and Arica, it will form a matter of little consequence from which of these ports she receives her foreign supplies as regards expense of transport.[1]

The distance from Buenos Ayres to Potosí is 540 leagues, and from Arica to the same town 150 leagues; but whilst every thing must be conveyed on the backs of mules, over bad roads, and through unproductive country from the shores of the Pacific, the Buenos Ayrian merchant can transport his goods in waggons for 420 leagues to Jujuy, whence they are carried at a comparatively trifling expense to the southern provinces of Upper Peru. From enquiries which I instituted at Chuquisaca, I have formed the following table showing the expense attending transport of merchandise from the ports of Buenos Ayres and Arica. The principal

[1] Such a comment reveals how steadfastly so many in Chuquisaca and Potosí continued to ignore the commercial dominance of La Paz and Cochabamba. Transport costs to these last two cities, as set out below, clearly favoured Arica, while time was vital factor. Merchandise could be pack-muled from Arica to La Paz in 7 or 8 days; the journey from Buenos Aires took at least 6–8 weeks.

data on which this comparison is founded were furnished by Mr Madero, the Bolivian Minster of Finance, who had been extensively engaged in the trade from Buenos Ayres to Bolivia before he entered the Ministry.

Expenses attending the transport of merchandise per 100 lbs:

Buenos Ayres to		Arica to	
Potosí	$16.4	Potosí	$16.4
Chuquisaca	$19.0	Chuquisaca	$16.4
Oruro	$22.0	Oruro	$13.4
Cochabamba	$25.0	Cochabamba	$13.4
La Paz	$26.0	La Paz	$ 7.0

The roads throughout Bolivia are only adapted for mules and llamas; a cart or carriage road does not exist in any part of the Republic, and with the exception of one or two carriages used in religious ceremonies at Chuquisaca, a wheeled vehicle does not exist in any part of Bolivia. Everything is therefore transported on mules, asses and llamas, the latter the most common and useful beast of burthen possessed by the aboriginal population. The bad state of the roads has occupied the attention of the Bolivian Congress, which has empowered the Executive to make roads connecting the different provinces of the Republic, and it is proposed to apply a portion of the expected excedent of the revenue during the present year to this useful purpose. It is projected to render the road from La Paz to Potosí fit for carts, an undertaking of little difficulty from the level nature of the intervening country.[1] From this road others will branch off leading to Cochabamba and Chuquisaca, but as they cross the Eastern Cordillera it will not be practicable to form roads for wheeled vehicles, except at an enormous expense. The same may be said of the roads from Potosí to Chuquisaca, and to Salta, but notwithstanding, much may be done in improving those roads which are already formed, by carrying them along the sides of the valleys instead of following the beds of torrents, a system generally adopted in the Departments of La Paz, Cochabamba, Santa Cruz and Chuquisaca, which renders them intransitable in the rainy season, when for months together all communication is often interrupted between the provinces of the interior.

[1] The first section of this route, along the *altiplano*, is level, but the trail continues through the Cordillera de los Frailes and the *sierras* surrounding Potosí, and is steep and gruelling. Pentland had followed the route, so would seem to have written 'Potosí' in error here instead of 'Oruro'.

INTERNAL NAVIGATION

I have already adverted to the advantages to be derived from the navigation of the river Desaguadero, as connected with the opening of the port of Cobija and facilitating the transport of merchandise from that port to the northern provinces of the Republic. This river, which is lost by evaporation and infiltration into a muriatiferous soil in the Province of Carangas, is navigable from the villages of Aullagas and Condo in the same Province, to its junction with the lake of Titicaca. This lake is also navigable as far as the river of Laja where it empties itself into the lake, whilst this latter river may be also rendered navigable to the village of Laja, by establishing three or four sets of locks, and by turning into it some neighbouring streams to increase its depth. Laja is situated seven leagues from La Paz, to which an excellent cart road can easily be made.[1]

The villages of Aullagas and Condo are situated at 85 leagues from Cobija, and the road is perfectly good and always open. In this way merchandise may be transported from the shores of the Pacific to those villages on mules, and from thence to La Paz, passing by Oruro, at an inconsiderable expense on the Desaguadero. The advantages resulting from the navigation of this river and of the lake from which it issues will also be great to the northern and western provinces of the Republic, and will be attended with a trifling expense. The principal outlay will be to construct a drawbridge on the Desaguadero where it rises in the lake, to deepen the river of Laja and to construct the necessary boats, for which wood may be obtained from the Provinces of Munecas and Larecaja. The current of the Desaguadero is throughout extremely slow, its waters are of sufficient depth for boats of large size as far as Oruro, and its navigation will be materially facilitated by the easterly and south-westerly winds which observe a kind of periodical regularity in the great valley which separates the two longitudinal branches of the Bolivian Andes. The scarcity of fuel must preclude the possibility of steam navigation on the river Desaguadero and on the lake of Titicaca for the present, but should the coal beds lately discovered near to Corocoro in the Province of Pacajes prove productive, as

---

[1] The possibilities of cheap transport by canal and canalized river for heavy, bulky commodities had always to be considered in this pre-railway age. There were even wholly impracticable schemes to negotiate parts of the Cordillera Occidental and the Eastern Cordillera by flights of locks. No system of linked canal transport on Lake Poopó and the rivers Desaguadero and Laja was ever implemented, although projects continued to be studied until well into the twentieth century, and dredging of the Desaguadero took place.

there is every reason to expect they will, the day may not be far removed from us when steam vessels may be seen navigating in the midst of the snow-capped Andes, at an elevation surpassing that of the Peak of Teneriffe [Pico de Teide, 12,270 feet] and of the most elevated summits of the Pyrenees.[1]

All communication with the extensive Province of Moxos is carried on by means large canoes which navigate the rivers Guapay [or Grande] and Mamoré, descending from Yuracares, and from the town of Santa Cruz de la Sierra, to the different missions. This navigation is chiefly conducted by the Moxos Indians who arrive with the productions of their province consisting chiefly in cocoa and wax, and with their cotton manufactures at Santa Cruz, in the season of the rains, when the great rivers are more easily navigated. The inhabitants of the Provinces of Yungas and Larecaja also navigate the many rivers which enter into the river Beni, but little is known of the facilities which those rivers offer for internal navigation. It does not appear that any attempt has been ever made to navigate the river Madeira, from the point where it receives the river Beni, until it empties itself into the Marañon, but there is little doubt that it will offer every facility for internal navigation, as it is not interrupted in its course by rocks or rapids.[2]

The navigation of the three great rivers which descend from the eastern side of the Bolivian Andes, the Guapay, Mamoré and Beni, is at the present day of little importance. But when the population of Moxos shall have increased and turned its attention to the varied and valuable agricultural productions which the soil of this province is capable of furnishing, and it shall have profited of the numerous wild herds which roam over its extensive savannas, the navigation of

[1] Steam navigation on Lake Titicaca began in June 1871 with the launching at Puno of a small steamer built by Cammell Laird. It had been taken to Peru under its own steam, dismantled at the coast and then hauled in part by rail (Arica-Tacna), and finally by mule up to the lake, where the vessel was reassembled. A second vessel was launched in March 1872. The railway reached Puno from Mollendo and Arequipa in 1874. Coal supplies were imported (*supra*, p. 187n). Nevertheless, the world's first commercial steam navigation had begun on the Hudson (1807) and the Clyde (1812), and by 1826-7 its future importance was recognized.

[2] Navigation of the Amazon-Madeira-Guaporé routeway to the Mato Grosso goldfields had been developed by the Portuguese in the eighteenth century, and their claims were strengthened by a series of frontier posts and forts along the banks, particularly of the Guaporé. This river and the upper Madeira formed part of the boundary between Spanish and Portuguese possessions in South America delimited by the Treaty of San Ildefonso, 1777.

Pentland's failure to record the interruption to navigation caused by the Madeira-Mamoré falls was a serious one, and reflected the Andean regions' ignorance of the continental interior. (See Figs. 2 and 3, and Introduction, p. 177).

the confluents of the river Madeira, and of this river itself will assume a vast importance, not only as connected with the interior, but with the foreign commercial relations of the Bolivian Republic.

IMPORTS

The articles of foreign manufacture imported into the Bolivian provinces may be classed under the following heads:—*Cotton manufactures, Woolen manufactures, Silks, Hosiery, Linens, Cutlery, Glass, Pottery, Saddlery, Wines, Iron and Mining utensils and Quicksilver.*

The *Cotton manufactures* consumed in Bolivia consist chiefly of the more ordinary description of printed cottons, of chintzes, of that quality of glazed calicoes called Madopolams, and of coarse grey cotton cloths of North American manufacture. The Madopolams are by far the article most in demand, having taken the place of the home manufactures, and driven the North American cottons out of the market. Their low price has made their consumption general among all classes, and I have been informed by the British agents at Arica that they form the most extensive and profitable article of British manufacture at the present day in Upper Peru. The consumption of printed cotton, chintzes and muslins is chiefly confined to the white population and mixed races. In all articles of cotton manufacture those from England are preferred; indeed until within the last twelve months they were the only sort imported. Since then, the Dutch, Germans and French have imported imitations of our cotton goods which have met with sales in the absence of those of British manufacture. It is certain that the coarser description of Indian cottons would meet a ready sale in the provinces of Upper Peru, and especially the blue Bengal calicoes which would replace the blue Cochabamba barracans, an article still of extensive consumption among the aborigines.

Woolen manufactures. Under this head are comprised the different descriptions of South Sea baizes, of serges, cloths, kerseymeres [cashmeres] and carpetings. The two first are exclusively of British manufacture, the French having completely failed in imitating them for the Peruvian market. Baizes and serges are among the most important articles of woolen manufacture, their consumption is general amongst all classes inhabiting the colder regions bordering on the Andes, and their importation equals in value that of the glazed cottons, or even surpasses it. The consumption of broadcloths is daily becoming more general; those of British manufacture are now in less demand than they formerly were, owing to large importations from France during the last and present year of a finer description of broadcloth, of a lighter texture and higher finish than those of

British manufacture. In the coarser description of woolens, however (those called starcloths, of which there is a very extensive consumption), the British manufacturer stands without a competitor. The use of the coarser description of broadcloth is now becoming general even among the Indian population, and to this is owing, as I have already noticed, the decadence of the woolen manufactories of Guamanga and Cuzco.

Within the last year considerable importations of rugs and carpetings of British manufacture have taken place, and met with a ready sale in Bolivia.

Silks. The consumption of silks, being confined to the better classes of society inhabiting the large towns, is necessarily very limited. Those of French manufacture are by far the most generally worn, but China silk goods would meet a ready sale in Bolivia as in other parts of South America. None, however, has been imported of late. Some parcels of British silks sent out as patterns to Arica and Arequipa in 1826 met with a ready sale and gave very handsome returns, and it is probable that before long the British manufactures will be able to supplant the French in respect of silk articles for consumption in the interior provinces of Peru and Bolivia.

Hosiery. The consumption of cotton hosiery is generally speaking trifling; that imported is chiefly composed of stockings of British and German manufacture. The demand for silk hosiery is very considerable, and here the British article is universally preferred, and bears a price fully 30 per cent above that of French and Dutch manufacture.

Linens. The use of linen is very limited in every part of Bolivia, arising from the climate, which is in general cold throughout the year. In the adjoining Provinces of Salta, Tucumán and La Rioja, however, large quantities of Irish and Silesian linens are consumed. Should the foreign trade of Bolivia ultimately pass through the port of Cobija, there will be a considerable demand for Irish linens from the northern provinces of the Argentine Republic.

Cutlery, Ironmongery. All the articles embraced under these heads may be said to be of British manufacture. Of late, however, the Germans have imported into Bolivia and Peru some cutlery, consisting chiefly of knives and other cutting instruments which from its very low price has met with a ready sale among the Indian population. The French and Prussians have also introduced some fire-arms and sabres, but these have met a very limited demand, and that only in the absence of arms of British manufacture which are universally preferred, and bring prices from 20 to 30 per cent higher than those of any other nation.

Glass, Pottery. The great distance at which the most populous

provinces of Bolivia are situated from the sea coast, and the consequent expense of transport, must preclude the more general use of
these two articles of European manufacture. There is, however, a
good deal of glass and Delftware carried from Arica into the Departments of La Paz and Chuquisaca. The major part of the glass
hitherto imported has been of German manufacture and of a very
ordinary description, but within the last twelve months considerable
importations have taken place from England, and as it has been sent
out in packages capable of being easily transported across the Andes,
it has met a ready sale. Blue Staffordshire ware is daily coming into
use among the higher classes, and the ordinary description of French
ornamental porcelain is much sought after. An article which is likely
to become one of extensive consumption is window glass. The trade
is confined to that of German manufacture, but it merits the attention of the British merchant.

Saddlery. A good deal of saddlery and military accoutrements
have been lately imported from France, and have given handsome
returns arising from the circumstances of the times, but further
importations of saddlery are not likely to turn out so well, since that
of European manufacture is totally unsuitable to the country.[1]

Wines. The French have imported also large quantities of inferior
Bordeaux wines, but their consumption is extremely limited in the
interior provinces, and the demand consequently very trifling.

Iron and Mining Utensils. Iron and steel are now articles of very
extensive consumption, chiefly in the mining districts, and will daily
become more so, with the increasing prosperity of the mines. The
iron hitherto used has been of British origin, and also the steel in
part, but of late the French and Germans have imported large quantities of the latter article, imitating that formerly sent from Spain,
which has been preferred, to the depreciation of the British article.

The mining utensils hitherto imported have been exclusively of
British manufacture and have realized in some instances enormous
profits. A great deal remains to be done under this latter head, and
the trade in utensils and machinery connected with the mining
industry of the country appears to me to offer one of the most
profitable branches of commerce to the British manufacturer which
Bolivia possesses at the present day.

Quicksilver. I have adverted in another part of this report to the

[1] Discussing French supplies, Ricketts had reported to Canning, Lima, 27
December, 1826 (F.O. 61/8, and Humphreys, *British Consular Reports*, p. 134)
that 'a merchant made an advantageous speculation by bringing a set of very rich
cavalry clothing and equipments for 400 men; the cost was, I learn, 200,000
dollars, and General Bolívar purchased it for the corps of Lancers in Bolivia'.

importance of the trade in this metal. The limited supplies imported into Arica by the French have met an instant sale, and have in every case given a profit of from 70 to 100 per cent. This most important branch of import into the Peruvian provinces has been hitherto neglected by the British merchant, whilst in the whole catalogue of imports there is not one which will meet so ready a sale, or give larger or quicker returns at the present day than quicksilver. The consumption of this metal during the year 1826 exceeded 2,000 quintals (or 100 tons), averaging 95 dollars per quintal, the price seldom exceeding during the same period 40 dollars in the European market. This consumption is likely to be increased considerably during the present and future years.

AMOUNT OF FOREIGN IMPORTS

It is difficult to ascertain the exact amount of the foreign importations during the two years which have passed since Bolivia has become independent, since during this period the trade has been carried on partly from Buenos Ayres and partly from the ports of the Pacific. The information to be derived from the Custom House returns is not to be depended on, considering the extensive contraband trade which prevailed, and the corruption which formerly reigned in every branch of the Financial Department of the Republic. From the best information which I have been able to collect from the Buenos Ayrian and native merchants of Bolivia, the importations of foreign merchandise from Buenos Ayres amounted to:

in *1825*	$1,300,000
1826	$1,000,000

According to the official returns of the duties levied on foreign imports at Arica, it appears that they amounted to:

in *1825*	$1,238,452
1826	$1,344,691

As the Custom House valuations at Arica, however, are admitted not to exceed on an average two-thirds of the invoice prices of the goods imported, and as a very extensive system of smuggling prevails in that port, especially in the more valuable and less bulky articles, the amount of the importations may be fairly estimated at one-half more than that deduced from the duties levied at the Custom House. There are also some articles of foreign import which are not subjected to any duty, such as iron, steel, quicksilver, books, and machinery in general, so that in drawing up a statement of the total amount of importations to the Bolivian provinces, it will be necessary to include these different items to arrive at a more accurate result:

Statement showing the amount of Foreign Importations to Arica in 1825 and 1826 for consumption in Bolivia:

	1825	1826
Imports chargeable with duties	$1,238,452	$1,344,691
Amount of Contraband trade	$ 619,226	$ 672,346
Iron imports ⎱ not chargeable	$ 60,000	$ 70,000
Quicksilver ⎰ with duties	$ 100,000	$ 100,000
Total amount of imports	$2,017,678	$2,187,037

The total amount of imports as contained in the preceding table agrees with a Statement furnished to me by the British agents in Arica, from which it appears that during the two years which have elapsed since the opening of that port,[1] the amount of sales effected has little exceeded four million dollars.

The total amount, therefore, of foreign importations to the provinces of Bolivia since their independence will stand as follows:

Importations by way	1825	1826
of Buenos Ayres:	$1,300,000	$1,000,000
Arica:	$2,017,678	$2,187,037
Total	$3,317,678	$3,187,037
	(£ 663,536)	(£ 637,407)

This valuation of the foreign trade of Bolivia corresponds with reports which I received from the native merchants throughout the Republic. It also corresponds nearly with the amount of the precious metals exported during the same period, and differs little from the amount absorbed in the foreign commerce of the provinces of Upper Peru, during the latter years of Spanish rule.

BRITISH TRADE

The British agents in Arica estimate that of the total amount of foreign manufactures imported, two-thirds are British and the

[1] Officially declared a free port by decree of 22 January, 1825.

C M—Q

remaining third composed of French, German and Dutch. The importations from the United States are comparatively trifling, and confined to coarse calicoes, and some China and Bengal goods. Adopting this estimate, the proportion of British goods consumed in Bolivia during the last two years will stand thus:

1825	$2,211,785	(£442,357)
1826	$2,124,691	(£424,938)
Average annual amount of Brtish manufactures	$2,168,238	(£433,648)

EXPORTS

The foreign exports of Bolivia consist chiefly in the produce of her mines, her soil furnishing in its present neglected state few articles suited for European market. The following are the most important exports: *Silver, Gold, Tin, Bark, Vicuña or Vigogna wool, Alpaca wool, Vanilla, Monkey, Panther and Chinchilla skins.*

Silver. This metal forms the most extensive article of export which the Republic possesses and one exceeding in value all the others united. I have shown in another part of this report that the produce of the silver mines of Bolivia has amounted to 2,619,918 dollars in 1826, of which the whole is exported, a fact proved by the gradually decreasing amount of the silver currency of the country. The whole of the silver exported is carried to Arica and Buenos Ayres in the state of *plata piña*[1] and of coinage, a very trifling proportion of the latter paying the legal duties on its leaving the Republic.

Gold. No coinage of this metal having been struck at the Bolivian Mint within the last two years, the whole of that obtained is exported clandestinely. The great mass of Bolivian gold is purchased by the merchants of La Paz, who remit it to the British agents in Arica, from whence it finds its way to Europe. The price varies from 15 to 16 dollars per ounce at La Paz, which is that at which it is remitted to the foreign agent on the coast, who derives a handsome profit on its arriving in the European market. With *plata piña*, native gold is considered the safest and most profitable remittance which can be procured in this country, in return for European manufactures. The amount of gold exported is fully equal to the produce of the mines, which I have shown exceeded 800,000 dollars in 1826.

---

[1] A mass of refined silver, moulded in the shape of a pineapple or cone, and usually weighing between 20 and 60 lbs.

Tin. This metal has formed an important article of export trade during the last 20 years. It is obtained at Oruro and from the mines of Huanuni, twelve leagues south-east of the latter town, as mentioned in the chapter of my mining report. The foreign markets for Oruro tin have been hitherto North America, France and Germany. During the past year, however, the North Americans have ceased to purchase this metal, so that this branch of trade may be said to be now exclusively in the hands of the French. Prior to 1824, the mines of Oruro have furnished as much as 10,000 quintals, or 500 tons, of tin annually, whilst in 1825 and 1826 the quantity has not exceeded 7,000 quintals, or 350 tons. The average price during the last two years has been 54 *reales* at Oruro, or 74 *reales* at Arica per 100 lbs, from which we may conclude that in 1826 the total value of the tin exported from Bolivia has not exceeded 64,750 dollars. All the tin produced in Bolivia is exported from Arica, where it pays a duty of 6 per cent like all other Bolivian produce. It is chiefly employed in Europe in forming alloys with copper in the fabrication of bronzes, bell and cannon metals.

Bark. Very large quantities of Peruvian bark have been collected in the Department of La Paz in 1825 and 1826 and from thence sent to Arica for the European market. The best qualities are those produced in the district of Zongo on the eastern side of the Andes, where a great variety of the genus *Cinchona* grows, and furnishes a bark equal, if not superior, to the Lloxa or Colombian. The description of bark now collected is that growing on the larger branches or even on the trunk of the plant, being better suited for the preparation of the salts of quinine than the smaller varieties called quill bark. The whole of this article hitherto exported from Arica and Quilca has been brought from the northern provinces of Bolivia, and has averaged 3,000 quintals in each of the two last years.

The price has decreased considerably in 1826, and is likely to continue to do so, arising from the limited consumption of this article, and the very large quantities which have been thrown into the European market.[1] The amount of exports in bark have been as follows:

1825	3,000 quintals, at 36 dollars per quintal	$108,000
1826	3,000 quintals, at 28 dollars per quintal	$ 84,000

The principal importers have been the Germans and French for the

[1] The demand and price for Peruvian bark were shortly to soar, however, to the benefit of La Paz and Arica which handled the Bolivian, and much of the Peruvian, trade. Cochabamba became an important subsidiary centre in the 1850s and 1860s. After that, wild South American bark ceased to be economic in competition with Indian and S.E. Asian plantation production developed from seeds and seedlings collected in Peru by Clements Markham, at the request of the India Office.

purpose of extracting the salts of quinine, which they are able to prepare to more advantage than the British chemist from the lower price of alcohol in their countries—an ingredient of the first necessity as facilitating the formation of these preparations.

Vicuña wool. A considerable quantity of this wool was formerly collected in Upper Peru and exported from Buenos Ayres, but not having been found to succeed in the European market, it has in a great measure ceased to be collected for foreign export. Its consumption in Bolivia, however, and the mountainous districts of Lower Peru is considerable, being employed in the manufacture of hats, ponchos, etc. In 1826, a parcel of nearly 9,000 lbs was purchased at 9 and 10 *reales* (4s. 6d. and 5s. 0d.) per lb and sent to France, so that the total amount exported has little exceeded in value 10,000 dollars in 1826.

Alpaca wool. This wool is produced by an animal of the genus *Llama* [*Lama*] inhabiting the most frigid and rigorous regions of the Andes, in the provinces of Oruro, Pacajes and Carangas. The animal is shorn annually and furnishes on an average from 4 to 5 lbs of wool. The general colour of the alpaca is black [often dark brown], and its wool is of a beautiful silky texture and long fibre, and appears admirably adapted for the manufacture of the very fine description of broadcloths. I am not aware that it has been yet tried in Europe, but I think it is likely to form a valuable article of Bolivian export when it becomes known to the European manufacturers; some parcels have been forwarded to Europe by the British merchants of Arica which cost 1s. 3d. per lb on the spot, so that it cannot be brought to the English market for less than 1s. 8d or 1s. 10d per lb under present circumstances.[1]

Vanilla. The discovery of the species of *Epidendrum* which furnishes the vanilla[2] only dates from 1826, when a small parcel was brought to La Paz from Apolobamba, where it grows in the deep humid valleys descending from the Eastern Cordillera. It has been since found in the Department of Santa Cruz de la Sierra, and there is little doubt that large quantities could be obtained, if there existed a demand for it; about 60 lbs have been offered for sale, and were purchased at the rate of 10 dollars per lb for the French market.

Chinchilla skins. A great number of those skins were formerly

---

[1] In 1836 machinery for handling alpaca wool was invented by Sir Titus Salt, the Bradford mill-owner, and hitherto unsaleable bales were quickly in demand.

[2] Species of *Epidendrum* (Dragon's-mouth orchid) are noted only for the beauty of their flowers. Vanilla comes from the seed pods of a different American orchid, *Vanilla planifolia* (syn. *V. fragrans*).

brought to Potosí from the neighbouring Provinces of Lipez, Chichas, and Atacama, and from thence exported through Arica and Buenos Ayres. At present the decreasing consumption and low prices of those skins in Europe has caused their collection to be neglected; in 1826, the entire amount of this species of peltry exported from the Bolivian provinces did not exceed 5,000 dollars. The exportation of panther [*i.e.* jaguar] and monkey skins has also decreased, and with the exception of a few of the latter, the export trade in peltries has been reduced to a mere trifle.

Table of the Foreign Exports of Bolivia in 1826

Silver and Gold	$3,420,000
Tin	$ 64,750
Peruvian bark	$ 84,000
Vicuña and Alpaca wools	$ 15,000
Vanilla and other drugs, about	$ 10,000
Peltries and Sundries	$ 20,000
Total　　Dollars	$3,613,750
(Sterling £	722,750)

In the review which I have taken of the commerce of Bolivia, I have experienced much difficulty in arriving at correct estimates of the amount of the several items of which it is composed, in a country where the Customs Department has been so carelessly and corruptly administered, and where contraband trade has been conducted on such an extensive scale. It would be idle to place confidence in the official returns as presenting the true state of the trade of the Republic. The valuations contained in the preceding Table of Exports I have obtained from enquiries among the native merchants concerned in the traffic of the different articles, and although I am fully aware that such valuations do not possess all the accuracy to be desired in a report of this kind, they do so in a sufficient degree to enable you to arrive at a more correct general view that has been hitherto presented of the commercial transactions of this infant Republic.

On comparing the amount of imports and exports, they will be found to agree within a few thousand dollars. In the comparison it will be necessary to include the amount of duties paid on merchandise imported from Lower Peru, which enhances its value and increases the amount of imports as given in the preceding pages. The following Statement will therefore present the real state of the commerce in foreign manufactures in Bolivia for the past year:

1826 Amount of imports, as above [see page 233] $3,187,037
    Duties levied on items at Arica $ 443,748

Total amount paid for imports $3,630,785
Total amount of exports $3,613,750

Excess of import trade $ 17,035

Notwithstanding the heavy duties to which all foreign manufactures are subjected before entering the Bolivian provinces, and the
great expense attending on their transport into a country situated at
so considerable a distance from the sea coast, their consumption has
gone on increasing, and their use has become more general among
all classes. The lower classes, chiefly composed of the aboriginal
Indians, were formerly excluded from articles of European fabric,
consequent on the monopoly of the trade, the limited supplies, and
the excessive prices of foreign manufactures. Their clothing was comprised of the coarse manufactures of the country, whilst the consumption of European manufactures, or as they were denominated
Ropa de Castilla, was exclusively confined to the more favored
creole population. At present, European cloths, cottons and cutlery
are in general use amongst all classes, to the exclusion of those
fabricated in the country, even amongst the aboriginal races, the
most averse to innovations.

LAWS RELATING TO COMMERCE

The Bolivian Congress and His Excellency General Sucre have
pursued a line of policy well calculated to increase the foreign commerce of the Republic, and to contribute to the comforts and wants
of every class of its population. In all the laws and decrees which
have been promulgated regarding the commercial relations of the
State, a spirit of liberality and of enlightened views of political
economy and of free trade will be found to reign, such views as are
rarely to be met with in the fiscal laws of the other newly constituted republics of South America. Of this, the new Bolivian tariff
may be adduced as a proof. Shortly after the Declaration of Independence, His Excellency General Bolívar, then vested with the
supreme power of the Republic, promulgated a Decree on the
24th of December 1825 regulating the duties on importations. These
duties were thereby fixed at 8 per cent on valuations determined by a
tariff published on the same date.

Several complaints having been received by the Executive on the exorbitant valuations placed on many articles in this first tariff, it appointed a commission of native merchants, presided by the Minister of Finance, to frame another for the consideration of the Congress when it came to regulate the entire financial system of the Republic. This tariff was adopted by the Congress and embodied in the Law of Customs of the 31st December, a copy of which I have the honour to enclose for your information. By this Law, all importations from beyond the seas are subject to a duty of 10 per cent on entering the Bolivian territory, except the following articles: quicksilver, iron and steel, mining utensils and machinery, books, scientific instruments, and instruments employed in the different arts and manufactures which may be imported free of duty. The importations from the neighbouring states pay 6 per cent, except mules, which may be introduced free of all charges. All productions of the Republic are free of export duty, except gold and silver coin, which pay 2 per cent *ad valorem*.

To afford every encouragement to the trade through Cobija, the Congress has passed a law reducing the duties on all foreign imports through that port to 2 per cent on the valuations of the above mentioned tariff. These different laws have given general satisfaction to the commercial interests of Bolivia, and to the British agents resident at Arica, and are likely to contribute in a considerable degree to the growing prosperity of the Republic.

I have endeavoured to embody in this part of my report, the principal information which I have succeeded in collecting during my residence in Bolivia, on her commercial relations. This information has been chiefly derived from the respectable native merchants inhabiting the large towns, and from the foreign agents established at Arica. The review into which I have entered does not possess the strongest claims to accuracy as regards the valuations or exact amount of the several articles of import and export, but in every case they may be considered as useful approximations in the absence of more correct data. In new countries like Bolivia, which has scarcely enjoyed a political existence or possessed a regular Administration for twelve months, every information on the subject of their commercial relations can only be looked upon as approximating to the truth, since those infant Governments are in possession of few documents relative to any part of their financial administration, and therefore are of so doubtful and unsatisfactory nature as to merit little confidence.

CHAPTER V

A SHORT VIEW OF THE PRESENT POLITICAL
STATE OF BOLIVIA, EMBRACING THE HISTORY
OF THE COUNTRY SINCE ITS INDEPENDENCE,
ITS GOVERNMENT, LAWS, AND INSTITUTIONS

THE Bolivian Republic having only established its independence within the last two years, its Government has been since then more of a
provisional than of a fixed description. His Excellency General
Bolívar, as Commander-in-Chief of the Liberating Army, having
been authorised by the Peruvian Congress in 1825 to establish a
Government in Upper Peru, was subsequently invested by the
General Assembly of these provinces with the supreme power of the
new State, until the assembling of a future Congress. His Excellency
on his departure from the Bolivian provinces at the commencement
of 1826 conferred on Don Antonio José de Sucre, General-in-Chief
of the Colombian army, the same power and authority as he had
received from the legislative bodies of the two countries, and ordered
that a General Congress of the Bolivian Republic should be assembled
in the course of 1826.

The General Assembly of the Provinces of Upper Peru was convoked by General Sucre on his entry into the provinces in February
1825. By a Decree promulgated from La Paz, fifty-four deputies were
elected, and met at Chuquisaca in July 1825,[1] for the purpose of
determining on the future form of Government to be adopted, in
furtherance of the desire manifested by the Buenos Ayrian and
Peruvian Congresses, that the inhabitants of Upper Peru should be
permitted to decide freely on their future political existence, without
any reference to their former annexation to, or connection with,
either of those Republics. The most important act of their first
Legislative Assembly was the Declaration of Independence promul-

[1] The February decree had placed the Assembly at Oruro, to begin on 29
April, 1825, but Royalist resistance in Upper Peru did not end until early that
month. Because of this, and also because of Bolívar's opposition to the 'self-
determination' decree, arrangements were postponed. Forty-eight, not fifty-
four delegates were elected to the Assembly, of whom thirty-nine had reached
Chuquisaca in time for the inauguration on 10 July, 1825. Indeed, of the two
elected delegates from Santa Cruz only one had arrived by 6 August, Independence Day, so that forty-seven delegates took part in the voting upon the future of
Upper Peru. See C. W. Arnade, *The Emergence of the Republic of Bolivia* (Gaines-
ville, Florida, 1957) pp. 183–205.

gated on the 6th of August 1825, by which the provinces known under the general denomination of Upper Peru, and formerly constituting the *audiencia* of Charcas, are declared to be for ever separated from the dominion of Spain, and independent of every other state, expressing a determination not to unite themselves either with the Argentine or Peruvian Republics.[1]

By a decree of the same Assembly, subsequent to the promulgation of the Declaration of Independence, the name of General Bolívar was given to the new republic thus constituted.[2] The other labours of the General Assembly were confined to enacting *pro tempore* regulations as to the interior administration of the country, and granting recompenses to the troops who had contributed to its liberation. On the 6th of October 1825 it dissolved itself, having previously appointed a permanent deputation of five of its members to co-operate with Generals Bolívar and Sucre in the administration of the Republic, and fixed the meeting of the Constituent Congress previously convoked by General Bolívar for the 25th of May 1826.

From the time when the united Colombian and Peruvian armies entered Upper Peru until the dissolution of the General Assembly, the affairs of the Republic were administered by General Sucre under the direction of General Bolívar who did not reach Upper Peru until September [18 August] 1825, whilst the latter continued to promulgate the several decrees in virtue of the power vested in him, and which were to govern the country until the assembling of the Constituent Congress. It was during this period that the Congress of the United Provinces of Buenos Ayres passed a resolution that the Provinces of Upper Peru, formerly annexed to that Viceroyalty, were left at full liberty to decide on the form of Government which might be judged as best suited to their interests and future happiness.

On General Bolívar's departure from Bolivia [in January 1826], His Excellency General Sucre continued to govern this infant Republic. The administration of His Excellency forms the most prominent feature in the existence of this new State; his efforts have been increasingly directed towards the promotion of its happiness and prosperity, and his conduct in gaining for him the suffrages of every citizen has mainly contributed to stifle party spirit and to establish and preserve tranquillity and order in a country where many elements

[1] Throughout the debate, no support was expressed for union with Argentina. Two delegates from La Paz, however, had voted for union with Lower Peru, giving Upper Peru's lack of a good seaport as one of their reasons for maintaining the old political ties. But both agreed to sign the Declaration of Independence in order to make it a unanimous document.

[2] The new State adopted the name *República Bolívar* on 11 August, 1825, amending it to *Bolivia* on 3 October, 1825.

of discord had previously existed. General Bolívar, prior to his departure, had laid the foundation of many of the reforms, and fixed regulations which were to serve until the administration had been ultimately established by the Legislature of the country. General Sucre during the time he possessed the unlimited power conferred on him by General Bolívar, and the Assembly of the Provinces, continued to promote the beneficient views of the Liberator.

In taking a review of the acts of His Excellency, the good which they have effected can only be appreciated by those acquainted with the state of the country when he assumed the reins of government, and the present peace and prosperity which pervades every class of its citizens. The last act of General Sucre when possessed of supreme powers, deserves to be noticed here. Bolivia had been divided into political parties as every newly constituted State must be at the termination of a lengthened Revolution, in the midst of which that composed of European Spaniards was marked out as an object of obloquy and vengeance. To protect a class of persons so respectable and at the same time possessing considerable wealth and influence, and to secure their residence in the Republic, he promulgated a decree declaring eternal oblivion on the score of past political principles, and that henceforward no person was to be held answerable for his past acts or political conduct during the struggle for independence. The effect of this decree has been to preserve to Bolivia a numerous and wealthy class of citizens, long established in the country and possessing powerful connections, who have been rendered by this act of generosity amongst the staunchest and most sincere supporters of the new order of things.[1]

CONSTITUENT CONGRESS

The General Constituent Congress assembled on the 25th of May[2] 1826, when General Sucre resigned into its hands the power conferred on him expressing his desire to be permitted to return to

---

[1] This drew attention to the contrasted situation in Peru. In December 1826, C. M. Ricketts had reported to Canning that 'the Spanish capitalists in Peru were all persecuted, and ultimately banished, and the consequence has been that the capital which existed has disappeared with its possessors, the European Spaniards' (F.O. 61/8). But Sucre's amnesty was not to survive long in Bolivia, *infra*, p. 248n.

[2] The 25 May became a significant day in Bolivia's history when at Chuquisaca, in 1809, the authority of the Viceroy of the Río de la Plata was openly challenged. Traditionally, this marks the beginning of the country's fight for independence, although the uprisings of 1809 were quickly put down.

Colombia, and to place the Government of Bolivia in the hands of her own citizens. At the earnest and often repeated solicitations of the Congress, he assented to remain at the head of the Administration until the meeting of the next Bolivian Legislature in August 1828, when it is his fixed and decided determination to retire with his Colombian Auxiliaries to his native country.

The Bolivian Constituent Congress continued its sittings until the 6th of January 1827, a period of seven months, during which its members have shown a degree of moderation and self-denial worthy of imitation, and offering a strong contrast with the tumultuous Legislatures of the other newly formed Republics of South America. During the time of its installation the Congress adopted the Constitution of the Republic which had been drawn up by General Bolívar, with some alterations and amendments in the original *projet* of which I shall speak hereafter.[1] It fixed the entire financial system of the Republic, enacted laws relating to the secularization of the monastic orders, and the suppression of several useless monasteries, and sanctioned and extended the decrees of Generals Bolívar and Sucre in the foundation of establishments of public education and charity. The general bases of the judicial system had been regulated by decrees of General Bolívar, and subsequently by the enactments of the Constitution. Codes of laws were, however, waiting to replace the voluminous collections of decrees and precedents contained in the *Recopilaciones* of Castile and of the Indies, on which all decisions of the Spanish colonial tribunals were founded. These codes were ordered to be drawn up, but the time only permitted of the Code of Procedure to be prepared and adopted by the Congress before its dissolution. In taking a review of the collection of laws sanctioned by this Assembly, they will be seen to be directed chiefly towards the extension and regulation of the enactments contained in the Constitution.

The Constituent Congress of Bolivia was composed of forty-three members of whom twenty-two were lawyers, ten ecclesiastics, six landowners, four military officers and one physician.

CONSTITUTION

The *projet* of a Constitution which had been drawn up by General Bolívar at the request of the General Assembly of the Provinces was

---

[1] Bolívar's draft Constitution for Bolivia, presented in May 1826, was designed as a model for other South American republics. The proposal for a life-time Presidency with strong, though not absolute, executive power was monarchy in disguise, and was one of the articles later rejected.

submitted to the Constituent Congress shortly after its installation, and was adopted with some alterations on the 6th November, 1826. On the 9th December of the same year it was promulgated throughout the Republic, and is now the fundamental law of the State. I do not here enter into a detail of its enactments, as you will of course have forwarded a copy of the original *projet* to England, and in transmitting to you the amended Constitution I shall confine myself to remarking on the more important amendments which it has undergone in its progress through Congress.

In the original *projet* as presented by General Bolívar you will recollect how studiously he avoided introducing any article on the subject of religious toleration, with a view of preventing the agitation of so delicate a question in the then infant state of the Republic. The wish of the Liberator was supported by that of General Sucre and of the Bolivian Executive, and it was expected that their united influence would prevent the introduction into the Constitution of any enactment on the subject of religion. In this expectation they were disappointed, an article being introduced by the Commission appointed to report on the *projet*, of which the Ecclesiastical Governor of Chuquisaca and a clever lawyer named Calvo[1] were the most active promoters. The amendment, or rather the proposed article, was of a most intolerant and illiberal nature. A cry that the Roman Catholic religion was in danger was raised at the same time throughout the country by the clergy, and whilst some of the members of Congress were frightened into assent, others feared that dangerous consequences might result on their return to their homes from the influence of the clergy and the lower orders, and were obliged to support the amendment.

The introduction of the question of religion into the Constitution was very strongly combatted by the members of the Executive, and by the liberal and enlightened part of the Congress, whilst it found its principal supporters among the clergy. The debates lasted for five successive days, when the Executive succeeded in putting aside the Article proposed and substituting for it another which only applied to the celebration *in public* of any worship different from the Roman Catholic. In other respects, toleration may be considered as full as before, since members of any other church or faith can inhabit Bolivia without being subjected to any disabilities on account of their religious belief, although their religion forms a bar to their holding certain employments of the State.

[1] Mariano Enrique Calvo, an influential creole lawyer of Chuquisaca, who at various times had been a prominent figure in both the Royalist and Patriot causes between 1809 and 1825.

The Article on religion as it now stands forms the 3rd Title of the Constitution and is as follows:

The Roman Catholic and Apostolic Religion is that of the Republic to the exclusion of every other public worship. The Government will protect it and cause it to be respected, on the principle that no human power can exercise a control over men's consciences.

It is worthy of remark that the Article thus worded was only adopted by a majority of two votes, and that the minority was composed chiefly of the lawyers and of the most influential members of the Congress. It may also be observed that this has been the only instance in the seven months during which the Congress remained sitting, in which the Executive and its friends were left in a minority; on every other question an almost perfect unanimity prevailed, and the several laws proposed by the Executive have met the support and approbation of the Legislative Assembly.

The blank left by General Bolívar in the original *projet* relative to the period which was to elapse before the Constitution could be reconsidered, and reforms introduced into it, has been filled up by the Congress, and fixed at *ten* years from the date of its promulgation.

The other amendments and alterations introduced into General Bolívar's Constitution are of trivial nature, consisting chiefly in verbal alterations, in the transposition of its Articles, or in the reglamentory enactments relative to the mode of election.

EXECUTIVE

The Bolivian Executive is composed at present of His Excellency Don Antonio José de Sucre as President of the Republic, and of three Ministers of State, Messrs Infante, Jeraldino, and Madero. The appointment of a Vice-President provided for by the Constitution has not yet taken place, nor is it proposed to nominate to this situation until the Meeting of Congress in August 1828.

PRESIDENT

General Sucre who now fills the Presidential chair is a [Gran] Colombian by birth, and General-in-Chief of the Auxiliary Colombian forces in Bolivia and Peru. He entered at a very early period into the patriot ranks during the War of Independence in Venezuela and New Granada, where he soon attracted the notice of Generals Miranda and Bolívar. He distinguished himself in the irregular warfare carried on in the plains of Cumaná and of Apure, and after having mainly contributed to the success which attended the patriot armies in the battle of Boyacá, he was appointed one of the Deputies sent by Bolívar to negotiate the armistice of 1820 with the Spanish General Morillo, which afterwards contributed so much to the liberation of Colombia. On the expulsion of the Spaniards from Venezuela, General Sucre was appointed to the command of the Colombian forces in the Province of Quito and Guayaquil, and in the campaign of 1821 he defeated the only remaining Spanish force throughout Colombia, in the battles of Riobamba and Pichincha. In 1823 he was appointed to accompany the auxiliary force which Colombia sent to liberate Peru, and during this and the following year he was actively engaged in that country where he won the esteem and respect of all parties by his moderation and humanity.

When General Bolívar took the field with the united Colombian and Peruvian armies in 1824, General Sucre continued to command, under the Liberator, the Colombian division and in that capacity was present at the battle of Junín in August of the same year. The disgraceful scenes which took place at Lima about this period having necessitated the presence of General Bolívar in the Peruvian capital, the command of the combined force devolved on General Sucre. He conducted the campaign in the midst of the Peruvian Andes and on the banks of the Apurimac, with much skill and vigour, and on the 9th December, 1824, he defeated at Ayacucho the united armies of Spain amounting to 11,000 men, commanded by the Peruvian Viceroy, and obliged it to capitulate after one of the most brilliant engagements, which shines in the military history of the lengthened struggle for South American independence. Two months afterwards, General Sucre crossed the river Desaguadero, the former limit of the two Perus, and from that time only can Bolivia be said to date her political existence.

During the two years which General Sucre has remained in Bolivia, he has gained the respect and love of all men, even of those who have most suffered from his reforms. His manners are most pleasing, his temper mild, unpossessed of that violence so common amongst those accustomed to command, possessed of a strong and vigorous mind and of great firmness of character. He is indefatigable as a man of business, and having received a careful education in his youth, he possesses great facility as a writer. His unremitting attention is directed towards the prosperity of Bolivia, and his greatest ambition, as he has often repeated to me, will be to leave this Republic at his departure free from external enemies, in the enjoyment of order, peace and contentment, having established the enactments of her

Constitution and introduced elements of harmony amongst her citizens. I have before remarked it is His Excellency's intention to quit Bolivia in 1828, when he shall have placed the Government in the hands of one of her own citizens, and to retire to Colombia to offer his services to his native country, should they be required. As a military man, General Sucre holds the first rank amongst those who have fought in the cause of South America; to Generals Bolívar and Sucre, Colombia and Peru owe the accomplishment of their liberties, and to General Sucre, Bolivia is mainly indebted for the commanding position which she now holds, and for the peace and tranquillity which reign throughout her territory, contrasting forcibly with the anarchy and disorder which surround her.

Among the other acts of General Sucre to promote the prosperity of Bolivia may be mentioned the establishment of schools and colleges throughout the Republic. The strict economy which he has introduced into every branch of the Administration has enabled this infant State at the end of the first year of her political existence to meet every pecuniary demand on her, and to equal her disbursements to the receipts, although surcharged during a great part of this time by a large military force. This will not appear less extraordinary when it is known that General Sucre on his entering Bolivia found not a dollar in the public Treasury. He has caused the laws to be respected, and has placed the administration of justice on a respectable footing, by rendering the members of the judicial administration independent of corruption, and of undue influence on the part of the Executive.

His Excellency possesses warm feelings of gratitude towards Great Britain; he looks upon the British nation as the model which the new states of South America should hold before them in their future political career, and as the nation to which they must look up for protection against foreign aggression. As an American, his feelings of gratitude are unbounded to the British who have so usefully concurred in the establishment of South American independence, and to the British Government for that confirmation of their political independence and existence which it has conferred on the new states of America, in its manly and disinterested acknowledgment of the independence of Colombia and Buenos Ayres.

MINISTRIES

(i) The Departments of the Interior and of Foreign Relations are filled by Don Facundo Infante, formerly a colonel in the service of Spain, and one of the distinguished members of the last *Cortes* of that country. On the dissolution of that assembly, Mr Infante was

proscribed and fled to Rio de Janeiro, from whence he traversed the
continent to Bolivia, where he has filled the high office as Secretary to
the Government since its installation. As such, he has contributed
with General Sucre to the reforms which have been introduced into
the Administration. Mr Infante has served in the Anglo-Spanish
army during the Peninsular War, and has imbibed a strong partiality
for our national character and institutions. As a literary man, he
possesses considerable abilities and talent; he has written a work on
Fortification, and is now occupied in a biography of Ferdinand VII.
He is General Sucre's bosom friend, and next to this illustrious
individual, no person has concurred in so great a degree to the present
prosperity of Bolivia as Mr Infante. His nomination to the post
which he holds has contributed to unite many of the European
Spaniards to the new Government who may be looked upon amongst
its sincerest friends. It is hoped that Mr Infante will continue in the
Ministry on General Sucre's retirement, as Bolivia does not possess
a more sincere friend, or a more conscientious and useful servant.[1]

(ii) Ministry of War and Marine: Don Agustín Jeraldino, who now
holds this appointment, is a Colonel in the Colombian army, and
was formerly secretary and chief *aide-de-camp* to General Sucre. He
is a young man possessed of considerable military talents, and has
acquired a good knowledge of military administration from his long
connection with General Sucre, and with the Colombian army.
Colonel Jeraldino, although a Colombian by birth, has become a
naturalized citizen of Bolivia by his marriage in the country, so that
he can no longer be considered in the light of a Colombian, or of a
foreigner. Here I may be permitted to remark that with the exception
of Colonel Jeraldino, and of some subaltern military officers who
have been lent from the Colombian regiments to discipline those
newly raised in Bolivia, the Prefect of Potosí, Colonel Galindo, is the
only other Colombian holding a responsible situation in the Republic,
and he is also a naturalized Bolivian citizen possessing property and
married in the Republic.

(iii) The Ministry of Finance or Hacienda. The present Minister is
Don Juan Bernabé y Madero, a native of Potosí, and possessing considerable property in the Republic. Mr Madero left his native country
early in life and fixed his residence at Buenos Ayres, engaged in com-

[1] Sucre's departure in 1828, however, was to put an abrupt end to local toler-
ance of his policy of selecting foreignersfornewandcritical Bolivian Government
appointments whenever such men appeared to him to offer the best, or only
prospect for competent, stable administration. Facundo Infante was among those
swept from office that year by a wave of xenophobia and intrigue, and by the
growing impatience of some to see Bolivians in senior administrative positions.

mercial pursuits. From thence he visited Europe where he remained for some years. On his return to Buenos Ayres, Mr Madero held official employment under the Government of that Republic and accompanied the army under Belgrano into Upper Peru as Commissary. In the breaking-up of that unfortunate expedition he returned to Buenos Ayres, where he continued to hold official situation. In 1825 he returned to Potosí, his native town, where he became known to General Sucre who appointed him Minister of Finance, founded on his long experience in this branch of the Administration, his known integrity, and his intimate acquaintance with the commercial relations of the Republic.

Mr Madero's long residence at Buenos Ayres has naturally caused a decided partiality on his part for the institutions of the Argentine Republic and has created a desire in him to introduce the financial reforms of that state into Bolivia. He possesses very liberal notions on free trade, and of the principles which should regulate the commercial intercourse of the Republic. He is a declared enemy of the privileges and systems of exclusion as referable to national industry and trade, and to the establishment of excluding duties on foreign importations. He is a strenuous advocate for encouraging foreigners to settle in Bolivia with their arts and industry. Mr Madero is the principal author of the laws and reforms adopted by the Constituent Congress in the financial system, and of the new Bolivian tariff of which I have spoken in another part of this report.

In speaking of the territorial division of the Republic, I have entered into a short view of the internal administration of the Departments which will complete what relates to the Executive and to the Government of Bolivia.

JUDICIAL ADMINISTRATION

The judicial system being regulated by the 7th Title of the Constitution, the Executive is now actively employed establishing it as an object of the first importance, considering the corruption and disorder which had crept into this department under the Spanish dominion. The administration of justice is composed at present of one Supreme Court of Judicature residing at Chuquisaca, the power and authority of which differ little from those possessed by the ancient *audiencia*, and two Courts of Appeal at Chuquisaca and at La Paz, which take cognizance of the acts of the Inferior Judges and decide on appeals from the decisions of those latter, and of Inferior Courts in the capitals of each province.

In addition to these three Courts, there are Judges or Justices of

C M—R

Peace in each canton, whose duties are more of a conciliatory than of a judicial nature, and who act as arbitrators in conjunction with a certain number of the inhabitants, in adjusting disputes in civil cases before they can be carried before a higher tribunal. Already those different courts have been established, and in order to render them more independent, the salaries of the judges have been augmented. Every branch of the Judicial Administration possesses a perfect independence of the Executive, whilst the Supreme Court exercises a strict vigilance over the the Inferior Tribunals, and by the examples which it has made since its installation, the corruption and ignorance which formerly reigned among the Inferior Magistrates will be ere long removed.

The laws which have heretofore governed Upper Peru are those contained in the *Recopilaciones* of Castile and of the Indies, and as many of them are necessarily in opposition to the present order of things, new codes have been formed by a Commission appointed to that effect by the Constituent Congress. Of those codes, that regulating the proceedings of the Courts of Justice has alone been promulgated, the others are in a considerable degree of forwardness and will be presented to the Legislature during the ensuing session. In the meantime the codes of law framed by the Spanish *Cortes* in 1812 are considered as those of the Republic until its own civil and criminal codes shall have been completed.

In the present state of ignorance which exists throughout the great mass of the population it has been judged prudent not to introduce immediately trial by jury in criminal or civil cases. Contraventions of the Press are the only points of which juries take cognizance according to the existing laws.

FINANCES

The revenues of the provinces of Upper Peru prior to 1825 were made up from a considerable number of taxes, some of a very trifling amount, which rendered their collection difficult and open to many frauds. According to the returns made to the Congress in 1826, the average revenue under the Spanish authority between the years 1820 and 1825 amounted annually to 2,023,009 dollars, or £404,601 16 shillings.

The present system of taxation has been regulated by various decrees of Congress during the past session, by which many of the former imposts have been abolished, and new ones established. The entire financial system has been placed on a more solid basis and the charges of the State borne more equally by all classes of the population. The principal sources of the revenue arise from the duties on foreign imports, on the precious metals, from the profits of the Mint, the Indian tribute or Capitation Tax on the aborigines, the direct contribution or taxes on lands, tenements etc, licences on trades and professions, and from a Stamp Duty. In addition, a proportion of the tithes belonging to the three vacant bishoprics, and from some canonries which have been suppressed in the Chapters enter into the receipts of the Treasury. The receipts during each of the years 1825 and 1826 have averaged 2,000,000 dollars, or £400,000 sterling.

The most vexatious tax which contributes to the revenues of the State is that levied on the Indian population under the name of Tribute or Capitation Tax.[1] The new Government has abolished this odious impost after the present year when a Census of Bolivia shall have been completed, and the Indian subjected to the same charges as the other citizens of the Republic. The effect of the direct contribution established by Congress will be to increase the resources of the Republic; it is estimated that this tax will produce from 1,000,000 to 1,200,000 dollars, and as it increases the public revenue, it is proposed to diminish in proportion the high duties on the produce of the mines, a branch of national industry which now suffers from the excessive charges to which it is subjected.

DISBURSEMENTS

The public expenditure during the two past years has not exceeded the receipts, notwithstanding the very large military force cantoned in Bolivia in 1825. The expenditure of the Republic may be assumed 2,000,000 dollars, or £400,000, whilst the estimated expenditure for the years 1827 and 1828, according to an official document drawn up by the Finance Minister, amounts to 1,800,000 dollars, or £360,000 sterling, composed of the following items:

Expenditure of the Congress and Supreme Government	$ 200,000
Expenditure attendant on the administration of the 6 Departments	$ 286,000
Expenditure of the military force of the Republic	$1,314,000
Total	$1,800,000

[1] Able-bodied male Indians, usually between the ages of 18 and 50, were required to pay tribute with the exception of chiefs (*caciques*), their eldest sons, and those who were senior local officials (*alcaldes*). Lynch, *Spanish Colonial Administration, 1782–1810*, pp. 128, 199–200, notes certain other exemptions within the Viceroyalty of the Río de la Plata.

To meet this, the Legislature has granted two million dollars to the Executive for each of the above mentioned years, and as it is not proposed to keep up the large military establishment decreed by Congress, a large balance will remain in the hands of the Government. This it is intended to apply to making roads, to placing the port of Cobija in a fit state to receive shipping, and to other works of public utility. It is expected that after defraying all charges of the State, and paying over 210,000 dollars to the sinking fund of the Public Debt, there will remain a balance of 300,000 dollars, or £60,000 sterling, disposable for the objects above mentioned. It is estimated that the expenditure of the Republic hereafter and in time of peace will not exceed annually $1,600,000, or £320,000.

DEBTS

The only debts due by the Republic consist of a balance of 200,000 dollars to Lower Peru, and 700,000 dollars forming the balance of 1 million voted as a recompense to the liberating army by the General Assembly of the Provinces of Upper Peru in 1825. It is proposed to pay off a part of the former in 1827 from the expected excedent of the revenue, and to meet the latter either by a loan raised in the country on the security of one-half of the mines and other property possessed by the State, or to sell a part of this property for the same purpose.

By a law of the Congress, a Public Fund has been created to the amount of three million dollars nominal value, with an issue of bonds or securities bearing an annual interest of 6 per cent. This fund, denominated the Public Credit, is intended to indemnify the losses sustained by individuals in the cause of independence, to discharge debts contracted by the armies which from 1809 to 1825 have been engaged in the Revolutionary struggle, and to pay the public debt due to the Spanish Government in Upper Peru prior to the commencement of the Revolution in 1809. The Congress has assigned a part of the national property possessed by the State as a security for the capital of this fund, and enacted that, in addition to the interest amounting annually to 180,000 dollars, the Treasury of the Republic will pay 210,000 dollars each year to form a sinking-fund for the redemption of the paper issued, and for extinguishing the capital of the debt.

These are the only debts which Bolivia possesses at the present day, and it is not probable that she will hereafter be obliged to have recourse to other loans or pecuniary assistance which she will not be able to raise amongst her own citizens.

CREDITS

To meet the debts above noticed, the Republic possesses a large amount in lands, tenements and mines, property which in more favorable times will more than suffice to meet her present exigencies. The property in lands, houses, etc. is valued at two million dollars, the mines have been valued at three million, but this valuation is exaggerated and is not likely to be realized from their sale under actual circumstances. The outstanding debts owing to the Treasury before the Declaration of Independence, amount to nearly four million dollars. Bolivia will possess on the credit side of her account:

Property in lands, tenements	$2,000,000
Property in mines, say	$1,500,000
Outstanding debts to the Treasury	$3,793,568
	$7,293,568

Whilst her debts amount to:

Debt to Lower Peru	$ 200,000
Balance due to liberating army	$ 700,000
Amount of securities of the Public Fund	$3,000,000
Total Debt	$3,900,000
Balance remaining to the Credit of the Treasury	$3,393,568
	(£678,713 : 12s)

Few countries in the New World afford so flattering a picture of their financial prosperity as Bolivia does at the present, a country abundant in her resources, her receipts equalling and even surpassing the amount of her expenditure, and without any foreign debt or incumbrance. The financial reforms which have been introduced have had for their object to place the burdens of the State more equally on all classes of its citizens, and to relieve the aboriginal population from the heavy taxation to which it was before subjected. The mode of collection of the revenue has been reformed, and the expense and frauds formerly committed considerably diminished. Whilst heavy and impolitic duties have been placed on foreign commerce in the surrounding states, the Bolivian Government has evinced in this respect a spirit of liberality and of enlightened views in the low duties imposed on foreign merchandise worthy of praise and imitation.

MILITARY ESTABLISHMENT

The Congress has fixed the Regular Army of the Republic at 5,600 men, formed into the following corps:

1 Regiment of Artillery, rank and file	205
9 Squadrons of Cavalry	1,000
5 Regiments of Infantry	4,012
Officers of the above corps and the staff	383
Total	5,600

At present the military force of Bolivia is composed as follows:

Bolivian or native troops	2,291
Colombian auxiliaries	2,283
Total	4,574

It is proposed to augment the native force according as the Colombian regiments shall retire from the country, so as to form an effective army of 4,000 men, it not being considered necessary in the actual state of peace of the Republic, to keep up the entire force voted by the Congress.

The Bolivian regiments are for the most part commanded by native officers, or by foreigners who have fought in the War of Independence. A few Colombian officers have been lent for a limited time in order to form the lately-raised Bolivian regiments. The troops are in general well disciplined, armed and clothed, and regularly paid; General Sucre has repeatedly assured me that no finer troops exist in South America than those of Bolivia. His Excellency is very attentive to the organization of the military force of the Republic as preparatory to withdrawing the Colombian auxiliary division.

In addition to the regular force, militia corps have been organized on the frontiers, but as General Sucre is averse to placing arms in the hands of the great body of the people, the formation of militia has not extended into the interior of the Republic.

The Colombian auxiliary force amounted in January 1827 to 2,285, including officers and staff corps. It exceeds a little the number (2,000) stipulated for between the Bolivian Government and that of Colombia. The Colombian troops are commanded by a General Officer of the same country under the orders of General Sucre; the Colombian regiments receive the same pay and allowances as those of Bolivia.

The only fortresses situated within the Bolivian territory are those of the Desaguadero and of Oruro, the former a defence placed on the frontier of Lower Peru of little importance as a military post, the second serves as a depot for the native Regiment of Artillery.

As a military position, Bolivia possesses some advantages over the states which surround her, from her smaller extent of territory and its more concentrated population, whilst in the neighbouring Republics of Peru and Buenos Ayres it must require a considerable time to unite an armed force on one of their frontiers owing to the great distance at which they are separated from each other. Bolivia can keep her troops in garrison until the moment they are required to act, without incurring the expenses and other inconveniences attendant on keeping an army in the field, and can in the space of twenty days concentrate her entire military force on either of her frontiers, an advantage which she alone possesses among the states of the New World. General Sucre is of the opinion that Bolivia, with a force of 5,000 men, will prove more than a match for any of the neighbouring states[1], and it is His Excellency's wish to place the Republic before his departure in such a state of defence, as will enable it to maintain a respectable position among the other South American states, capable of resisting every aggression from without, and of preserving its internal order and tranquillity.

General Sucre has founded a military school at Chuquisaca for the education of the officers for the Bolivian regiments, an institution which promises to be attended with considerable advantage to the native troops.

ECCLESIASTIC ESTABLISHMENT

The Republic is divided into three Sees: one Archbishopric (that of Charcas) and two Bishoprics (those of La Paz and Santa Cruz de

[1] Such reasoning by Bolivian authorities at this time reveals the controlling influence of former colonial ties with the Viceroyalties of Peru and the Río de la Plata, underlined by a familiarity only with the more densely settled Andean regions. Frontier defence is thought of exclusively in terms of Peru and Argentina. In future years, however, it was with Chile, Brazil and Paraguay, on the lowland perimeter, that the most serious boundary conflicts were to develop.

la Sierra). Their revenues, as well as those of their respective Chapters, have been derived from the tithes. The three Sees are now vacant, and the ecclesiastical affairs are in the meantime placed under the administration of an Ecclesiastical Governor in each diocese, who acts under the direction of the Minister of the Interior or other civil authorities.

The parochial clergy are nominated for the most part by the Executive, and receive their confirmation from the Ecclesiastical Governors of their respective dioceses. They are paid entirely by their parishioners and receive in general a handsome income: the curates from 1,500 to 5,000 dollars, the vicars from 200 to 500 dollars,[1] according to the fertility and population of the districts which they are placed over. The influence of the parochial clergy amongst the lower orders, and especially among the aborigines, has decreased considerably of late years, and at present the Government has little to fear from ecclesiastical intrigues. It has sedulously applied itself to liberate the Indian population from the extortion and tyranny which the clergy formerly exercised over it, and the enactments to that effect, as they tend to diminish the influence of the clergy and to protect the aboriginal race, have met with general approbation. During the Revolutionary struggle, the parochial clergy manifested a strong predilection for the cause of independence. To this feeling is in some measure to be attributed the decided conduct displayed during the early struggles by the Indians of Upper Peru, who have not ceased to manifest a partiality throughout for the patriotic cause. At the present day, the great mass of the parochial clergy may be considered as strong partisans of the new order of things, and many members of the ecclesiastical body have displayed in the late Congress a strong degree of liberal feeling and of national independence.

The Church Establishment properly speaking, and separated from the monastic clergy, has never possessed in Upper Peru landed or other entailed property to any considerable amount. The greater part of that which it did possess has been added to the fund of Public Education and Charity.

The tithes which belonged exclusively to the prelates and canons of the Chapters amounted, on an average, to 400,000 dollars (or £80,000) per annum which was divided among the bishops, deans and canons of the respective cathedrals. Abuses having crept into the collection of this revenue, the Executive has taken it into its own hands, reserving for the use of the State the proportion belonging to the three vacant mitres, and that resulting from the suppression of

[1] Pentland uses the term 'curate' here in the sense of parish priest (*cura*), and 'vicar' as his substitute or representative.

several canonries. These, with economies effected in the collection of the tithes, will add about 150,000 dollars annually to the public revenue of the Republic.

MONASTIC ORDERS

On the installation of the present Government there existed in Upper Peru thirty-four monasteries containing 190 Brothers, and nine convents peopled by 340 Sisters, the former possessing property in lands and tenements to the amount of 3,000,000 dollars, and the latter 3,800,000 dollars. By a law of the Congress, the regular clergy having been permitted to secularize themselves and to quit their monasteries, the number of monks and friars has been thereby reduced to eighty. Many of these monasteries have become deserted, and others ceased to contain the necessary number of inmates according to the rules of such establishments. Many of them have been suppressed and this property applied to purposes of Public Charities and Education. Of the thirty-four monasteries which existed two years ago, only six now remain, and a further reduction is soon likely to take place by the secularization and death of their remaining inhabitants. The property handed over to the fund of Public Education and Charities from the twenty-eight suppressed monasteries amounted to 2,700,000 dollars at the commencement of 1827.

The convents, although fewer in number than the monasteries, possess more considerable property, and notwithstanding that the nuns have been permitted to abandon their cells, this permission has been seldom profited of. The Executive has not judged it prudent to suppress any of the nunneries, but has preferred dictating such rules and regulations concerning the mode of taking vows as must eventually cause those establishments of laziness and vice to die a natural death, when their immense property will ultimately revert to the fund of Education and Charity.

The immorality and vices which have reigned through the monastic orders have caused them to be looked down upon and despised; their destruction has therefore met with the general approbation of all classes. The execution of the laws dictated for their suppression has been effected throughout the Republic without a murmur: the better classes applaud it as a measure which will mainly contribute to the foundation of establishments well calculated for the general good, whilst the lower orders, and especially the Indian population, are glad to see the destruction of that tyranny and oppression to which they were formerly subjected by the monastic orders.

PUBLIC EDUCATION AND CHARITIES

The only establishments of education which the present Government found on its formation were a Seminary for Ecclesiastical Studies, a School of Law, and a few ruined scholastic institutions left behind by the Jesuits. The public charities were nearly in a similar state and their funds dispersed. These important objects formed one of the earliest cares of His Excellency General Bolívar on his arrival in Upper Peru; by various decrees he ordered the organization of these establishments, assigning funds for their support. Both General Sucre and the late Congress have zealously followed up the steps of the Liberator, and in the space of twelve months not only have colleges and hospitals been founded in the more populous towns, but schools for the education of the lower orders in the most remote villages of the Republic.

With the exception of an inconsiderable income possessed by the Ecclesiastical Seminary, and the dispersed funds of one or two hospitals, the Executive of Bolivia found no means to forward at the commencement its beneficient views. The late Government had in a measure proscribed every species of education save those of jurisprudence and divinity. The clergy had during a long series of years introduced into the charities which had existed the greatest abuses, and had converted a part of the property to their own uses. There existed also in the clergy's hands considerable property which had originally been bequeathed for the support of charitable institutions, but which had been diverted from the use intended by the testators, whilst several churches possessed dotations [endowments] to a considerable amount for performing certain ceremonies and feasts at stated periods. The secularization of two-thirds of the monastic clergy having led to a reduction in the number of the monasteries, a large income was left without a possessor, and to render the suppression of those bodies still more popular, it was judged prudent and necessary for the public good to assign their revenues, as well as the others above mentioned, to the foundation of establishments of public charity and public education.

The funds have been consequently placed in the hands of Commissions or *juntas* created in each Department, where they are exclusively to remain without any direct interference on the part of the Executive. These *juntas* were established in the capitals of the Departments and had accumulated at the commencement of 1827 an available income of 130,000 dollars, or £26,000. The amount belonging to this fund will go on increasing from the suppression of the monastic establishments which remain, and from the increasing value of its landed and other property. When the whole of the property assigned to these foundations shall have been consolidated by the Departmental *juntas*, it will be formed into one general purse from which all public charities and establishments of education will receive the funds necessary for their support.

His Excellency General Sucre, during the time which he has filled the office of President, has founded the following establishments of gratuitous education:

i. An Ecclesiastical Seminary at Chuquisaca, for the education of those destined for the Church. It admits 24 gratuitous pupils, and possesses professors on every branch of ecclesiastical science, with an income of 9,000 dollars for its support.

ii. Colleges of Arts and Sciences have been established in the chief towns of the Departments admitting in all 130 gratuitous pupils, of whom nearly one-half are chosen among the aborigines. Each college possesses from 10,000 to 12,000 dollars income. The course of study in these colleges embraces Foreign Languages, Rhetoric and the more elementary moral sciences, Jurisprudence, Medicine, and in the colleges of the capital that of the transcendent sciences. It is the intention of the Government to introduce foreign professors into the college of Chuquisaca, where the professors destined to teach in the other colleges of the Republic will receive their education. In March 1827, these colleges were established in all the Departments except in that of Santa Cruz de la Sierra.

iii. More elementary or central schools have been formed in the chief towns of each province, in which the course of study embraces the more elementary physical sciences, mathematics, writing, drawing, etc.

Primary or Lancasterian schools have been established in each parish, where reading, writing and elementary arithmetic are taught in the Lancasterian system. When I quitted Bolivia in [April] 1827, the formation of these primary schools had been attended with complete success, and in those Departments where I myself had an opportunity of judging, and which embrace the most populous and civilized part of the Republic, the schools had been well received by the lower orders for whose benefit they were principally intended. In corroboration of this, I cannot adduce a better proof than what passed under my own observation in the extensive Department of Cochabamba which I traversed in March last. I did not visit a village or hamlet where I did not find a primary school established, and where forty or fifty boys were seen learning to read and write, where formerly scarcely an inhabitant could be found who knew to do either.

Mining schools have been established at Potosí and La Paz which, as I have mentioned in another part of this report, are likely to be attended with great advantage in furthering the mining prosperity of the Republic.

The hospitals and other public charities were in a most deplorable state on the establishment of the new government in Upper Peru. Under General Sucre's administration, hospitals and Poor Houses have been founded in the Departmental chief towns, and also houses of reception for orphans, where they will receive a careful education and will be ultimately provided for.

It can scarcely be supposed that in the short space of one year which has passed over since the foundation of these establishments of Public Education and Charity, that they have attained that perfect organization to which they may ultimately arrive. Such can hardly be expected in a country where these are the first foundations of the kind which I may say have existed, and considering the prejudices of a people long debarred from similar advantages. To no class will such establishments prove more beneficial than to the aboriginal population who have been ever excluded by their former rulers from the advantages of education; in no branch of his Administration has General Sucre employed greater zeal and with greater success, than in that relative to public education. To his efforts Bolivia is mainly indebted for those institutions of learning which they possess and which give her the foremost rank as a literate country among the newly constituted states of the American World.[1]

PUBLIC AND POLITICAL FEELING

Public feeling may be said to be exclusively confined in Bolivia to the white or creole population, since the aborigines who have scarcely enjoyed a political existence heretofore, cannot be supposed to possess any other feeling beyond that which regards their immediate interests.

The four principal classes of the white population: the landowners, merchants, lawyers and clergy, may be said to be warmly attached to the present Government. Where a different feeling might have been expected to exist was amongst the clergy, but from what I have

[1] Despite the inaccuracy of this statement, after such a promising start it is saddening to record Bolivia's present adult literacy still, at only c. 32%, one of the lowest in Latin America.

been able to collect from others, and from what has passed under my immediate observation, I am of opinion that scarcely a voice will be found in the entire extent of the Republic, in favor of a return to Spanish rule, and that the Bolivian parochial clergy will be found in the event of an attack on their national independence to support and defend it. Strong feelings of dissatisfaction against the Government are, however, to be found among the monastic clergy, who have suffered by the suppression of their monasteries, and from the enactments respecting the secularization of the members of their order. The state of vice, laziness and immorality which have disgraced those institutions had caused them to be despised, and their members to be generally excluded from the society of the higher orders of the community. They have long ceased to possess any influence on the minds of the people, and their intrigues or dissatisfaction are likely to prove innocuous should they be directed against the present order of things in the Republic.

If Bolivia possesses enemies to her independence amongst her own citizens they are few, and little to be feared, since all classes of her population already begin to appreciate the acts of the Congress and of the Executive, and to profit by the reforms which have taken place in the enjoyment of tranquillity and peace. In every branch of her commerce and industry prosperity is gradually diffusing itself; a dissentient voice is seldom to be heard against the acts of the Government notwithstanding the entire liberty of sentiment and expression possessed by her citizens, and the enactments of her fundamental law are gradually coming into operation to the advantage of all.

During my sojourn in the Bolivian Republic, I have inhabited for a certain time its principal towns.[1] I have traversed the Departments in different directions, and I have endeavoured to ascertain the general feelings on the acts of the Government. I have universally met with returning prosperity and contentment, and on my departure from Bolivia in the early part of April of the present year, I had the gratification to learn in my last communication with His Excellency General Sucre, that in the midst of the political frenzy, disorder and anarchy which surrounded Bolivia on the sides of the Republics of Peru and Buenos Ayres, the laws continued to be obeyed and respected, and the most perfect tranquillity and order continued to reign among her citizens in every point of the Republic.

As to the illustrious individual now at the head of the Bolivian Executive, I may add that one feeling towards him exists throughout the Republic: every one looks to General Sucre as the person to

[1] Excepting Santa Cruz de la Sierra and Tarija. *Supra*, p. 179 n. 1.

whom Bolivia is indebted for her present commanding position, coupled with the prayer that he will not abandon her before he shall have banished any scattered elements of discord which may yet remain, and until he has consolidated her institutions by the establishment of the fundamental enactments of her Constitution. I cannot in conclusion adduce a more convincing proof of the popularity enjoyed by the President of the Republic, than by stating that his election by the Bolivian Congress was unanimous, and in opposition to his own wish. On his election being submitted to the approval of the electoral bodies, there was not a dissentient voice to the nomination, and this by no preconcerted measure, since the elections took place and were completed on the same day from one extremity of the Republic to the other.

With regard to the political feelings of the people of Bolivia towards the two neighbouring Republics of Buenos Ayres and Lower Peru, I have already transmitted to you a note from General Sucre on the projected federation between Bolivia, Buenos Ayres and Chile.[1] It is certain that a federation of that description would meet the assent and approval of the majority of Bolivians as far as it went to cement the friendly intercourse between these states, to put an end to the disorders which prevail in some of them, and to strengthen the political existence of each state individually. But I am convinced that in her present state of prosperity, Bolivia would not assent to a close union with any of the neighbouring Republics to the sacrifice of her own independence, or to form a province of any other state, since she possesses within herself almost everything which can constitute her existence as a prosperous independent state. Her citizens are contented under the present system, her taxation is considerably less than that which is borne by the inhabitants of the neighbouring Republics, and the resources of her territory are in no wise inferior to those of any republic of South America. What then has Bolivia to gain by annexing herself to either the Peruvian or Argentine Republics? Nothing, and I am persuaded such a union would be attended with many disadvantages and evils to Bolivia, and if attempted would produce serious discontent in the country. I may here add that General Sucre in the formal rejection of the bases proposed by Lower Peru for the consolidation into one federal state of the Bolivian and Peruvian Republics, had expressed his fixed determination

[1] This was formally proposed by Sucre in April 1827, but rejected. Bolívar had favoured a union with Peru, while between 1836 and 1839 the Peru-Bolivian Confederation was to be established under Andrés Santa Cruz. In common with all such projects for, or attempts at, federation, however, for the majority it proved unpopular in theory and unworkable in practice.

to preserve to Bolivia the independence which she now possesses, and to resist every attempt which may be made on the integrity of her territory.

In bringing this report to a close I have to apologise for its great length arising from the many details into which I have entered. I have endeavoured, however, to convey to you in it, and as concisely as I could, all the information which I have succeeded in obtaining on the actual state of Bolivia, in obedience to your instructions. As my report comprises a greater variety of subjects than are generally embraced in similar documents, I trust that this diversity of matter will be received by you as some excuse for its apparent prolixity.

In conclusion it becomes my duty to make known to you the many obligations under which I have been placed to His Excellency General Sucre, to the members of the Executive, and to the other authorities of Bolivia, to whom I am indebted for much of the information contained in the foregoing pages. During my journey in Bolivia I have always experienced unlimited hospitality from every class of her citizens. The reception and kindness which I experienced from the President of the Republic were of the most flattering description, and the many marks of favor shown to me by that illustrious individual were received by me with pride, and shall be remembered with gratitude.

I have the honor to be be, Sir,
With great respect,
Your very obedient
and humble servant
J. B. Pentland.

London, 2nd December 1827

Charles Milner Ricketts, Esq.,
His Majesty's Consul General for Peru.

[APPENDIX I]. Statement showing the quantity of silver produced by the mines of Upper Peru from the earliest period, exhibiting the amount of duties paid to the Crown of Spain on this metal, and the amount of silver registered at the Treasury of Potosí from 1545 to 1824, compiled from official documents.

YEARS	AMOUNT OF DUTIES		AMOUNT OF SILVER		AVERAGE ANNUAL PRODUCE	
	Duties in dollars of 8 reales rs	Rate %	in marks of 8 ozs.	in dollars of 8 reales rs	in marks ozs.	in dollars rs
1545–1556	$ 13,846,300. 0	20%	7,800,734. 0	$ 69,231,514. 0	709,158. 0	$6,293,683. 0
1556–1578	$ 15,928,667. 6	20%	8,973,897. 2	$ 79,643,338. 6	390,149. 0	$3,462,754. 0
1578–1736	$129,509,939. 0	21½%	67,872,880. 0	$602,371,809. 2	429,575. 0	$3,812,479. 0
1736–1800	$ 18,618,927. 0	11½%	18,242,683. 0	$161,903,800. 0	276,404. 3	$2,453,088. 0
1800–1809	$ 2,549,786. 0	11½%	2,668,864. 0	$ 23,686,168. 0	296,540. 4	$2,631,796. 0
1809–1824	$ 3,027,153. 3	11½%	3,156,144. 6	$ 28,010,778. 0	210,409. 4	$1,867,384. 0
TOTAL: in dollars	$183,480,773. 1		108,715,203. 0	$964,847,408. 0		
in British money	£36,696,154 . 12s. 6d.			£192,969,481. 12s.		

NOTES: 1. The accounts of the provincial Treasury of Potosí, having been kept in dollars of 13½ reales until the year 1778, I have reduced them in the foregoing table to dollars of 8 reales, the currency of the country at the present day.

2. As the accounts of silver produced have been generally kept in Castilian marks, I have deduced the value in dollars by supposing the mark of pure silver to furnish 7½ reales, or 8⅞ dollars, when converted into coinage.

J. B. Pentland

earliest period, including the amount estimated to have been exported by contraband, and the quantity furnished by the other mines of those provinces not included in [Appendix I].

YEARS	MARKS OF 8 OUNCES	VALUE IN DOLLARS OF 8 *Reales*	AVERAGE ANNUAL PRODUCE	AMOUNT OF DUTIES PAID
	ozs.	*rs*	*rs*	*rs*
1545–1578	16,774,631. 2	$148,874,852. 6	$4,511,359. 2	$ 29,774,967. 6
1578–1736	67,872,880. 0	$602,371,809. 2	$5,718,718. 0	$129,509,939. 0
Exported clandestinely during the same period of 158 years, estimated at ½ of the silver registered	33,936,440. 0	$301,185,904. 5		
1736–1800	18,242,683. 0	$161,903,800. 0	$3,794,620. 4	$ 18,618,927. 0
Exported clandestinely during the same period . . . ½	9,121,341. 4	$ 80,951,900. 0		
1800–1824	5,825,008. 6	$ 51,696,946. 0	$3,231,059. 0	$ 5,576,939. 3
Exported clandestinely during the same period . . . . ½	2,912,504. 7	$ 25,848,473. 0		
Silver produced in the other mines of Upper Peru not included in [Appendix I], but which was registered at the other provincial treasuries, estimated at ¼ of that registered at the Potosí Treasury	27,178,801. 0	$241,211,852. 0		$45,870,194. 0
TOTAL	181,864,290. 3	$1,614,045,537. 5		$229,350,966. 1
Value in British money		£322,809,107. 10*s*. 6*d*.		£45,870,193. 4*s*.

J. B. Pentland

[APPENDIX III]. Statement exhibiting the amount of the precious metals coined at the Mint of Potosí from 1800 to 1826.

	SILVER	
Years	Marks of 8 ounces	Value in dollars of 8 *reales*
	ozs.	rs
1800	457,537. 0	$3,889,064. 4
1801	481,268. 0	$4,090,778. 0
1802	466,852. 0	$2,268,242. 0
1803	276,793. 0	$2,352,740. 4
1804	367,720. 0	$3,125,620. 0
1805	381,173. 0	$3,239,970. 4
1806	370,923. 0	$3,152,845. 6
1807	432,126. 0	$3,673,071. 0
1808	404,233. 0	$3,435,980. 4
1809	365,576. 0	$3,107,396. 0
1810	383,261. 0	$3,257,718. 4
1811	409,419. 0	$3,480,061. 4
1812	293,789. 0	$2,497,206. 4
1813	no returns	no returns
1814	315,643. 0	$2,682,965. 4
1815	111,059. 0	$ 944,885. 4
1816	222,660. 0	$1,909,610. 0
1817	228,916. 0	$1,945,186. 0
1818	199,036. 0	$1,691,806. 0
1819	182,676. 0	$1,552,763. 0
1820	170,249. 0	$1,442,116. 4
1821	152,688. 0	$1,197,842. 0
1822	193,011. 0	$1,640,593. 4
1823	199,676. 0	$1,697,246. 0
1824	188,391. 0	$1,601,323. 4
1825	162,614. 0	$1,382,219. 0
1826	186,242. 0	$1,583,075. 0
TOTAL	7,603,531. 0	$62,842,326. 6
Average annual amount	292,443. 4	$2,417,012. 4
		£483,402. 10s.

GOLD		
Years	Marks of 8 ounces	Value in dollars of 8 *reales*
	ozs.	rs
1800	3,357. 0	$ 455,828. 0
1801	3,501. 0	$ 476,204. 0
1802	2,409. 2	$ 372,688. 0
1803	2,083. 0	$ 283,288. 0
1804	2,647. 4	$ 360,060. 0
1805	5,771. 2	$ 784,890. 0
1806	4,550. 4	$ 618,868. 0
1807	4,593. 3	$ 624,716. 0
1808	4,203. 0	$ 571,608. 0
1809	2,649. 4	$ 360,332. 0
1810	2,797. 0	$ 380,390. 0
1811	2,797. 0	$ 380,390. 0
1812	925. 0	$ 125,834. 0
1822	3,171. 2	$ 431,290. 0
TOTAL	45,455. 5	$6,226,386. 0
Average annual amount	3,246. 7	$ 444,741. 7
		£88,948. 7s. 6d.

There exists no account of the gold coined at Potosí from 1812 to 1822, when the coinage of this precious metal ceased.

J. B. Pentland

INDEX

Abbot, Charles, M.P., Speaker of the House of Commons, 166, 167
Aberlady (E. Loth.), 61
Addington, Henry, M.P., 166
administration, Bolivian (1825-7), 179-81, 207, 240-63; constitutional, 183n 243-5; ministerial, 245-9; judicial, 249-50; fiscal, 250-4, 262; military, 254-5; ecclesiastical, educational, charitable, 255-60
Admiralty, 49
agricultural produce, Bolivian, 178-9, 213-14, 216-19, 223, 235-7
Alcester (Warws.), 104
Alderney (Channel Is.), 35
Aleyn (Alen), Sir John, Chancellor of Ireland, 15
Alost, letter from, 56
alpaca, 179, 192n., 236, 237
Alva, Fernando Alvarez de Toledo, duke of, 40
Andrews, Capt. Joseph, 208n
annates, 127
Antonio de Toledo, Don, 107
Antwerp, news from, 53
Apolobamba (or Caupolicán, prov., Dept of La Paz), Bolivia, 214, 221, 236
Appleby (Leics.), 104
Aquitaine, duchy of, 124
Ardres, 81, 83, 107, 108, 114
Arequipa, Peru, 171, 175n, 218n, 220, 222n, 228n, 230
Arica, Peru, 171, 172, 175n, 180, 189, 206, 209-10, 212, 215, 217, 218n, 219-39 *passim*
Arkendale (Yorks.), 19
army, English, behaviour of captains in, 31; payment of, 87
Arras, Antoine Perrenot, bishop of, eldest son of Nicholas (*q.v.*), 36
Arras, 38, 40, 47-52, 56, 57, 63-5, 66, 68-75, 107, 108, 109, 110
Arundel, earl of, *see* Fitzalan, Henry, 115
Ashley, Katherine, 25
Atacama (desert littoral prov. and

mining district), Bolivia, 171, 182, 196, 221, 223n, 237
Aucher, Sir Anthony, 19, 89; letter to, 88
Audley, Master, 82
Augallas (town and mining district), Bolivia, 182, 196-8, 204, 227
Augmentations, court of, chancellor (Sir Edward North), 27
Ayacucho (Guamanga), Peru, 171, 175, 218, 230, 246

Baker, William, M.P., 166
Balcarres, lord, *see* Lindsay
Banda Oriental (Uruguay), 197n, 220n
bark (Peruvian), 235-6, 237
Barré, Isaac, M.P., 164
Barthe, Paul de la, seigneur de Thermes, 34
Barton, Mr, chaplain to House of Commons, 167
Bassett, James, letters to, 117, 119; letter from, 139, 141
Bath, Margaret, countess of, letters to, 120, 122
Bathurst, Henry, 2nd earl Bathurst, lord chancellor, 159-60, 160
Bavaria, duke of, 23
beacons, 25
Bedell, Master, servant of William, Lord Paget, 80, 120
Bedford, earl of, *see* Russell
Begg, John, 184-5, 211-12
Belgrano, General Manuel, 197
Bell, Ralph, 152-3
bell metal, 46
Bellamy, Mr, deputy housekeeper to House of Commons, 166
Bellay, cardinal du, letter to, 100
Bellingham, William, lord deputy of Ireland, 15
bells, 21
benefices, 100, 134
Beni (river, prov., later Dept), Bolivia, 171, 183n, 215n, 228
Bennyngcourt, monsieur, 107, 111
Berenguela (town and mining district), Bolivia, 182, 186